DOCUMENTARY HISTORY

OF

The Protestant Episcopal Church,

IN THE

UNITED STATES OF AMERICA.

CONTAINING NUMEROUS HITHERTO UNPUBLISHED DOCUMENTS CONCERNING THE CHURCH IN

CONNECTICUT.

Vol. I.

FRANCIS L. HAWKS, D. D., LL. D.,
WILLIAM STEVENS PERRY, A. M.,
EDITORS.

New-York:
JAMES POTT, PUBLISHER,
No. 5 Cooper Union, Fourth Avenue.

1863.

PREFACE.

In offering to our brethren this first volume of "Church Documents," the editors are sensible that little need be said as to the nature and purposes of the work. They speak for themselves, and were, beside, fully explained in the commencement of our undertaking.

It is equally unnecessary to speak of its value as furnishing authentic materials for the early history of the Protestant Episcopal Church in our country.

We ask support from our brethren not from any expectation or desire of pecuniary return, to either the editors or the publisher. The labors of the first named are gratuitous, and the last but asks that he may be reimbursed the moneys expended by him in producing the work. A second volume, now in press, will complete Connecticut; and the next diocese that will engage our attention will, probably, be Maryland.

In the hope that their plans and efforts may be favorably viewed by their brethren, the editors commend the undertaking to their sympathies and kindness; and, without violating propriety by a profusion of promises, ask leave to say no more than that they will faithfully give to their brethren such documents as they have, with an occasional explanatory note such as, in their view, may help to a better understanding of the documents themselves. The principle that prompts us to our present labour is—"*pro Deo, pro Ecclesiâ, pro hominum salute.*"

CHURCH DOCUMENTS.

CONNECTICUT.

What was called New-England, in the times of our early history, comprised the colonies of Connecticut, Massachusetts Bay, Plymouth and Rhode Island, with Narragansett; and very little was there to be found, in it, of tendencies toward the Church of England. Episcopacy had, at first, few or no friends in New-England. The land had been settled, from 1620, by Protestant Dissenters of various names, Brownists, Independents, Presbyterians, &c. Here and there, indeed, might be found one who was bold enough to avow his preference for "Lords Bishops," rather than for "Lords Brethren;" but the country was soon made so uncomfortable a residence for him, that he was commonly glad to leave it for a more quiet home. Still, some remained, and from one cause or another, which it is not necessary here to detail, Episcopalians increased, insomuch that, in 1679, a considerable number of that class, who lived in Boston, petitioned King Charles II. "that a Church might be allowed in that city, for the exercise of religion according to the Church of England." The petition was granted, King's Chapel was established, and thus the Episcopal Church obtained foothold in New-England, surrounded with a numerous body of as bitter enemies as it has ever encountered on this continent. For years it fought hard for every inch of ground it gained. But for the Venerable Society for Propagating the Gospel, it had probably been entirely vanquished in the contest. This society was chartered in 1701, and the first help it afforded, in New-England, was in Connecticut. This help was rendered through the aid of agents, both clerical and lay, who belonged to one of the society's missions in New-York, on the borders of Connecticut; in which latter colony there was not a solitary congregation of Episcopalians, while the inhabitants (as one of these agents writes) were, almost without exception, "very ignorant of the constitution of our Church, and, therefore, enemies to it." To this agent we now beg leave to introduce our readers.

No name is more honorably conspicuous in the early history of the Church, both in New-York and Connecticut, than that of Colonel Heathcote. Our Church MSS., of both these States, will present letters enough from his pen to verify our statement. Caleb Heathcote, the first lord of the Manor of Scarsdale, was the sixth son of Gilbert Heathcote, Esq., in the county of Derbyshire, and hundred of Scarsdale, England. The family is an ancient one, of great worth and respectability in Derbyshire. Col. Heathcote was born at Chesterfield, in the year 1663, and by his talents and industry in mercantile pursuits, "with God's blessing, obtained both influence and a good estate." He came from England to New-York in 1692; and the circumstances which caused his emigration were not of an ordinary kind. It is stated in the "Documentary History of New-York," vol. iv., p. 1039, that he was engaged to a very beautiful English lady, to whom he introduced his eldest brother, Gilbert. The lady soon found that she preferred the elder brother, and broke her engagement with the younger.

Col. Heathcote immediately left England, and made his future home in America. He settled in New-York, and his career in this country is thus sketched by Mr. Bolton, in his interesting history of the Church in Westchester County: "He became a leading man in the colony; was Judge of Westchester, and Colonel of its militia all his life; first Mayor of the borough of Westchester; a counsellor of the Province; Mayor of New-York for three years; for a time, commander of the colony's forces, and, from 1715 to the time of his death, Receiver-General of the customs in North America. He was also one of the founders of Trinity Church, New-York; his name heads the list of its first Vestrymen, in 1697, and he remained in office till 1714. He was elected a member of the Venerable Society for the Propagation of the Gospel in Foreign Parts, in the year 1704, and embraced every opportunity of doing service to the Church, and, through the blessing of God, never let slip one fair occasion therein, when the Provincial Government would give him leave."

"St. George Talbot, Esq., writing to the Secretary of the Venerable Society, January 10th, 1707–8, says: 'I wish the report were true, that he (Caleb Heathcote) were appointed Governor; it would be the best news, next to that of the Gospel, that ever came over.'"

"Some time prior to 1704, he erected a stately brick manor-house in the village of Mamaroneck, upon what is still called Heathcote Hill, where he continued to reside for the remainder of his life. From this place most of the letters are dated which he addressed to the Venerable Society. Here he was reverenced by the poor, esteemed by the Colonial Governors, and respected by all. His death, which was very sudden and unexpected, took place in the spring of 1721. He was buried near the southwest corner of Trinity Church, New-York. The following obituary notice appeared at the time of his decease:"

"NEW-YORK, *March 6th*, 1721.

"On the 28th day of February last, died the Hon. Caleb Heathcote, Esq., Surveyor-General of His Majesty's customs for the Eastern District of North America, Judge of the Court of Admiralty for the Provinces of New-York and New-Jersey and the Colony of Connecticut, one of His Majesty's Council for the Province of New-York, and brother of Sir Gilbert Heathcote, of London. He was a gentleman of rare qualities, excellent temper and virtuous life and conversation, and his loss lamented by all who knew him; who, the day of his death, went about doing good in procuring a charitable subscription, in which he made a very great progress."

We gather a few more particulars concerning this most worthy gentleman from Mr. Bolton's truly valuable history of Westchester County. We have seen that Col. Heathcote came over in 1692. In 1696 he obtained, by purchase of Anne Richbell, relict of one John Richbell, a right to certain lands, which Richbell had derived from the Dutch West India Company in 1661; and in 1701 he purchased of the Indian proprietors, for a valuable consideration, their right and title to a large body of land lying on the Bronx and Mamaroneck Rivers; and the lands included in these two purchases united, constituted the manor or lordship of Scarsdale, for which a royal charter was granted to Col. Heathcote in 1701. The territory thus acquired was larger than several of the smaller principalities of Germany, some of its boundaries running uninterruptedly for a length of eighteen miles; and within this little empire the proprietor and lord was empowered to erect his court leet and court baron, appoint his stewards and deputies, impose amercements, issue the customary legal process of such courts, distrain for rents, services, &c., enjoy all waifs, estrays, deodands and forfeited goods of felons; and, in short, to be as near an approximation to the ancient lord of feudal times as the more modern laws of England, at that day, would permit.

Extensive, however, as were these powers of the lord of Scarsdale, there is no evidence that he abused them to the oppression or injury of any one; for he seems to have been a common benefactor, and a very public-spirited, conscientious and useful man, ready for any good work that would benefit the community in which he lived. And in no particular was this latter trait more conspicuous than in his efforts to make permanent the institutions and teachings of Christianity. There is an amusing account, given by himself, of some of the measures to which he resorted for accomplishing his object. He thus writes: "I shall begin the history of the Church from the time I first came among them, which was about twelve years ago. I found it the most rude and heathenish country I ever saw in my whole life, which called themselves Christians—there being not so much as the least marks or footsteps of religion of any sort. Sundays were the only times set apart by them for all manner of vain sports and lewd diversions, and they were grown to such a degree of rudeness, that it was intolerable. I, having then the command of the militia, sent an order to all the captains, requiring them to call their men under arms, and to acquaint them that in case they would not in every town agree among themselves to appoint readers, and to pass the Sabbath in the best manner they could, till such time as they should be better provided, that the captains should, every Sunday, call their companies under arms, and spend the day in exercise. Whereupon it was unanimously agreed, throughout the country, to make choice of readers, which they accordingly did, and continued in those methods for some time." This was certainly a novel illustration of the "*Church Militant.*"

After Col. Heathcote's settlement in New-York, (but of the precise date we are ignorant,) he married Martha, the daughter of Col. William Smith, of Long Island, who was commonly known as "Tangier" Smith, from the fact that he had been Governor of Tangier, in Africa. This lady was the mother of several children, all of whom died without issue, except two of the daughters, Anne and Martha, who became the co-heiresses of Col. Heathcote. Of these, Anne married the Hon. James De Lancey, Lieut.-Governor of New-York, son of one of the Huguenots, Etienne De Lancey, whom the revocation of the edict of Nantz had driven to America. One of their sons was John Peter De Lancey, who married Elizabeth Floyd, and these were the parents of the Right Rev. William Heathcote De Lancey, the present able and much esteemed Bishop of the diocese of Western New-York. The other daughter, Martha, married Lewis Johnston, Esq., M. D., of Perth Amboy, New-Jersey. They had four children, John, Anne, Margaret and Heathcote. Of these, Margaret married, according to Mr. Bolton, the Hon. Bower Reed, "Governor" of New-Jersey;* their daughter Maria married Joshua McIlvaine, and these were the parents of the Right Rev. Charles Petit McIlvaine, the gifted and zealous Bishop of Ohio. It will thus be seen, that two of our pres-

* Mr. Whitehead, in his "Contributions to East Jersey History," says that Mr. Bolton is in error in the statement that Mr. Reed was *Governor* of Jersey. He never held that office. He was a highly respected lawyer of Burlington County, Mayor of Burlington, Register-General and Secretary of State of New-Jersey, from the Revolution to the time of his death, in 1794.

ent Bishops are direct descendants of Colonel Heathcote, and by their pious labors have faithfully endeavoured to perpetuate and extend that Church, for which, in the beginning, their honored ancestor did all that he could, in laying the foundation. Nor is this all; according to Mr. Bolton, the Rev. William Walton, D. D., of New-York, is a great grandson of Chief Justice De Lancey, and has, therefore, the blood of Col. Heathcote in his veins. We have, therefore, among our clergy, three descendants of this worthy gentleman, who gave so much of his time and means to the establishment of the Church in which they minister. But it is time to let Col. Heathcote speak for himself.

[*Colonel Heathcote to the Secretary. Extract.*]

Manor of Scarsdale, Nov. 9th, 1705.

Sir,

I have been so long wandering from one subject to another, that I had almost forgot to give you my thoughts of Mr. Muirson, whom my Lord of London has sent for this parish. He has been here about three months, in which time he hath, by much, outdone my expectation; having very fully retrieved all that unfortunate gentleman, Mr. Pritchard, lost; and if he continues so faithful in the discharge of his trust, I have not the least doubt but he will be able to give as large an account of his services as any that has been sent over to this Province; and I must do him the justice to own, that he is deserving of the Society's favours. For, as some of his parishioners told me, and which I know in a great measure to be true, that although they have had a great many Ministers among them since the settlement of their town, yet Mr. Muirson did more good amongst them the first six weeks after his coming, than all they ever had before; and I question not, but when you have the particulars of his proceedings transmitted, you will find what I have said of him to be true.

My principles and natural temper lead me to do the

Church all the service I can, everywhere; but I dare not promise for more than this county at present, and my best endeavours in the westernmost towns in Connecticut Colony, when the Church is well rooted here. And it has always been my opinion, and is so still, that there is no part of this Province, or even America, that will be of greater use or service to have the Church thoroughly settled in; for it is not only large in extent, and the land very good, but near the city. So, consequently, it will in time be a great settlement. But, bordering on Connecticut, there is no part of the continent from whence the Church can have so fair an opportunity to make impressions upon the Dissenters in that government, who are settled, by their laws, from Rye Parish to Boston Colony, which is about thirty-five leagues, in which there are abundance of people and places. As for Boston Colony, I never was in it, so can say little about it. But as for Connecticut, I am and have been pretty conversant with it, and always was as much in all their good graces as any man; and now that I am on that subject, I will give you the best account I can of that colony.

It contains, in length, about 140 miles, and has in it about forty towns, in each of which there is a Presbyterian or Independent Minister, settled by law, to whom the people are all obliged to pay, notwithstanding many times the Ministers are not ordained, of which I have known several examples. The number of people there is, I believe, about 2,400 souls. They have abundance of odd kind of laws, to prevent any dissenting from their Church, and endeavour to keep the people in as much blindness and unacquaintedness with any other religion as possible, but in a more particular manner the Church, looking upon her as the most dangerous enemy they have to grapple withal, and abundance of pains is taken to make the ignorant think as bad as possible of her; and I really believe that more than half the people in that government think our Church to be little better than the Papist, and they fail not to improve every little thing against us. But I bless God for it, the Society has robbed them of their best argument, which was the ill lives of our clergy that came into these parts; and the truth is, I have not seen many good men, but of the Society's sending; and no sooner was that honourable body settled, and those prudent measures taken for carrying on of that good work, but the people of Connecticut, doubting of maintaining their ground without some further support, with great industry went through their colony for subscriptions to build a college at a place called Seabrook; and the Ministers, who are as absolute in their respective parishes as the Pope of Rome, argued, prayed and preached up the necessity of it, and the passive, obedient people, who dare not do otherwise than obey, gave even beyond their ability. A thing, which they call a college, was prepared accordingly, wherein, as I am informed, a commencement was made about three or four months ago. But notwithstanding their new college here, and an old one in Boston, and that every town in that colony has one, and some two Ministers, and I have not only heard them say, but seen it in their prints, that there was no place in the world where the gospel shone so brightly, nor the people lived so religiously and well as they; yet I dare aver, that there is not a much greater necessity of having the Christian religion, in its true light, preached any where, than amongst them—many, if not the greatest number of them, being little better than in a state of heathenism, having never been baptized or admitted to the Communion. And that you may be satisfied what I tell you herein is not spoken at random, nor grounded on careless observation, Mr. Muirson's parish, which is more than three-fourths composed of two towns, viz., Rye and Bedford, which were first settled under the colony of Connecticut, and by the people bred and born under that government; and some time before my coming they had a Minister, one Mr. Denham, and had afterwards two more, Woodbridge and Bowers, at Rye, and one Mr. Jones, at Bedford, and the people of Rye only had of this county the care to provide a parsonage house; and notwithstanding all those great shows of religion, and that at such times as they were destitute of a Minister.

Greenwich and Stamford, the bounds of the former of which places join upon theirs, and the other is not above ten miles distant, where they were always supplied, so that they could not be said to want the opportunity of having the Sacraments administered to them; yet I believe twenty of them had never received the Communion, nor half of them been baptized, as Mr. Muirson will more fully inform you.

And now I have given you an account of the state of that colony, what will in the next place be naturally expected from me is, to know my opinion of the best and most probable way of doing good amongst them. There is nothing more certain than that it is the most difficult task the Society have to wade through. For the people are not only not of the Church, but have been and are trained up, with all the care imaginable, to be its enemies. That to make an impression, under all these disadvantages, is very difficult, though I hope not impossible; and though, at first view, the prospect of doing any good upon them is very little, yet no doubt but the most proper measures ought to be taken, leaving the event to Almighty God.

Now, to give you my thoughts in what way this great work may best be endeavoured at, so as it may be done with little expense, I believe, for the first step, the most proper way would be, that one of the Ministers in this County should be directed, by my Lord of London, to inform himself where there are any in that government that profess themselves to be of the Church, and to know if they or any of their neighbours have any children to baptize, or desire to partake of the Sacrament; and inform them that he will come to the town where they live, and after having given them a sermon, will perform those holy rites. There need, I think, no more be done in this matter at present; but the Society may, if they please, leave the rest to me, and I won't only give him the best advice and directions I can therein, but will, God willing, wait upon him in his progress, and persuade some useful friends along with me. And when this essay has been made, I shall be much better able to guess at the state of that government, and what is fitting to be done next.

Now, the person that I would advise them to pitch upon, by all means, for this expedition, is Mr. Muirson; he being not only posted next those parts, and so it will look less like design; but he has a very happy way of delivery, and makes little use of his notes in preaching, which is extremely taking amongst those people; and for argument, few of his years exceed him.

The chief end I have in this projection is to have the people of that government undeceived in their notions concerning our Church—there being, I believe, fifteen thousand in that colony who have never heard, or scarce seen a Church of England Minister; and I have the charity to believe that, after having heard one of our Ministers preach, they will not look upon our Church to be such a monster as she is represented; and being convinced of some of the cheats, many of them may duly consider of the sin of schism. However, let the success be what it will, to me the duty seems plain. I have not only mentioned this to you, but in my letter to my Lord of London, and shall patiently wait for his and the Society's commands therein.

CALEB HEATHCOTE.

The tour of observation suggested in this letter was, ere long, made by Col. Heathcote, in company with the Rev. Mr. Muirson, of whom he speaks in terms of such high commendation in the former part of the preceding extract. But Mr. Muirson deserves at our hands something more than the mere mention of his name, and we therefore ask leave to tell our readers somewhat concerning him; after which he, also, like Col. Heathcote, shall speak for himself.

The Rev. George Muirson, A. M., was born in Scotland, (in Ayrshire, probably,) about the year 1675, and received his education, as it is supposed, in some one of the colleges of that country. In 1703 he was sent to the Province of New-York, by the Venerable Society, as schoolmaster at Albany. When Lord Cornbury afterward established a Latin free-school in New-York, he appointed Mr. Muirson its master; and for some time he discharged the duties of that office successfully. The Rev. William Vesey (of whom our New-York documents, when published, will furnish more particular information) was, at that time, the Rector of New-York, which had in it no Episcopal Church but Trinity; and in

1704, Mr. Muirson, who was seeking the appointment of Catechist in Trinity, was spoken of as a fit person to be ordained, and to become assistant to Mr. Vesey in his ministerial labours. He was strongly recommended by Lord Cornbury, the Rev. Mr. Vesey, the Church Wardens and Vestrymen of Braintree, (now Quincey,) in Massachusetts, and by the Rev. Evan Evans of Philadelphia, of whom our Pennsylvania documents have much, that is good, to say. This last named gentleman thus wrote to the Bishop of London, in October, 1704: "This comes by the hands of the ingenious Mr. George Muirson, to receive holy orders from your Lordship, by the approbation of his Excellency, my Lord Cornbury. I find that he is very well beloved and esteemed by all sorts of people, a man of a very sober and blameless conversation. He seems to be endued with great humility of mind, and has the character of being very prudent in his conduct. I give him this recommendation not to gratify himself, nor any body else, but because I sincerely believe he may be very instrumental of doing much good in the Church."

With such testimonials, Mr. Muirson found no difficulty in obtaining orders from the hands of Dr. Compton, the Bishop of London; and, returning to America, he reached New-York in July, 1705. Though he had been spoken of as a suitable assistant to Mr. Vesey, from some satisfactory cause Lord Cornbury thought it best, soon after his arrival, to appoint him to the Church at Rye, which had been much injured under a year's ministry of the Rev. Mr. Pritchard. He soon revived the drooping prospects of the Church at Rye, and, "by the aid and assistance of the good Colonel Heathcote," as he expresses it, persuaded the parish to build a good Church edifice. In the same letter, from which the above words are quoted, he says: "I have lately been in the government of Connecticut, where I observe some people well affected to the Church; for those that are near, come to my parish on Sabbath days; so that I am assured an itinerant Missionary might do great services in that Province. Some of their Ministers have privately told me, that had we a Bishop among us, they would conform and receive holy orders; from which, as well as on all the Continent, the necessity of a Bishop will plainly appear."

Colonel Heathcote, who, as we have seen, was the leading man of that day in Westchester County, as well as of great and deserved influence in the Province at large, had, we are persuaded, much instrumentality in causing Mr. Muirson to be sent to Rye. He had the interests of the Church in view. Scarsdale embraced a great part of Mr. Muirson's parish at Rye, and, indeed, Col. Heathcote may almost be said to have founded the parish there; he was one of its first wardens, and for some time its chief supporter. He was, by much, the richest man in Westchester; very decided and ardent in his attachment to the Church of England; extremely liberal in the use of his fortune for its extension; so that not only did the Church at Rye owe almost its existence (as it certainly did its preservation) under God to him, but all Westchester County is indebted to his efforts and to his means for nearly every one of her ancient parishes, which are now among the oldest in this country. The object of Col. Heathcote was two-fold: first, to plant the Church securely in Westchester, on the borders of Connecticut; and, secondly, from that point, to act upon Connecticut, which was wholly Puritan, and, withal, not a little bigotted and uncharitable. After Mr. Muirson was settled at Rye, the Colonel commenced the execution of the second part of his plan. Mr. Muirson frequently crossed the border, "holding services, preaching, baptizing and distributing prayer-books and devotional works;" and, as Mr. Bolton states, in his History of the Parish of Rye, "on these expeditions he was invariably accompanied by Col. Heathcote. They rode on horseback, with their saddle-bags full of books, and the Colonel always went *fully armed*, as, in those tolerant times, it was as much as a man's life was worth even to talk of 'the Church' in Connecticut, without the means of self-defence."

Mr. Muirson must have possessed a peculiar aptitude for this itinerating duty in Connecticut, and he was much blessed in his labours. It pleased God, however, to take him to himself when he was yet but a young man, of but little more than thirty years. He died in October, 1708, deeply lamented by all who knew him. One who had studied his character well, thus speaks of him: "He was a most zealous, devoted and truly good man; a sound Churchman in his principles, and bold and fearless in advocating his views; cool in judgment, winning in manners, and possessed of great natural eloquence, he was well fitted for the position in which he was placed, and admirably calculated to introduce the Church into the then benighted government of Connecticut."

His friend and patron, Col. Heathcote, who probably knew and understood him better than any other man did, thus expresses himself, in a letter to the Secretary of the Venerable Society, dated not long after his death:—"I must, in the first place, give you the melancholy account of Mr. Muirson's death, who was a very industrious and successful Missionary, and had it pleased God to have preserved his life, he would have been able to have given a wonderful account of his labours. By his constant journies in the service of the Church, and the necessary supply of his family, he expended every farthing he got here and of the Society." The testimony of his clerical brethren, to the worth of such a man, should not be omitted. It is equally honourable to him and to themselves. In a joint letter which they sent to the Bishop of London, dated November 24th, 1709, they thus write:

"May it Please your Lordship,

"We think ourselves obliged by the ties of humanity and sacred relation of paternity, as well as those of Christian charity to the indigent, to make this representation to your Lordship, our most worthy Diocesan, and the Venerable Society for the Propagation of the Gospel, in the behalf of the virtuous relicts of our late deceased reverend brethren, Mr. Muirson and Mr. Urquhart, whose present difficult circumstances, as they extort this our petition, so we humbly hope will render them proper objects of your commiseration. The former was Missionary of Rye, a parish bordering on Connecticut Colony, where God was pleased to bless his painful labours with suitable success; and that he might not fall under the censure of avarice, or give the least occasion of any reflection amongst his people, (who were for the most part proselytes to the Church,) he not only frequently parted with what, by law, was his just demand, but out of his Missionary allowance of £50 per annum, endeavoured to support himself, that he might make the Gospel as little burdensome to them as possible, one of the most effectual means to establish the Church in these parts, and by his frequent journeys to Stratford, a town in that Province where he was invited to preach, and had a very good prospect of erecting a Church for the worship of God, according to the form and manner of the Church of England, he was put to more than ordinary charges, which, (had God granted him a longer life,) he might have reaped so much advantage from, as to have made a settlement there for the service of our Church, and, in a great measure, repaired the voluntary poverty he had brought upon himself in his endeavours to effect this good work; but it pleased God to remove him in the midst of his labours and dawning of our hopes, by which his poor widow, and one son, born since his death, are left to struggle with some difficulties, which we hope the pious zeal of your Venerable Society will remove, by an allowance of £50 sterling, to commence from his death, for one year, to pay his just debts contracted in that service," &c.

This letter was signed by the following reverend gentlemen: *Evans* of Philadelphia, *Talbot* of Burlington, *Thomas* of Hampstead, *Barton* of Westchester, *Sharp*, Chaplain to the Queen's Forces, *Bridge* of Rye, and *Myles* and *Harris* of Boston.

On the 20th of June, 1707, Mr. Muirson married Georgiana, the youngest daughter of the Hon. William Smith, of St. George's Manor, Long Island, Chief Justice and President of the Council of New-York. The posthumous son alluded to in the foregoing letter was George Muirson, Esq., M. D., of Setauket, L. I. Mrs. Muirson survived her husband but two years. The posthumous son, Dr. George Muirson, married Anna Smith, and their descendants are still, we believe, living on Long Island.

[*Mr. Muirson to the Secretary. Extract.*]

Honored Sir,

Please to communicate to your Society that I have lately been in Connecticut Colony, and found some persons well-disposed towards the Church. I preached in Stratford to a very numerous congregation, both forenoon and afternoon. I baptized about twenty-four persons the same day. I intend another journey thither again quickly, being invited to baptize their children, and hope (by the Divine aid) to make a fair beginning for the establishment of the Church, in a considerable part of that government. There are, I'm informed, some thousands of persons in that colony unbaptized, and the reason is this, most of their Ministers refuse to admit any children into Christ's Church by baptism, but those whose parents are in full communion with them. The Independents threaten me, and all who are instrumental in bringing me thither, with prison and hard usage. They are very much incensed to see that the Church (Rome's sister, as they ignorantly called her) is likely to gain ground among 'em, and use all the stratagems they can invent to defeat my enterprises. But, however, since I hope my superiors approve of my undertaking, I shall not fail to visit as often as the affairs of my parish will permit; neither shall all they can do or say discourage me from prosecuting (to the utmost of my ability) so good a design. I shall be glad to receive the instructions of your Honourable Corporation by the next opportunity, which I shall always think myself happy in obeying. In the mean time shall continue to proceed in this method till I receive further orders. The Hon. Col. Heathcote (who always studies and endeavours the good of the Church) has been very diligent and industrious in carrying on this great work. The eminency of his station, and withal his favouring and countenancing my attempts of this nature, is of so great consequence among the people that, truly, what success I have hitherto had, either at home or abroad, is owing more to his prudent conduct than to the best of my weak labours. He honours me with his good company in all such progresses, and exerts his utmost endeavours to settle the Church wherever he goes, which will recommend him to the esteem and regard of all good men, but especially (I'm persuaded) of your worthy members.

Honor'd sir,

Your most faithful,

Humble servant,

GEORGE MUIRSON.

RYE, *October* 2*d*, 1706.

[*Colonel Heathcote to the Secretary.*]

October, 1706.

Sir,

I gave you the trouble of a very long letter by Mr. Talbot, and another by the Virginia fleet, both which I hope are come to your hands, and have not since been favoured with any from you, tho' am in daily expectation thereof. I have not lately heard any thing of or from Mr. Clayton; and since he does the Society no service, I hope he is in no charge to them. I have a proposal to lay before the Board concerning schooling, in which I propose a considerable service without any very great charge, and am apt to believe it may be approved of. I have it now upon the anvil, and hope to have it ready to transmit to you in my next, which shall be with the first opportunity, God willing, that presents after this. I told you, in my former letter, that I intended to accompany Mr. Muirson into Connecticut, to try what impression could be made on those people. We accordingly paid them a visit about six weeks ago, and had done it sooner, but the expectation we were under of the French making an attack on this Province, obliged me not to leave until those fears were over. We found that Colony much as we expected—very ignorant of the constitution of our Church, and, for that reason, great enemies to it. All their towns are furnished with Ministers, (as I formerly told you,) who are chiefly Independents, and denying baptism to the children of all who are not in full communion; there are many thousands in that government unbaptized. The Ministers are very uneasy at our coming amongst them, and abundance of pains was taken to persuade and terrify the people from hearing Mr. Muirson, but it availed nothing; for, notwithstanding all their endeavours, he had a very great congregation, and, indeed, infinitely beyond my expectation. The people were wonderfully surprised at the order of our Church, expecting to have heard and seen some wonderful strange things, by the account and representation of it that their teachers had given them. I am in hopes, upon the whole matter, that our journey was not lost; but that we have done service to the Church in our progress, in which I shall be able to give a better guess after our next visit, which we intend, God willing, to pay them about a month or six weeks hence. Mr. Muirson baptized about twenty-four, mostly grown people; and when he goes there next, I hope many more will be added to the Church. He is, truly, very well qualified for that service, having a very happy way of preaching; and, considering his years, wonderfully good at argument, while his life is without blemish. I've not any thing further at present worth the while to trouble you with, save my most humble regards and duty to the Society, so remain, sir,

Your most affectionate servant,

CALEB HEATHCOTE.

[*Col. Heathcote to the Secretary.*]

Sir,

I wrote you a letter by the last fleet, since which I have not been favoured by any from you, which I attribute to the misfortune of the Resolution Galley. I therein gave you an account of some small progress we had made toward settling the Church in Connecticut. Since which, we have made another journey amongst them, when Mr. Muirson baptized four or five more, mostly grown persons, and administered the

Sacrament to about fifteen. He met with more opposition this time than the last, the justices having taken the freedom to preach, giving out at the same time, amongst the people, that he and all his hearers should be put in gaol. But, notwithstanding all their threats to some and persuasions to others, he had a handsome congregation; and I believe the next visit that is paid them, it will be found that their struggling to stifle the Church will be a great means to forward its growth, for I hope, with the blessing of God, in as short a time as can reasonably be expected, there won't only be a fine congregation gathered, but ways will be found by our projection, or otherwise, to have a handsome Church for them to worship God in—for the effecting of which, my hearty endeavour shall not be wanting. Those there in the interest of the Church are very desirous to have a Minister sent amongst them, in which, if the Society shall think fit to assist them, more than common care must be taken that they have one of an exemplary life, and in all respects qualified to answer that great work; for a miscarriage at our first setting out would ruin all, and it would afterwards be extremely difficult to make any steps toward settling the Church in that colony. It would be absolutely necessary, for the better and more easy effecting this great and good work, that an order be procured from Her Majesty, requiring the government of that Colony not to force any of her subjects to pay for maintenance of the Ministers settled by their laws, and to repeal that act whereby they pretend to refuse liberty of conscience to those of the established Church. If those grievances were redressed, which in itself is very reasonable and proper, and not much more than hath been granted the Quakers, on their petition against the same government, it would be of greater service to the Church than can at first sight be imagined. I acquainted you, in my former letter, that there was a very ingenious gentleman at Stratford, one Mr. Reed, the Minister of that place, who is very inclinable to come over to the Church; and if the charge can be dispensed with, he is well worth the gaining, being by much the most ingenious man they have amongst them, and would be very capable to serve the Church. By reason of the good inclination he shews for the Church, he has undergone persecution by his people, who do all which is in their power to starve him, and being countenanced and encouraged therein by all the Ministers round them, they have very near effected it; so that if any proposal could be made to encourage his coming over for ordination, his family, which is pretty large, must be taken care of in his absence. I thought fit to lay this matter before the Society, and leave it to their wisdom and judgment to move therein, as they think proper and convenient.

I hear nothing of Mr. Cleator, so suppose that he is either dead or hath declined the service, as having since better considered that matter. If the Society will be pleased to allow the £15 he was to have for schoolmasters in this country, I believe I could, for that money, encourage the settling of four, by having it sent over in goods, as I shall direct; and the Society shall have no trouble, nor run any risque therein, for I will be answerable if any misfortune happen to it in coming over; for, though 'tis but a small sum, I will give directions to have it insured. If this projection answers my expectation, as I am very much of opinion it will, it may be of great use and service to the Society on many other accounts.

The bearer hereof, Mr. Evans, who has a very fair character, and is clothed with the reputation of having done very great service to the Church in Philadelphia, is going home to receive my Lord of London's directions for settling the Church at that place, which is very much rent by some unhappy differences, and I don't doubt his Lordship will find out effectual ways for healing their wounds, for it's a great pity the Church should be hurt by any divisions amongst her own members; but especially in that place, where she is, in a more than ordinary manner, surrounded with enemies. Mr. Evans will be able to give you some account concerning the state of this parish, which Mr. Muirson hath, as I formerly told you, got into very great order. They are now busy in ceiling their Church, and it is, I believe, the first country Church in America that ever had that cost bestowed on it; and I question not but we shall persuade them to finish it in all other respects decently and well. Mr. Muirson, the next journey he makes to Connecticut, intends to settle his Church at Stratford, by making choice of Churchwardens and Vestry, as Mr. Evans will more fully inform you. I was not mistaken when I formerly told you that he was the most proper of all the Missionaries hereabouts to go on that great undertaking, having performed that work with a wonderful deal of prudence and discretion. When the Church hath got footing in Connecticut, it will in the next place be advisable to try what is to be done with the east end of Long Island, where there are several considerable towns, concerning which, when I have informed myself better, I shall give you my thoughts therein. I have not at present any thing further worth your notice, so with my most humble duty to the Society

I remain, sir,

Your most obedient servant,

CALEB HEATHCOTE.

NEW-YORK, 24 *Feb'y*, 1707.

[*Mr. Muirson to the Secretary. Extract.*]

Much Honor'd Sir,

I received yours, dated May 2, 1706. The instructions you sent along with it, I'm informed, are at York, which will come to my hands quickly. I understand by yours that the Society expects an account of all the subscriptions and contributions I receive from the Government or inhabitants, of which this is an exact statement. That there is £50, N. York money, settled by act of Assembly upon Rye Parish; but the people being very poor, I've received only about £10 or £12 since I've been their Minister. It's true I could compel 'em, by law, to pay the whole; but such proceedings, I'm well assured, would have been very hurtful to the interest of the Church, in a place, especially, surrounded with Dissenters of all sorts; and, therefore, I thought it better to have patience with them till they are more able, than that our glorious work should anyways suffer. They are all new converts, and so I must bear with 'em in many things, tho' to my present disadvantage; but I hope, when our Church is finished, they will consider my circumstances, and make my life more comfortable than hitherto it has been. As to the present circumstances of my parish, I've nothing new to offer; only, since my last, I've baptized several persons; that the number of communicants increases; that the people duly frequent the Church, excepting a few Quakers and Anabaptist families. There is a considerable number of growing persons not yet baptized; but I intend to admit them after they are instructed into the principles of that religion of which their baptism makes them members; for I think it necessary that the adults be first taught what they are to promise and perform in that covenant.

I have been thrice in Connecticut Colony, and, in one town, have baptized about 32, young and old, and administered the Holy Sacrament to 18, who never received it before. Each time I had a numerous congregation. Col. Heathcote has taken abundance of pains among 'em, and I find that many of the people are well disposed to the Church, but dare not, at present, show themselves, being under great discouragement from the Government, for the Independents threaten 'em with prison and punishment for coming to hear me preach; and not only so, but one of their magistrates, with some other officers, came to my lodgings, on Saturday, and, in the hearing of Col. Heathcote and a great many people, read a long paper; the meaning of it was to let me know that theirs was a charter government; that I had done an illegal thing in coming among 'em to establish a new way of worship, and to forewarn me from preaching any more. This he did by virtue of one of their laws, entitled ecclesiastical, page 29. The words he made use of are these, as the said law expresses them: "Be it enacted by the Governor, Council and Representatives, convened in General Assembly, that there shall be no ministry or church administration entertained or attended by the inhabitants of any town or plantation in this Colony, distinct and separate from, and in opposition to, that which is openly and publickly observed and dispensed by the approved ministers of the place." Now, whatever interpretation the words of the said law may admit, yet we are to regard the sense and force they put upon them, which is plainly thus, to exclude the Church from their Government, as appears by their proceedings with me; so that hereby they deny a liberty of conscience to the Church of England, as well as to all others that are not of their opinion, which, being repugnant to the laws of England, is contrary to the grant of their charter; and which, I humbly presume, if our Gracious Queen was acquainted with, her Majesty would be pleased to disannul the same, or, at least, make it ineffectual against the settling of the National Church. Till this be done, or some other method taken to remove these hindrances, I cannot expect my endeavours should be so successful as otherwise they might be; for though the people are very inclinable, yet they are afraid of the penalty annexed to the law. It's very remarkable how industrious both ministers and magistrates are to frustrate my undertaking; for, wherever they come, they busy themselves from house to house to keep the people away. Among many others, I shall offer only one particular instance of their spight and malice against the Church. I was lately invited to preach, and baptize some children, in a town called Fairfield; upon which, I sent a letter to the minister and magistrate of said town, entreating the use of their meeting-house, supposing they would readily grant it, being on a week-day; but they refused it, and told me they would discountenance such new ways. A gentleman was so kind as to invite me to his house, where (notwithstanding all the stratagems they had used to hinder the people from coming) I had a large congregation; but so cruelly was the Independent party set against us, that they railed and scoffed at the Church, making her as idolatrous as Rome, and denied us the liberty of ringing the bell, or beating a drum, to give the people notice. The Reverend Mr. Evans was there along with me. He was pleased to travel almost 200 miles, that, being acquainted with the particular circumstances of that Colony, he might be the more capable of giving you a true and full information. He has their law book; he can show you what laws they make use of against the Church, and how they force our people to pay to their Ministers, and take their estates by distress. By those and such intolerable oppressions, the people are disenabled to contribute to the support of a Church of England Minister, and therefore have petitioned home that one may be sent, with a sufficient maintenance, from the Honourable Corporation. He had need be a man very prudent in conduct, and exemplary in life and conversation, (for being the first,) the advancement of the Church in after ages depends, in a great measure, upon his good behaviour; for the people generally judge a man's principles by his life.

Sir, it would make my letter too tedious, should I enumerate all the attempts they make against us. I shall therefore desist from this subject, desiring only you would be pleased to enquire more particularly of Mr. Evans, as also to consult those letters which the people, from time to time, have sent to me, by which you will see the necessity there is of a Missionary among 'em, and how desirous these good men are of receiving the sacred ordinances, and worshipping God in the way of our holy mother, and yet what sore grievances and hardships they labour under for the same.

It would be a great service if the Society would be pleased to send over some Common Prayer-Books and some small treatise in defence of the Church; for our adversaries have mustered up all the scandalous and reviling pamphlets they can get, and have dispersed them among the people in order to prejudice 'em against us.

I want books very much for my own use, having only a few I bought before I came from London, but I hope the Society have been pleased to consider my request before this time.

I heartily beg your prayers, that all my endeavours may answer the glorious ends of my mission, the advancement of God's Glory in the due edifying of his people.

That Almighty God may be pleased, (out of the immense treasury of His riches,) so to increase your stock and bless all your laudable designs, that you may, for the further good of

His Church and people, send forth more labourers into His Harvest, shall ever be the fervent prayer of

Honor'd sir,
Your most faithful friend and
Very humble servant,
GEORGE MUIRSON.

RYE, 4 *April*, 1707.

[*Colonel Heathcote to the Secretary.*]

Sir,

After I had furnished my other letter by the bearer, Mr. Evans, he, resolving to tarry a month or six weeks longer than he first proposed, gives me the opportunity to send what new matter hath since occurred. And to begin with Connecticut:—About 14 days ago, Mr. Muirson paid his congregation in those parts a visit, and had the happiness to be accompanied by Mr. Evans, who, out of his zeal to serve the Church, though of a weakly constitution, undertook that troublesome journey, so that, being an eye-witness to those affairs, he might be the more able to give a more satisfactory account concerning the state of the Church there, to whom I shall make bold, in a great measure, to refer you. I bless God for it. Every thing has almost outgone my first hopes, and I am very much of opinion that, if that matter is pushed on with care, a wonderful deal of service may be done the Church in that government. The people having been kept in perfect blindness, as many of them now declare, and as I told you in mine by the Jamaica fleet, it cannot be an act of greater charity to undeceive the Indians, than those miserable blinded people; and where there are such vast numbers debarred from the benefit of God's Holy Ordinances, concerning which I was so full in the letter before mentioned, that it will be needless to enlarge on that head.

I did, in my last two letters, acquaint you that there was a very ingenious Minister in that Colony, who showed great inclination to come over to the Church, and I was of opinion he would be well worth the recovery. I also told you that his affection for the Church had created him many enemies; and that he has undergone a sort of persecution on that account; but now his enemies have done their worst to him, having turned him out of his living, as Mr. Evans can more fully inform you—he having seen and discoursed with him—that, as I really believe, it will conduce very much to the service of the Church, and also, in justice to the poor gentleman, who has a large family of small children, who must come to ruin and misery, and become a sacrifice to the cause of the Church, which would be a great dishonour, should he not be relieved by us. I did, therefore, make bold to assure him of the Society's favours; and that upon his going to England, and making a solemn declaration, that he will receive orders from the Bishop of London, so soon as he can with conveniency do it; that to enable him to maintain his family during his absence, I would pass my word that he should be entitled to the usual Missionary allowance of £50 a year, from the time of his going off; and that in order thereunto I would give him my best recommendations to the Society. So it is my humble request they would be pleased to allow it if he comes; and in case they do not think it proper to settle a salary upon him before such time as he is actually in orders, that it may be considered him under some other name; because my promise to him is such; and I am not under the least doubt but he will merit it by his service to the Church.

This sudden turn, concerning Mr. Reed, has put upon me new thoughts, which are, to have Mr. Muirson removed from this parish, and that his mission be for Connecticut Colony in general, the place of his residence being at Stratford, or at such town as he shall judge to be most for the service of the Church. This will, in my opinion, not only be the most effectual way for carrying on that great work; but the Society will be put to no difficulty in getting a proper person, in which, if the least mistake should happen as to the qualifications of a Minister, the whole Mission would be endangered by it; and as experience hath fully satisfied us how fitting Mr. Muirson is for that undertaking, by what he hath already done, I am humbly of opinion that for that reason it would not be proper to put that matter to a new risk; and, in the next place, it will be of absolute necessity not only to have a very good man in this place, being on the frontiers of that government, but also one who will be zealously assisting to Mr. Muirson, in which none will be more proper than Mr. Reed. And in case there is a removal, according to the advice given herewith, it is my desire it may be so; and then as to Mr. Muirson, if he goes on that mission, he cannot have less allowed him than 100 pounds sterling a year; because, at the first setting out, nothing must be expected from them, nor, indeed, any offers made toward it; and as his Mission will be four times as large as any other, so he must consequently be in a perpetual motion, which will be chargeable and troublesome. I have not had much talk with him about it, but I doubt not in the least, if my Lord of London and the Society directs his removal, I can persuade him to be easy under it.

I have, since writing my other letters, taken some pains to inquire concerning the character and behaviour of the bearer, Mr. Evans, and, upon the whole, find him to be an extraordinary good man, and one that hath done very great service to the Church, not only in Philadelphia, but in other neighbouring towns, so that I am very much concerned that there should be any misunderstanding betwixt him and any of his parish, as he represents things; and being a very honest, good man, I can't help giving credit to it. The Church and he have had hard usage offered them, though I am past a doubt that upon his making out those things to my Lord of London he will find means to settle and complete their differences, and will return him to his parish; and, so far as it may be proper for the Society to concern themselves in that matter, I could wish they would give their assistance therein, because, whilst they are in that broken condition, the Church can't but receive many wounds by it. I can't think of any thing further of moment at this time. So remain, sir,

Your obed't servt.,

CALEB HEATHCOTE.

NEW-YORK, *April* 14, 1707.

[*Mr. Muirson to the Secretary. Extract.*]

Honor'd Sir,

I entreat your acceptance of my most humble and hearty thanks for the kind and Christian advice you were pleased to tender me in relation to Connecticut. Such measures as you proposed I have all along observed, and I am sure no man in that Colony can justly accuse me of the contrary. I know that meekness and moderation is most agreeable to the mind of our blessed Saviour, Christ, who himself was meek and lowly, and would have all his followers to learn that lesson of him. It was a method by which Christianity was at first propagated, and it is still the best policy to persuade mankind to receive instruction. Gentleness and sweetness of temper is the readiest way to engage the affections of the people; and charity to those who differ from us in opinion is the most likely to convince them that our labours are intended for the welfare of their souls; whereas passionate and rash methods of proceeding will fill their minds with prejudices against both our persons and our principles, and utterly indispose them against all the means we can make use of to reclaim them from their errors. I have duly considered all these things, and have carried myself civilly and kindly to the Independent party, but they have ungratefully resented my love; yet I will further consider the obligations that my holy religion lays upon me, to forgive injuries and wrongs, and to return good for their evil. Thus I hope, by God's assistance, I shall behave myself, and avoid the doing any thing that may bring blame upon that godly Society, whose Missionary I am, or hinder the progress of that glorious work they have undertaken; and ever since I have been invited into that Colony I have been so far from endeavouring to entrench upon the toleration which Her Majesty has declared she will preserve, that, on the contrary, I desired only a liberty of conscience might be allowed to the members of the National Church of England; which, notwithstanding, they seemed unwilling to grant, and left no means untried, both foul and fair, to prevent the settling the Church among them; for one of their Justices came to my lodging and forewarned me, at my peril, from preaching, telling me that I did an illegal thing in bringing in new ways among them; the people were likewise threatened with prison, and a forfeiture of £5 for coming to hear me.

It will require more time than you will willingly bestow on these lines to express how rigidly and severely they treat our people, by taking their estates by distress, when they do not willingly pay to support their Ministers. And though every Churchman in that Colony pays his rate for the building and repairing their meeting-houses, yet they are so maliciously set against us, that they deny us the use of them, though on week days. They tell our people that they will not suffer the house of God to be defiled with idolatrous worship and superstitious ceremonies. They are so bold that they spare not openly to speak reproachfully, and with great contempt, of our Church. They say the sign of the cross is the mark of the beast and the sign of the devil, and that those who receive it are given to the devil. And when our people complain to their magistrates of the persons who thus speak, they will not so much as sign a warrant to apprehend them, nor reprove them for their offence. This is quite a different character to what, perhaps, you have heard of that people. That they are ignorant, I can easily grant; for if they had either much knowledge or goodness they would not act and say as they do; but that they are hot-heady, I have too just reason to believe; and as to their meaning, I leave that to be interpreted by their unchristian proceedings with us. Whoever informed you so, I may freely say, that he was not so well acquainted with the constitution of that people as I am, who gave you the contrary information. I beg that you would believe that this account (though seeming harsh and severe, yet no more than is true) does not proceed from want of charity, either towards their souls or bodies, but purely for the good of both. And to give you better information concerning the state of that people, that proper remedies may be taken for curing the evils that are among them, and that our Churchmen in that Colony may not be oppressed and insulted over by them, but that they may obtain a liberty of conscience, and call a Minister of their own Communion, and that they may be freed from paying to their Ministers, and may be enabled to obtain one of their own. This is all these good men desire.

Honored sir, your most assured friend
And very humble servant,
GEO. MUIRSON.

RYE, *9th January*, 1707–8.

We have already printed a joint letter from the clergy of the Northern and Middle Colonies, addressed to the Lord Bishop of London as their "most worthy *Diocesan*." The document we shall give as coming next in sequence of time, is an address to the same prelate, from the Churchmen in the Colony of Connecticut, reciting their grievances and seeking redress. As we shall have to present, from time to time, many similar documents, and as there will be frequent allusions in our pages to this claim of ecclesiastical allegiance, as due from the American Colonial Church to the Bishop of London, it may be well, ere we proceed, to give in brief some explanation of this close connection of our fathers with the See of London.

The earliest traces of this superintendence of the Bishop of London over the Colonial Church we have been able to find, is the application of the Virginia Council, early in the seventeenth century, to Bishop King, whose interest in the work of colonizing and Christianizing America was already well known, for assistance in providing "pious, learned and powerful Ministers" for that Colony. The choice of the good Bishop as a member of the Council followed; and, as Anderson, in his "Colonial Church," (I. 261,) expresses it, "so far, one channel of direct authoritative communication was established between himself and the clergymen whom he nominated, and over whom he was to exercise, as far as it was practicable, Episcopal control." From this kind interest in the new settlement, and the zealous efforts to which it gave birth, seems naturally to have grown up the connection of the Colonial Church with the Diocese of London. At the close of this century, the Governor and Assembly of Maryland petitioned the King and Queen for the transfer of the "Judicial Office of Commissary" from the Governors of Colonies, in whom it had at first been vested, to the Bishop of London; and from this time the Bishop either took out a commission from the King for this purpose, and delegated the commissarial authority to a suitable clergyman in the Colonies, or, as was the case with Bishop Sherlock, declined to take this course, from the conviction that he could not do justice to the American Church, and consequently ought not to undertake the nominal oversight of it. Whichever was the case, the American clergy learend from the first to look to Fulham as the seat of their ecclesiastical allegiance, and commissaries, acting under the authority of the Bishop of London for the greater part of a century, exercised their delegated power over their brethren in the Colonies, and the successive Bishops at home sought in every way to promote the interests of the infant American Church.

It was this bond of union with the See of London, on the part of the scattered Churches of America, that was broken at the Revolution; and the broken links of the chain were of course never re-united; but, by the adoption of the ecclesiastical constitution of 1789, the Church at large was organized by the federation of the separate and independent Churches of the various States, in one Protestant Episcopal Church in the United States, thus making a *union* among themselves. The *unity* of faith between the Church of England and the American Episcopal Church, as contra-distinguished from the *union* of the Churches, was not affected by the Revolution.

With this parenthetical explanation, we proceed to give the address, to the Lord Bishop of London, from the Connecticut Churchmen.—[Editors.]

[*Address to the Lord Bishop of London from Connecticut Colony.*]

RIGHT REV. FATHER IN GOD:

May it please your Lordship,

We, your Lordship's humble petitioners, living in Stratford Town, in the Colony of Connecticut, do, with all submission, crave leave to represent before your Lordship our present condition, which briefly is as followeth: We are members of the National Church of England, but having no minister of our own communion in this colony, have sent, some time ago, unto the Rev. George Muirson, who, in compliance with our request, hath been twice amongst us, and administered the holy sacrament of Baptism and the Lord's Supper to us. We praise God for his goodness in giving us an opportunity, at last, of receiving his holy ordinances in the way which, of all others, we believe to be most pure and agreeable to the Holy Scriptures. There are many in this colony who are well-disposed to our Church, but being under the same circumstances with ourselves, are not capable of maintaining a minister of our Church, by reason of some laws which compel us to pay our money to the support of Dissenters, and empower them, as sometimes they do, to take our goods by distress. They have another law, by virtue of which they hinder many persons from coming to hear Mr. Muirson preach; they threaten us with imprisonment and severe usage, and though we have proceeded regularly in asking their magistrates' leave before we did meet together to worship God, yet they carried it so far as to forewarn Mr. Muirson from preaching in their Charter Government; and told him that he did illegal things; but what relates to all the particulars contained in these laws we shall not at present offer your Lordship any trouble in mentioning, but refer ourselves to Mr. Muirson to inform your Lordship by letter, and also to the Rev. Mr. Evans, Minister of Philadelphia, who hath been pleased to give us a visit, and, being bound for England, we present to your Lordship, by him, one of the law books of this colony. He can acquaint your Lordship what laws they make use of against the Church, and what hardships and grievances we labour under because of them.

Now we humbly request that your Lordship would be pleased of your zeal, which always moves your Lordship to extend a fatherly care to the distressed members of the Church, to take this our case into your serious consideration; and because by reason of the said laws we are not able to support a minister, we further pray your Lordship may be pleased to send one over with a missionary allowance from the Honourable Corporation, invested with full power, so as that he may preach and we hear the blessed Gospel of Jesus Christ, without molestation and terror. We live in the midst of the rigidest Presbyterians and Independents, and we doubt not but your Lordship will be pleased to send us one exemplary in his conversation, fluent in preaching, and able in disputation, that he may silence the cavils of our enemies. The Hon. Colonel Heathcote hath been pleased to come along with Mr. Muirson; his presence has had no small influence upon the people; we have prayed him to add to all the rest one favour more, that is, to present to your Lordship our case, which we, hoping he will do, shall not offer you any further trouble. We humbly beg your Lordship's fatherly benediction and prayers, that our infant Church may be daily enlarged for God's glory and men's good; and that your Lordship, for its further prosperity and happiness, may long preside over the same, shall be the constant prayers of,

My Lord, your Lordship's most obedient sons
and humble servants,

Stratford, April 1st, 1707.

Richard Blacklath,	Isaac Snell,
Daniel Shelton,	Wm. Rawlinson,
Jonah Pitman,	John Peat,
Saml. Gaskill,	Samuel Hawley,
Will. Smith,	John Skidmore,
Timothy Titharton,	Archibald Dunlap,
Thomas Edwards,	Isaac Beint,
Daniel Bennett,	Rich'd Blacklath, Jr.,
Tho. Brooks,	Isaac Stiles,

Samuel Henery,

(in behalf of the rest.)

[*Col. Heathcote to the Secretary.*]

Stratford, 1 *January*, 1707-8.

Worthy Sir,

I have given you the trouble of so many letters by this Fleet that I am ashamed you should hear further from me; however, I shall depend upon your good and generous temper, and the cause I am upon, to plead my pardon; the occasion of this is, Mr. Muirson and I, being at this place, where the people's zeal hath carried them so far that they are resolved of building themselves a Church, with which be pleased to acquaint the Society;—they intend to build and furnish it very regularly, and are in hopes to have it fit to preach in before next September. I intreat the favour of your care concerning the enclosed, that to his Grace is to give him the best account of the state of this colony I can; in which I do not only beg the delivery with your own hands, but that you would be pleased to speak your thoughts of me to him, and recommend me to his favours. As to our proceeding in this place, I desire the Society would believe that every part is managed with all the temper and moderation they can desire, and they may be assured it shall never be otherwise where I am concerned; for I abhor heat and violence on any account whatsoever, but especially in matters of religion, and Mr. Muirson is very much of my opinion; and not only that, but it would be the greatest breach upon prudence and discretion to act otherwise, for we are here in an enemy's country, and, by the laws, they pretend to govern themselves. Independency and Presbytery are the established Churches, and the Church of England the only dissenters, and indeed the only people they unwillingliest would admit to have liberty of conscience amongst them;—that all the ground we can propose to gain amongst them must be by soft and gentle means, for should the friends of the Church do otherwise, the whole country would soon be in a flame; for the ignorant, blind people believe already that, by virtue of their charter, Independency and Presbytery are as firmly established here, as the Church is in England. I am sorry that anybody should be so unjust in giving the Society an account of the people of this colony, as that they are a well-meaning and not heady people, nothing being more true than the contrary, concerning which I will be more full and particular in my next. In the mean time, I beg leave to assure you that I am, unalterably,

Worthy Sir, yours, &c.,

CALEB HEATHCOTE.

[*Rev. Mr. Talbot to Mr. Keith.*]

Westchester, 14*th Feb'y*, 1707–8.

Reverend and Dear Sir,

I came to this Province before Christmas, but the winter set in so hard that I could go no further than New-York; so I came back again and preached about in several places, and dispersed such books as I had in this and the next colony, Connecticut;—*Mr. Leslie's Five Discourses, The Poor Man's Help and Young Man's Guide*, by Mr. Burket. The Independents say, if they don't get some books soon to answer them, they will convert the colony. Mr. Muirson is the first that read the Common Prayer in that place, in Stratford; when he set up first, the Honourable Col. Heathcote came along with him, or else I believe their justices would have put him in prison. Gov. Winthrop is dead, and was buried at Boston when I was there, and they of Connecticut have chosen Mr. Salstonstall, Preacher at New-London, to be their Governor. He called his council lately of Milford, and showed them his letter that he had written home to answer the Quakers' complaint, and also to get power to hinder the progress of the Church in the Province; but I hope we shall have as much toleration as the Quakers have obtained there, which is all that we expect or desire. Mr. Muirson deserves a double salary for the great pains and prudence he has shown in that matter.

The people of several towns, by the way, as Norwalk and Fairfield, are ready to break open their meeting doors and let him in, if he would suffer it;—they have taken measures at Stratford to build a Church, which never was seen in that country before. I pray God send them an able minister of the New Testament, for they have been long enough under the old dispensation. I wish their case were well known and considered at home, for I'm sure that no man that has any ears or bowels of compassion can resist their importunity. I saw Mr. Bradford at New-York; he tells me mass is set up and read publicly in Philadelphia, and several people are turned to it, amongst which Lionel Brittain, the Church-warden, is one, and his son another. I thought that Popery would come in amongst Friends, the Quakers, as soon as any way. An Anabaptist meeting it seems is set up at Burlington, and another Independent is come to Elizabeth Town. So that for lack of a good Governor we lose our time and the Society their money, and the last state of America will be worse than the first, if the rest of the missionaries go away before more come. I suppose you have heard of Mr. Brook and Mr. Moore, two of the best hands that were there; they are gone, and upon what account? purely for want of a Bishop to direct and protect them. I pray God help us, for we have nobody to apply to, and nobody cares for our souls.

Your loving friend and servant,

JOHN TALBOT.

P. S.—Poor Mr. Honyman is much disturbed at Rhode Island by Mr. Bridge, who says he has a letter from my Lord of London to take his place; if so, he will ruin two Churches at once. Pray help your countryman what you can, for he is worthy.

[*Mr. Evans' Memorial relating to Connecticut Colony.*]

To the Most Honorable Society for the Propagation of the Gospel in Foreign Parts.

I being desired, by those honourable members of the committee of last Monday, to lay before you what I know relating to the Church in Connecticut Colony, and what disposition the people are in to receive it, as also what may probably tend to its advancement there, do humbly beg leave to inform you—

That, immediately before my parting from America, I accompanied Mr. Muirson to Stratford, a town in that colony, where we preached; had a considerable number of hearers, and administered the holy Sacraments of Baptism and the Lord's Supper to many pious persons.

That we found a considerable number of people in a ready disposition to be received into the Church, they being flexible to our invitations, and only wanting occasions of instruction.

That Mr. Muirson seems to be the most proper person to be employed in their service, he having done them so many good offices, and they deservedly having a great esteem of his piety and virtue.

That it would undoubtedly tend to the honour and increase of the Church, in those American parts, if the laws compelling Church of England members to maintain dissenting ministers were repealed, and especially that called the Ecclesiastical Law, in that colony.

That Mr. Read, a dissenting minister in the said Stratford, who is willing to receive holy orders in the Church of England, and who has suffered extremely, by his countrymen, for his inclinations to the Church, not only seems to deserve your compassion, but encouragement, if he can be prevailed on to take orders in England, and receive a Mission from the Venerable Society.

EVAN EVANS.

June 18, 1708.

[*An Account of the Sufferings of the Members of the Church of England at Stratford.*]

A true narrative of the late persecution, which hath been lately cruelly acted by the authority of the Colony of Connecticut in New England, upon and against the members of the Church of England, being professors of the same faith, and Communicants of the same Church of England, as by law established; the said government of Connecticut being, at present, in the hands of Independents, (viz.:)

Firstly.—Whereas, there hath been, for twenty or thirty years past, a considerable number of Freeholders, inhabitants of the town of Stratford, professors of the faith of the Church of England, that are desirous to worship God in the way of their forefathers, but have hitherto been hindered from enjoying the holy ordinances of Jesus Christ, until the year 1705; by which means our children and many others, grown persons, have remained without the administration of the holy ordinance of Baptism, (there being at this day in the town of Newhaven to the number of near 900 unbaptized persons,) and so throughout the government, proportionably.

Secondly.—The above said town of Stratford, in the fore mentioned year 1705, being destitute of a minister, and the professors of the said Church of England having hitherto lived peaceably and quietly, paying all rates and taxes proportionably with our neighbours, considering the deplorable state we were like to be in with our posterity, the professors of the Church of England made their application to the Rev. Mr. Vezie [Vesey], Minister of Trinity Church in New-York, the 14th of September aforesaid, to come and preach to us, and also to administer the holy ordinance of baptism; but by reason of the distance of places, the Rev. Mr. Vesey interceded with the Rev. Mr. Muirson, Minister of the Church of England at Rye, being considerable nearer. To which Mr. Muirson readily complied, and accordingly, on the 2d Sept., 1706, came to Stratford, accompanied by the Honourable Col. Caleb Heathcote, a member of the Honourable Society for the Propagation of the Gospel in these Foreign Parts; and then, in order for the carrying on the worship of God decently, the professors of the Church of England made their application to the authorities, viz.: Mr. Joseph Curtice, one of the Council, and Mr. James Judson, a justice of the peace, and also to the Selectmen of the town of Stratford, to allow liberty for the use of the publick meeting-house of said town, either before, after, or between their exercise, alledging that they were fellow-builders with them, and had paid their full proportion towards the same; yet, notwithstanding all these arguments, could not at all prevail; yet, blessed be God, though not so convenient as we desired, notwithstanding we met with such difficulties, the Rev. Mr. Muirson, finding in Stratford so great a Congregation, and such a great number to be baptized, that, at the request of those who first sought after him, he gave encouragement for a future support, and a promise of a second visit upon the same account.

Thirdly.—As yet the Independents kept themselves veiled, and did not openly appear until such time as the Rev. Mr. Muirson, before his second coming, sent to the professors of the Church of England to prepare themselves, for he intended to administer the holy Sacrament of the Supper of our Lord Jesus:—this being known, the Independents immediately began to bestir themselves, and soon after the Rev. Mr. Muirson, in company with the Honourable Col. Heathcote, arrived a second time at Stratford, and on Saturday, in the evening, came to the house where the said Mr. Muirson lodged, (where were assembled several of the communicants,) the abovesaid Mr. Joseph Curtice and said James Judson, Justice, and read of a paper containing a whole sheet of paper writ on both sides, in which was contained several threats, that if we should proceed to worship God or administer the Sacrament, otherwise than what was agreeable to the law of this colony, that then they would proceed against them by fine or imprisonment, as their law directed; and did forbid them to worship God in any such way they well knew was the worship of the Church of England: upon which, the honourable Col. Heathcote and the Rev. Mr. Muirson demanded, of the said Curtice and said Judson, a copy of said paper, which they refused; and moreover, Mr. Joseph Curtice abovesaid, the day following, being the Lord's day, stood in the highway himself, and employed several others, to forbid any person to go to the assembly of the Church of England, and threatened them with a fine of five pounds, as the law directed; nevertheless, the people were not wholly discouraged, by reason that the Rev. Mr. Muirson, being encouraged by the earnest desire of his auditory, did promise to assist them as often as he possibly could.

Fourthly.—The Rev. Mr. Muirson, at the request of the communicants of the Church of England in Stratford, took advice of the gentlemen of the Honourable Society, and also the Rev. ministers of the Church of England to the west, and some time after having taken their advice, in company with Col. Heathcote, came to Stratford, and advised us to embody ourselves into a Society, which accordingly we did, and made choice of Churchwardens and Vestrymen, which occasioned the Independents to be more enraged against us.

Fifthly.—Not long after the Rev. Mr. Evans, minister of the Church of England at Philadelphia, being bound for England, came in company with the Rev. Mr. Muirson to Stratford, to visit the Church, and see what state we were in; the Church, understanding that Mr. Evans was bound for England, did request of him that he would be so kind to us, as to take care of, and present a petition of ours, to the Rt. Rev. Father in God, the Bishop of London: and also to the Honourable Society for the Propagation of the Gospel in Foreign Parts, that they would be pleased to take pity on us, and consider our sad condition, and the necessity we stand in of an able minister of the Gospel; and, if it might stand with their honour's pleasure, that the Rev. Mr. Muirson might be our minister, which we understand was granted to us, for which favour we, as in duty bound, shall ever pray for their honour's weal and prosperity.

Sixthly.—Before we had any return from England, it pleased Almighty God, in his providence, to bereave us of the Rev. Mr. Muirson, by taking of him to himself, by reason whereof we remain as sheep without a shepherd, notwithstanding the great kindness we have received from the Rev. ministers to the west of us, viz., the Rev. Mr. Talbot, the Rev. Mr. Sharpe, who was near a month amongst us, and took much pains, and baptized many, (amongst whom was an aged man, said to be the first man-child born in the colony of Connecticut,) and the Rev. Mr. Bridge, who have administered the holy Sacraments and ordinance of Jesus Christ, to our great comfort and consolation. Nevertheless, by reason of their great distance from us, we remain as sheep having no shepherd, are exposed the more, as a prey to our persecutors, the Independents, who watch all opportunities to destroy the Church, both root and branch.

Seventhly.—But as yet we received no other persecution but that of the tongue, until the 12th day of December, 1709. Some of their officers, namely, Edmund Lewis, Jonathan Curtice, and Francis Griffith, having a warrant from the authority, viz., Joseph Curtice and James Judson, abovesaid, to levy by distress of estate, or imprisonment of the bodies of such person or persons as should refuse to pay to them such sums of money as were by them demanded, they no sooner having power but put it vigorously in execution; and on the 12th of December, 1709, about midnight, did apprehend and seize the bodies of Timothy Titharton, one of our Churchwardens, and John Marcy, one of the Vestrymen, and forced them to travel, under very bad circumstances, in the winter season and at that unreasonable time of night, to the common gaol, where felons are confined, being eight miles distant, not allowing them so much as fire or candle-light for their comfort, and there continued them until they paid such sums as by the gaoler was demanded, which was on the 15th day of the same month.

Eighthly.—Notwithstanding all this, they still persisted with rigor to continue their persecution, and seized the body of Daniel Shelton, at his habitation or farm, being about eight miles distant from the town, and hurrying of him away toward the town in order to carry him to the county gaol; passing by a house, he requested of them that he might go in and warm him, and take some refreshment, which was granted; but they being in a hurry bid him come along, but he desiring a little longer time, they barbarously laid violent hands on his person, and flung his body across a horse's back, and called for ropes to tie him on the horse; to the truth of which several persons can give their testimony, and are ready when thereunto called; and, having brought him to the town, they immediately seized the bodies of William Rawlinson and Archibald Dunlap, and carried them, all three, to the county gaol, it being the 16th day of January, 1709, and there confined them until such time as they disbursed such sums of money as the gaoler demanded of them, which money was left in the hands of the Lieut. Governor, Nathaniel Gould, Esq., he promising them that the next general court should hear and determine the matter, and that the money left in his hands should be disposed of as the court should order, and they were at present released, being the 17th day of the same instant.

Ninthly.—Several others of the Church had their estates distressed on the same account, and rended from them, particularly William Jeanes, having money due to him in the hands of the town treasurer, the above Edmund Lewis, distressed of his estate that which was in said treasurer's hands on the same account, for the maintaining the Dissenting minister the year 1709, and left no copy of his so doing; and also the treasurer detains all the rest that remains in his hands, telling him that he will keep it for his rate, which rate is chiefly for the purchase of a house for their Dissenting minister, which house and land cost £180: and so are our estates rended from us. Notwithstanding this, the said Wm. Jeanes did, for himself in person, go to a town meeting convened in Stratford, (being empowered by the Society of the Church of England,) when they were ordering a rate to raise money to pay for the said house and land, and did, publickly, in behalf of himself and Society, declare and protest against any such proceedings, and tendered money to the town recorder to enter said protest, but he refused so to do.

Tenthly.—When the general court of said Colony of Connecticut was assembled at Hartford, in May, 1710, the Society of the Church of England empowered William Jeanes, their lawful attorney, to address said general court for a determination and issue of what should be done with said money committed to the abovesaid Lieutenant-Governor, and also to see if we should, for the future, enjoy peace amongst them: our said attorney, in order thereunto, tendered an address to said court, dated May 20th, 1710, but could obtain no positive answer, but was detained there by dilatory answers, until the 26th day of the said instant, (May,) when one of the members of the lower house brought to the said Jeanes the address and power of attorney, and told him the thing had been often moved, but they see cause to give no answer, and so we find no relief for the poor distressed Church, nor the members thereof.

Eleventhly.—The poor Church at Stratford, being left in a deplorable condition, destitute and without hope of any relief in this colony under this government, several of our Society have already, of necessity, fled their persecution finally, being such an additional one as was seldom heard of; for finding that some of our Society, being tradesmen and handicraft, and such as had dependence upon working at their trades for other people, they combined together not to set them to work, saying that by that means they should weaken the interests of the Church; by which subtle stratagem of Satan's to persecute the Church of Christ, we are likely to be brought low, for some are already gone, and others looking out where to shelter themselves from their cruelty, and must inevitably fall, if God, of his infinite mercy, do not raise up some goodly, compassionate friends for us: and we, the subscribers, do assert the truth of what is here written.

TIMOTHY TITHARTON, } *Church*	RICHARD BLACKLATH,
WILLIAM SMITH, } *Wardens.*	DANIEL SHELTON,
WILLIAM RAWLINSON,	ARCHIBALD DUNLAP,
WILLIAM JEANES,	JAS. HUMPHREYS,
JOHN JOHNSON,	JAMES CLARKE.

[*Address from Stratford for a Minister.*]

To the Right Rev. Father in God, the Lord Bishop of London, and to the Honourable Society for the Propagating the Gospel in Foreign Parts:

WE, the Churchwardens and Vestry of Stratford, in the Colony of Connecticut, in New-England, have long lain under very great grievances from the Independents of this colony, as may be seen in the narrative of our case, which comes with this our address; but above all, from the want of a minister to furnish us with ghostly advice, and to administer the bread of life to us in our miserable and deplorable loss. It is the less matter that we suffer persecutions and afflictions in this life, if we could but see, with a comfortable prospect, into the other world. What signifies what becomes of the body, if our precious souls, for which Christ vouchsafed to die, be saved? And it is not without great affliction that we reflect on the bad success so many addresses for a minister have met with. We hope God has not altogether forsaken us; neither the patrons of our holy religion at home quite laid us aside; and therefore we presume, once more, to address your Lordship and the Honourable Society for a minister; and, were he to be a travelling missionary through the colony, we doubt not but in a short time the best of churches in the world would flourish even in this government, where they are strangers to the happy constitution.

We leave the further representation of our case to be made by the faithful and worthy labourer in God's vineyard, the Rev. Mr. John Talbot, who has visited us sometimes, and often by letters given us great comfort and courage, who is going home in the service of the Church, and is always ready to venture his life for it. The Lord reward him for his labour of love which he hath showed to all the Churches; and, indeed, had it not been for the visits we have received from the clergy to the west, and the encouragement we had from the Honourable Colonel Heathcote, who hath ever been a true friend to us and the Church, we should not have been able to get through the trouble and grievances we have met with, and are yet likely to meet with, if not relieved. We pray God preserve your Lordship, and grant that the many souls that have been relieved by the charity of your Lordship and the Honourable Society, may be your and their crown of rejoicing in the world to come. We beg your Lordship's prayers, and are your Lordship's most dutiful and obedient humble servants,

Timothy Titharton, } *Church*
William Smith, } *Wardens.*
Richard Blacklath,
William Jeanes,
John Johnson,
William Rawlinson,
Archibald Dunlap,
Edward Burrough,
James Humphreys,
James Clarke,
Daniel Shelton.

[*Address to the Queen from Stratford.*]

To the Queen's Most Excellent Majesty, the humble address of some members of the Church of England, residing at Stratford, in Connecticut, in the Province of New-England:

May it please your Majesty,

We have, for a long time, been oppressed and persecuted by the government of this colony; some of our estates taken from us, some imprisoned for refusing to pay money to buy a house and farm for their minister, and to pay a yearly stipend to him, and all of us menaced and threatened with several punishments if we presume to meet together to have the Church of England service performed to us, when it pleased God to order a minister of the said Church our way; and, besides, all do lie under their daily reproaches, scoffing and mockings, without the advantage of a minister to give us comfortable and ghostly advice, and to administer the bread of life to us.

These have been our grievances for many years, and we should not have been able to bear them, had we not received some visits from the Clergy of the west, and especially several from the Honourable Col. Heathcote, who hath ever been a true friend both to us and the Church, and has always encouraged us not to swerve from our holy profession, notwithstanding the difficulty and trials we met with, and the bad success we had in our frequent addresses for a minister to the Right Rev. Father in God, the Lord Bishop of London, and the Honourable Society for the Propagating the Gospel in Foreign Parts. And indeed, the want of a minister is the greatest of our afflictions, which, with the rest of our grievances, we presume humbly to lay before your Majesty, and pray your Majesty to use some means for our relief, and that your Majesty may long and happily live to reign over us; and when you lay aside this earthly crown, that you may receive a crown of glory, is the continual and fervent prayer of, may it please your Majesty, your Majesty's most loyal and faithful and obedient subjects and servants,

TIMOTHY TITHARTON,	} *Church*	WILLIAM RAWLINSON,
WILLIAM SMITH,	} *Wardens.*	WILLIAM JEANES,
JOHN JOHNSON,		DANIEL SHELTON,
ARCHIBALD DUNLAP,		EDWARD BURROUGH,
JAMES HUMPHREYS,		JAMES CLARKE,

RICHARD BLACKLATH.

[*Mr. Philips to the Secretary.*]

Philadelphia, Sept. 9th, 1713.

Sir,

It is with more than ordinary concern I am forced to give you this trouble to desire the favour of you to acquaint the Honourable Society with my reasons for leaving Stratford, in

Connecticut Colony, in New-England. During my abode there, which was till the 19th day of August last, I used my utmost endeavours to answer the end of my mission, as appears by a certificate signed by the Churchwardens and Vestrymen of that place. I made it my business to ride from place to place, to preach to and instruct those that showed the least inclination to become members of our Church, in the extremity of heat and cold, which has indeed very much impaired my health; but the dissenting party being very numerous, and being likewise encouraged by the Governor there, who is a rigid Independent, and finding the greatest part of those who pretended to be of the Churchway, were only so to screen themselves from the taxes imposed on them by Dissenters, I must beg leave to inform the Venerable Society that there is little success, and less encouragement, to be expected from the labours of the most painful divine which shall be sent to that place, whilst the government remains in the hands it's in, than almost any other part of America. The consideration of which, together with my unwillingness to put the Honourable Society to so great an expense to very little purpose, made me look out for some other place, where, in all probability, I might be capable of doing much more service; which, I hope, will in some measure help to plead my excuse with that venerable body that I did not let 'em know of my removal before I did remove; but the shortness of the time and the necessity of the present circumstances of the Church, which laid Mr. Evans under necessity to hasten home, could not possibly admit of it; otherwise, I should not have presumed to have taken any one step without first consulting that learned body, for which I have the greatest esteem imaginable; besides, I thought that no missionary now abroad could be so well spared from their cure, as myself. Therefore, when I heard of Mr. Evans' design of visiting Great Britain, I made my application to him, and by the persuasion of my friends and of the request of his Churchwardens and Vestrymen, as appears by the copy of their minutes, I, with much difficulty, prevailed upon him to accept of me for his curate during his absence; in doing which (though I have been guilty of a breach of my instructions) I beg that the Honourable Society will please to pardon it. I sent home bills of exchange for £20 sterling, payable to Mr. Nathaniel Simpson, or his order, bearing date May 2d, 1713; and since that, I have sent other bills of exchange, payable to the Rev. Mr. Gardiner, for £20 sterling, which is all that remains due to me from the Honourable Society. Pray, sir, please to order that it may be paid, and you will much oblige,

Sir, your very humble servant,
FRANCIS PHILIPS.

P. S. Had we a Bishop here to apply to in that and other exigencies that will happen when a Church begins to increase, there would be no need of troubling the Society with things of this nature; but where this guide is wanting, it can't possibly be but that some things that are done may be looked upon as irregular; but I humbly beg the Society's acceptance of my most grateful acknowledgments of their undeserved favours.

[*Extract of a Letter from Colonel Heathcote to General Nicholson.*]

New-York, April 19th, 1714.

May it please your Excellency,

I happened to be detained in the country out of the post-road, when the postman went last from home, and so was disabled from the keeping my promise in writing to your excellency then, and giving those accounts you desired, or acknowledging your excellency's favour of the 5th past. As to the Church of Stratford, I send your excellency the state thereof as it was transmitted to me by the Churchwardens and Vestry of that place; those poor people have hitherto been very unfortunate, but I hope it won't be always so with them. When I went first amongst them with Mr. Muirson, there seemed to be as fair a prospect of settling the Church as in any part of America, he having, in a very few journies, increased his communion to forty; and had he not unhappily died, or had the Society, upon the first notice of his death, been expeditious in supplying that place with another good, diligent missionary, it had still been recoverable; but they delayed it so long that the enemies of the Church had time to fortify themselves against us, for the effecting whereof the Presbyterians and Independent ministers, both in Connecticut and Boston, were consulted, and, among many other resolves to prevent the Church's growth, determined that one of the best preachers that both colonies could afford should be sought out and sent there; and one Mr. Cutler, who lived then at Boston or Cambridge, was accordingly pitched upon. As to Mr. Philips, the Society made a wrong choice in him; for that missionary being of a temper very contrary to be pleased with such conversation and way of living as Stratford affords, had no sooner seen that place but his whole thoughts were bent and employed how he should get from it, and to be employed either at Mr. Vesey's lecture, or to be settled at Philadelphia, the latter whereof he brought about.

[*Churchwardens and Vestry of Stratford to Colonel Heathcote.*]

Stratford, April 9th, 1714.

Honored Sir,

These are to inform you of the deplorable state of our poor Church, which we labour under by reasons of Mr. Philips leaving of us. Our Church was on a likely way to have flourished, and several persons, the masters of considerable families, were leaving the society of Dissenters, and coming over to us, but, by reason of his desertion, it all failed, and left us a scorn and reproach to the enemies of the Church; and as touching his behaviour whilst among us, the greatest thing we have to charge him with was his not attending his orders and commission; for when he first arrived he stayed weeks at New-York, and came not to Stratford until the 19th day of December, and then was with us but nine Sabbaths, and went again to New-York and stayed five weeks, and then was with us five Sabbaths more, and went again to New-

York and stayed about two weeks, and then stayed two Sabbaths, and then finally left us wholly, as at this day; but before he went the first time to New-York he desired us to sign for him a letter of recommendation to send to the Honourable Society, which we, like innocent sheep, did; he having it ready drawn; himself wrote it. The second time he left us we discoursed whether he designed to leave us, and he said he would never leave us until such time as we should have a supply, and another minister settled amongst us. But having no regard to his promise, he left us, as you are sensible, and carried away with him the books, which we understood since, were sent by the Honourable Society for the use of our Church. He also promised that he would receive what money he could for us to assist in the building of our Church, for which (though long first) we have at last got the timber felled, and do hope to get it raised in three months' time. Nothing else, but with hearty thanks and praises to God for a blessing on your faithful endeavours, and for the settling of the Church amongst us, we rest,

Your most humble servants,

RICHARD BLACKLATH, } *Churchwardens,*
WILLIAM SMITH, } *and others.*

Endorsed by Col. Heathcote: "Copy of this letter was sent to Gen. Nicholson."

[*Mr. Bridge to the Secretary.—Extract.*]

Rye, Oct. 14th, 1714.

Sir,

I am heartily sorry that I have occasion to inform the Honourable Society that the interest of the Church in Stratford seems to be declining; there are there an honest and sober people, truly zealous for the Church; but they live among neighbours who despise and misuse them for their loyalty to the crown and zeal for the Church, and they have met with so many discouragements and disappointments that they are almost wearied out; they are frequently calling on me to assist them, and I go as often as my health and the affairs of my parish will allow me; but they are at such a distance that it is both difficult and expensive to me, and I have not put them to any charge for my coming among them, and shall always be willing to assist them what I can, till a minister be sent to settle with them, if the Honourable Society be pleased to direct me so to do.

I am, sir, &c.,

CHRIS. BRIDGE.

[*The Churchwardens and Vestry of Stratford, in Connecticut, to the Honourable Society.—Extract.*]

Stratford, September 30th, 1718.

To the Honourable Society for Propagating the Gospel in Foreign Plantations:

The humble address of us, the subscribers, members of the Church of England, in Stratford, in the Colony of Connecticut, in New-England, on behalf of ourselves and Society,

HUMBLY SHEWETH:

Hoping your honours will consider that we have been an embodied society these twelve years, and you have so far considered us at first, to send a Commission to the Rev. Mr. Muirson to be our minister, but his deceasing, we remained destitute at least five years; then your honours considered us a second time, and sent us a minister, Mr. Phillips; but he not answering your expectations, nor ours neither, soon left us destitute as before, and much worse; for those who liked not the Church would often flout us and say, we might never expect another minister. So we remained in this deplorable state more than five years, as a scoff and by-word to the enemies of the Church. We have cause to doubt we have been represented to your honours as inconsiderable, few in numbers and not worth minding; and, indeed, as to our outward estate, it may very well be said that we are inconsiderable, it being the interests of our government so to make us; but as to our number, we have had at least a hundred baptized into the Church, and have had at one time thirty-six partakers of the Holy Communion of the Lord's Supper, and have several times assembled in our congregation between two and three-hundred persons; and if encouraged by your honours, may be as flourishing a Church as any country Church in America. We humbly beseech your honours to consider that there is not any government in America but what has our settled Church and ministers, but this of Connecticut.

[*General Nicholson to the Secretary.—Extract.**]

Charles City and Port, [*Charleston*,] *S. C.*, *Jan.* 11*th*, 1722.

Sir,

The affairs of the Reverend the gentlemen of Yale College, in Connecticut Colony, if rightly managed and encouraged, may be of great service to our holy mother, the Church of England, as by law established; and with submission I think that the ministers and people of those parts cannot, with justice or reason, blame the Church of England for taking care and encouraging those Reverend gentlemen who, out of conscience, left their communion. I am in hopes that the three Reverend gentlemen who are gone from New-England will receive Episcopal ordination, and 'tis probable that, according to their encouragement with you, others may follow their example; and it may be a very good way for the So-

---

* General Francis Nicholson, who was, at different times, in high authority in more than one of the colonies, and always very zealous in the cause of the Church, was, when this letter was written, Governor of South Carolina.

ciety, or My Lord Bishop of London, to send missionaries to these parts, the procuring of whom hath been so very difficult and chargeable to the Society.

I herewith send you the copy of a paper which I had when I was in New-England, in the year 1687, given me by the Honourable John Wart Winthrop, grandson to John Winthrop, who was the first governor of Massachusetts Bay, and his father was first governor of Connecticut Colony, having obtained their charter from King Charles the Second soon after the Restoration. Richard Saltonstall was a knight, and the Honourable Gurdon Saltonstall is the present governor. Isaac Johnson, I think, married with my Lady Arabella, daughter to the Earl of Lincoln. Thomas Dudley, I think, was steward to that family, and some time governor of Massachusetts Colony, and father to Joseph Dudley, Esq., deceased, late governor of that province. With submission I think this paper may be made good use of at this juncture, concerning the Reverend gentlemen desiring Episcopal ordination, &c.

I herewith send you the letter I received from Boston concerning the Rev. Mr. Cutler, &c.; and I desire you'll please to wait on my Lord Bishop of London concerning it, and I hope, in God, he will be sent over for the new Church of England in Boston, towards the furnishing of which I design, God willing, to send them something by the next safe opportunity of writing to them, which I am afraid will not be till March; and I am in hope that the Society and the Bishop of London will provide for the Rev. Mr. Brown and Mr. Johnson, either in those parts or here; and if the Society or Bishop of London send them, for the encouragement of those Reverend gentlemen, I desire the Society will please to advance £7 sterling each for paying their passage, and it shall be most thankfully repaid by me. This affair of those gentlemen has made a great noise and bustle in New-England, and I herewith send you some of their public prints.

I herewith send a letter I received from the Narragansett Country, which affair I earnestly recommend to the Society and the Bishop of London; and I intend, God willing, by the first opportunity to send them something. I likewise send you a letter from one Mr. Gabriel Bernon; and the affair he writes about I earnestly recommend to the Society and the Lord Bishop of London, and I design, God willing, to send them something.

I also send you a letter I received from Marblehead, and I hope, in God, that Church will do well, and most earnestly recommend them to the Society; and, if they should want, I shall, God willing, send them something, as likewise the Church of England at Newbury, [Newburyport,] and I hope, in God, they will do very well there.

I most earnestly recommend these affairs to the Society and the Lord Bishop of London; and pray give the humblest of my duty to the Bishop, and my service, &c., to the rest. I am now daily in hopes of having the good fortune of hearing from you, and that all the affairs of the Society prosper in all respects; and for the accomplishment whereof nothing shall be wanting that lies in the power of

Your affectionate friend and humble servant,

FR. NICHOLSON.

I herewith send you a letter which I had formerly from the Rev. Mr. Cutler, and a letter for you from Mr. Commissary Bull.

[*The Churchwardens of Stratford, in Connecticut, to the Secretary.*]

May 29th, 1722.

Sir,

After a long expectation we are supplied from the Honourable Society with a Missionary, for whom we do hereby return our most grateful acknowledgments. As to Mr. Pigot's care over us we are well satisfied that it will be to the advantage of the Church of England, and the edifying of all of us who belong to that Church, as far as can be guessed by his deportment hitherto. We received a letter with him from you, and should be glad, sir, to comply therewith, if our abilities would permit us to do it; for our number indeed is great, but we have no leading men to support us under our difficulties in a country resolved to fleece all of our persuasion as long as their charter continues. We are about to build a Church at our own expense, and should be extremely happy if the Honourable Society would bestow the same allowance on Mr. Pigot as they did on Mr. Philips, especially since he so much more deservedly merits it, and promises so much satisfaction therein. We also render our hearty thanks for those necessary books he has brought among us, and shall always retain in our memories a sincere affection for the auspicious Society who sent them, and therefore beg leave gratefully to subscribe ourselves, in the behalf of the whole Church,

Their, and, sir,

Your obliged humble servants,

JOHN JOHNSON, } *Church*
WILLIAM JEANS, } *Wardens.*

[*Mr. Pigot to the Secretary.*]

Stratford, August 20th, 1722.

Sir,

In my last of the 4th of June, by the hands of Mr. William Gardner, whose receipt I have, I gave you some account of my progress in the ministry here; but I am now more capable of guessing at the aims of the people about me. Since Trinity Sunday, when I first gathered a Church, (though by mistake I mentioned the Sunday following in my former,) I have administered the Communion to thirty persons, and baptized twenty-seven infants, as you may perceive by the enclosed, which is my *notitia parochialis* thereof. The leading people of this colony are generally prejudiced against their mother Church, but yet I have great expectations of a glorious revolution of the ecclesiastics of this country, because the most distinguished gentlemen among them are resolvedly bent to promote her welfare and embrace her baptism and discipline, and, if the leaders fall in, there is no doubt to be made of the people. Those gentlemen who are ordained pastors among the Independents, namely, Mr. Cutler, the President of Yale College, and five more, have held a conference with me, and are determined to declare themselves professors of the Church of England, as soon as they shall understand they will be supported at home; they complain much, both of the necessity of going home for orders, and of their inability for such an undertaking; they also surmise it to be entirely disserviceable to our Church, because, if they should come to England, they must leave their flocks, and thereby give the vigilant enemy an opportunity to seize their cures and supply them with inveterate schismatics; but if a Bishop could be sent us, they could secure their parishes now and hereafter, because the people here are legally qualified to choose their own ministers as often as a vacancy happens, and this would lighten the Honourable Society's expenses to a wonderful degree. I am informed, also, by these, that there are other gentlemen disposed to renounce their separation, not only in this colony, but also in other provinces of North America, and those a body, considerable enough to perfect a general reformation. Sir, the Honourable Society will perceive by this, that many sound reasons are not wanting to inspirit them to procure the mission of a Bishop into these Western parts; for, besides the deficiency of a Governor in the Church, to inspect the regular lives of the clergy, to ordain, confirm, consecrate Churches, and the like, amongst those that already conform; there is, also, a sensible want of this superior order, as a sure bulwark against the many heresies that are already brooding in this part of the world. I shall say no more on that subject till I have your and my Lord of London's sentiments on this affair. I have distributed what books I brought, and have reason to bless God for the good influence they have had on the people. I hope the Honourable Society will be pleased to order me some Common Prayer-Books and Catechisms, than which nothing, (besides a Bishop) can be more advantageous to the successful ministry of, sir, your and the Honourable Society's very humble servant,

George Pigot.

P. S.—I have frequent invitations to come to Providence, in Rhode Island Government, where I am a proprietor, and do humbly crave the patronage of the Honourable Society for that residence, when they are determined to send a missionary thither, whom it may suit as well to come to Stratford.

[*Mr. Pigot to the Secretary.*]

October 3d, 1722.

Sir,—I write this from New-York, where I am soliciting for subscriptions towards the building a Church at Stratford, for the glorious work we have already undertaken, notwithstanding the poverty of the oppressed inhabitants. I have not been idle since my dismission; and as I made quick dispatch on my setting out from home, so I've been diligent in promoting the good of our Church in this country. I shall, before Christmas, according to appointment, preach thrice at Fairfield, which is eight miles distant from my abode—as often at Newtown, which is twenty-two miles from Stratford—thrice, also, at Ripton, at the same distance—in which places I have and shall take care to improve the festivals of our Church to such purposes; and where these do not intervene, on other week-days. On the 4th of the last month, at the desire of the president, I repaired to the Commencement of Yale College, in New-Haven, where, in the face of the whole country, the aforesaid gentleman and six others, hereafter named, declared themselves in this wise, that they could no longer keep out of the communion of the Holy Catholic Church, and that some of them doubted of the validity, and the rest were persuaded of the invalidity, of Presbyterian ordination in opposition to Episcopal. The gentlemen fully persuaded thereof are the five following, viz.: Mr. Cutler, president of Yale College; Mr. Brown, tutor to the same; Mr. Elliot, pastor of Killingsworth; Mr. Johnson, pastor of West Haven, and Mr. Wetmore, pastor of North Haven. The two gentlemen who seemed to doubt are Mr. Hart, pastor of East Guilford, and Mr. Whittlesy, pastor of Wallingford. These seven gave in their declarations in writing, and, at the same time, two more; and these pastors of great note gave their assent, of whom the one, Mr. Buckley, of Colchester, declared Episcopacy to be *jure divino*, and the other, Mr. Whiting, of some remote town, also gave in his opinion for moderate Episcopacy.

This great outset towards a reformation in this deluded country has brought in vast numbers to favour the Church of England. Nay, sir, Newton and Ripton, if not Fairfield, do intend to petition the Honourable Society for Church ministers. The gentlemen above mentioned design, some of them, to go home for orders, and the rest will tarry till a Bishop comes, if ever it should please God to inspire those in authority to promote him. I mention this, sir, that those of the worthy gentlemen I have been writing about, who make application, may not be disappointed at their coming to England; but may, with the Honourable Society's good approbation, be sent back into the colony and parts adjacent at the same time.

Sir, I hope the Honourable Society will consider me, and grant me, according to a former vote, entered into their minutes, the preference of Bristol, if they shall dispose of Providence to another.

I shall now inform you, sir, of what obstructions I meet with in my ministry, and they are several, viz.: that of Lieutenant-Governor Nathan Gould, who is a most inveterate slanderer of our Church—charging her with popery, apostacy and atheism—who makes it his business to hinder the conversion of all whom he can, by threatening them with his authority—and who, as a judge of the courts here, disfranchises men merely for being Churchmen; also, that of living under a *charter* government, in which there is not the least mention of ecclesiastical affairs; so that they have boldly usurped to themselves, and insultingly imposed on the necks of others, the power of taxing and disciplining all persons whatsoever, for the grandeur and support of their self-created ministers; also, that of lying slanders, continually spread against our Mother, as if she were a persecutress, and gaped for the tenth of the country's increase; and, though these deceivers pretend a firm attachment to the illustrious house of Hanover, yet they are frequently oppugning the king's supremacy. Lastly; another great obstruction is the want of Common Prayer-Books and Catechisms. I shall, in a short time, inform my Lord of London of the result of the affairs, after a meeting of a General Assembly some time this month, when the fate of these gentlemen and myself, in relation to the resentment thereof, will be determined.

I remain, Sir,
With all due regard to the Honourable Society,
Their and your very humble servant,
GEORGE PIGOT.

[*Mr. Cutler's Representation.*]

To the Honourable Society for the Propagating the Gospel in Foreign Parts, in Conjunction with the Church in Boston, in whose name, as well as in his own, he appears, is:

1. That the Church now erecting there may have the support and protection of the Honourable Society, there being an apparent and universally allowed necessity of a new Church in that town, the old Church not being capable, in any manner, to accommodate all that are disposed to attend the Communion of the Church of England in that town, and many greatly disadvantaged by their remote situation from it.

2. That the Honourable Society would make yearly additions to the salary their minister may have from them, and particularly to my salary, who am invited by them, and intend their service, if I may receive orders and be disposed there; and to enforce my desires, I humbly offer these things to consideration, respecting the Church and town of Boston and myself.

1. The present slenderness of their number, of whose increase, though there is a great probability, there is no certainty.

2. The many difficulties which now lie upon them in build-

ing an house, &c., are very heavy for them to go through with.

3. The expensive living, which a town of such concourse and note as Boston is, requires.

4. The numerousness of my family.

5. The absolute dependence I have on a support from my services there, my own estate being very inconsiderable, and that also diminished by a free and voluntary resignation of £90, which I made to the College that I left, that I might not give disaffected persons any handle for reflection upon me; but these I propose with submission, and hope God will learn me in every state wherein I am, or may be, therewith to be content.

TIMOTHY CUTLER.

[*Mr. Johnson's Representation.*]

18*th Jan'y*, 1722.

The representation which I hereby desire to make of my case and request to the Honourable Society, is as followeth:

That whereas, I found myself obliged in duty, upon a serious and deliberate examination of the matter, to separate from the people which I had the care of, to join myself to the most pure and primitive Church of England, though I have hereby lost the good will of the greater part of that people, yet there is a very considerable number of the most serious of them that have an earnest desire of my return to them again, at least as near as possible, and who, if I should, would never submit to the administrations of any Dissenting teacher; and on my part, as I have a compassionate concern for that people, so I am earnestly desirous of having them still under my care, and for that reason of being placed as near to them as possible. Stratford (where I am well known) is within ten miles of them, so that if I were there I should be under advantage of doing service (according to my slender ability) among them as at Stratford.

The Rev. Mr. Pigot (who is now missionary at Stratford) is desirous (as his letters testify) of being removed to Providence.

Providence is a place which extremely suffers for want of the means of religion; and the people are so far disposed to the Church of England that they are building a Church, and are able to do considerable to the support of it, and will shortly, in all probability, address the Honourable Society for an interest in its case.

In case they should not, or the Honourable Society should not think fit to grant their request, there is another place, viz., Ripton, within 14 miles of my former people, who are addressing the Honourable Society for its favours, where I would gladly be ordered, (at least for the present,) if their request should be granted.

If this be not practicable, I should be thankful if the Honourable Society would permit me to succeed Mr. Dean, Catechist, at New-York; and finally, if nothing can be done whereby I might be enabled to serve the designs of the Honourable Society in or near my own country, though I must confess it would be with the greatest reluctance that I should leave it, yet such is my affection to the Church of England, and especially to the glorious designs of that venerable body, that I hope I shall be contented, (if it should admit me into its service, which is what I humbly desire,) wheresoever it shall be pleased to send me.

SAMUEL JOHNSON.

[*Letter from Rev. Joseph Webb to Rev. Dr. C. Mather.*]

FAIRFIELD, *October* 2, 1722.

Reverend and Honoured Sir,

The occasion of my now giving you the trouble of these few lines is to me, and I presume to many others, melancholy enough. You have perhaps heard, before now, or will hear before these come to hand, (I suppose,) of the revolt of several persons of figure among us unto the Church of England. There's the Rev. Mr. Cutler, rector of our College, and Mr. Daniel Brown, the tutor thereof. There are also of ordained ministers, pastors of several Churches among us, the Rev. Messieurs following, viz.: John Hart, of East Guilford,

Samuel Whittlesey, of Wallingford, Jared Eliot, of Kennelworth, (Killingworth,) Samuel Johnson, of West Haven, and James Wetmore, of North Haven.

They are, the most of them, reputed men of considerable learning, and all of them of a virtuous and blameless conversation. I apprehend the axe is hereby laid to the root of our civil and sacred enjoyments, and a doleful gap opened for trouble and confusion in our Churches. The Churchmen among us are wonderfully encouraged and lifted up by the appearance of these gentlemen on their side, and how many more will, by their example, be encouraged to go off from us to them, God only knows. It is a very dark day with us; and we need pity, prayers and counsel. And I am humbly of opinion that the Churches and pastors in your colony are concerned, (though something more remotely,) as well as we, in the present threatenings of Divine Providence; and I cannot but hope some measure will be concerted by yourself in this juncture, for the preservation of the good old cause, so signally owned by God and witnessed unto by the practice and suffering of so many eminent ministers and Christians. There is with you the advantage of age, learning, experience, books, &c., and therefore we cannot but earnestly desire your assistance in all that is proper on the sorrowful occasion. As for the gentlemen who have declared themselves in favour of the Church, some of them declared themselves much in doubt about the validity of Presbyterian ordination; others of them have (if I remember rightly) declared their satisfaction as to the invalidity thereof. As to this we value them not so much, as long as Acts xx. 19–23; Phil. i. 1; 1 Pet. v. 1, 2, 3, and other texts, are a part of Holy Scripture; though I should be glad of the help of some good arguments used by those who are skilled in the controversy, and have acted well therein; but if our antagonists should not be able to answer what may be alleged from Scripture, &c., concerning the powers of presbyters to ordain, they will, I conclude, allege that the ordinations among us were not Presbyterian, because several pastors in our colony, in the more ancient days of it, were ordained by laymen, and those pastors so ordained have acted in the latter ordinations among us. This the Churchmen among us improve, and fling every now and then about the leather mitten that was laid on the head of the Rev. Mr. Israel Chauncey, of Stratford, many years since deceased, by one of the brethren acting on his ordination. It is also suggested, that the Rev. Mr. Andrew, of Milford, was ordained by laymen, in part at least. What there is of truth in it, I cannot tell. I heard nothing of this latter instance till within about the compass of a week ago. And as to what is alleged relating to the Rev. Mr. Chauncey, of Stratford, deceased, I heard nothing thereof, (that I remember,) till many years after my ordination. I know the Rev. Messieurs Chauncey and Andrews abovesaid were actors in my ordination; together with the Rev. Mr. Walker, of Woodbury, deceased. What led those eminent men, who first settled the country, to allow laymen to act in such an affair, is not for me to say. But what I would in this case is, how we shall be able to justify ourselves if this article be insisted on by our antagonists. The notion of these ordinations by laymen will, I fear, do us more damage than all the arguments that can be brought for the necessity of Episcopal ordination. Our condition I look upon as very deplorable and sad. Please to communicate the contents of my letter to your venerable and honoured father, and to as many of the ministers of Boston, &c., as you judge meet. And let me (though unworthy) have, as soon as may be, what comfort, light and strength is needful in our sad circumstances, from as many of you as will please to engage in the cause. Thus desiring an interest in your prayers for us, I subscribe,

Reverend and honoured sir,

Your humble servant,

JOSEPH WEBB.

[To the Rev. Mr. Andrew and Mr. Woodbridge and others, our Reverend Fathers and Brethren, present in the library of Yale College, this 13th of September, 1722.]

Reverend Gentlemen,

Having represented to you the difficulties which we labor under, in relation to our continuance out of the visible communion of an Episcopal Church, and a state of seeming opposition thereto, either as private Christians, or as officers, and so being insisted on by some of you (after our repeated declinings of it) that we should sum up our case in writing, we do (though with great reluctance, fearing the consequence of it) submit to and comply with it, and signify to you that some of us doubt the validity, and the rest are more fully persuaded of the invalidity of the Presbyterian ordination, in opposition to the Episcopal; and should be heartily thankful to God and man, if we may receive from them satisfaction herein, and shall be willing to embrace your good councils and instructions in relation to this important affair, as far as God shall direct and dispose us to it.

TIMOTHY CUTLER, JOHN HART, SAMUEL WHITTELSEY,
JARED ELIOT, JAMES WETMORE, SAMUEL JOHNSON,
DANIEL BROWN.

A true copy of the original.
Testify, DANIEL BROWN.

[*Letter from Rev. Joseph Moss to Rev. Dr. C. Mather.*]

[Mr. Moss was the Congregational minister at Derby, Conn.]

Derby, *October* 2*d*, 1722.

Reverend Sir,

I presume, though unacquainted, to humbly ask your advice and help in a matter of great weight and moment, at which we are all amazed and filled with darkness, in our parts of the country, viz.: no less than five ordained ministers (all but one of our association of New-Haven) have declared before the trustees of the College, in the library, where many others also were present, that they were fully persuaded that only an Episcopal ordination was valid, and according to Divine institution; and therefore, inasmuch as their own ordination was by Presbyters only, they esteemed it invalid. Three of them said that, notwithstanding, they should go on to administer Sacraments, &c., as before, for awhile, waiting for further light; but if they could get no better light than now they had, thought that, in time, it would come to that pass with them that they should proceed no further to minister at the altar, without a re-ordination by a Bishop: two of them pretended to be conscience-bound at present to cease all sacred administrations until they had further light or an Episcopal ordination. The aforementioned three are, Mr. John Hart, Mr. Samuel Whittelsey, Mr. James Wetmore; the two abovesaid are, Mr. Jared Eliot, Mr. Samuel Johnson. And after these, both the rector and tutor of our College declared themselves for Episcopacy; and that they scrupled communion in sacred things with any other but the Church of England, because of the invalidity of a Presbyterian ordination. I cannot pretend to have set down the very words in which these gentlemen declared themselves, but to this purpose (though in many more words) they did declare themselves, in the audience of a large assembly of ministers and scholars. Now, reverend and learned Sir, two things I crave your advice and help in: 1st. Your advice on what we shall say to the people over whom these gentlemen were ordained pastors, (the people are uneasy, and come to us neighboring ministers for advice); they would choose to have their ministers rather desist their ministry, and have their pulpits free for others that may be ordained; but the ministers, I perceive, are willing to hold their posts still. What advice shall we give these people in their darkness and distress? 2d. I having not read much upon this controversy, should be very glad to have some books that do nervously handle this point concerning ordination by Presbyters, whether good or not? I have, according to my mean ability, studied the Scriptures upon this point for many years past, and have been, and now am, fully satisfied in my own mind that the truth is on our side, and that there is no difference between a Bishop and a Presbyter, *Jure Divino*. And there is no such superior order of Church officers as the Diocesan Bishops are, by Divine institution. But it is now a time with us that we must put on our armour and fight, or else let the good old cause, for which our fathers came into this land, sink and be deserted. I pray, Sir, that you would furnish me with some such books, as, with most strength of reason and argument, plead our cause, especially in this point, of the validity of Presbyterian ordination, and shall be very much obliged; and if the books that may be sent come as lent, I will safely and seasonably return them; but if they come as sold, (which I rather choose,) I will quickly send the money for them. There is at Boston, I suppose, Mr. Jeremiah Atwater, of New-Haven, who is my brother-in-law, and by whom there may be a conveniency of sending to me, or by any of our coasting vessels that come to any of the towns neighbouring to New-Haven. I humbly ask your pardon, Sir, that I have been so prolix in my writing, and for my presumption in requesting such favours from you as above desired, which I dare not have done to so great a superior, if it had [not] a reference to the advancement of the kingdom of our great Redeemer, for which I know you are evermore greatly concerned, and are always ready to spend and be spent; and in endeavours for its growth and flourishing estate, you have been in labours more abundant than any of us.

I subscribe, Sir, your very humble servant and unworthy fellow-laborer in the Gospel,

JOSEPH MOSS.

[*The Rev. John Davenport and the Rev. Stephen Buckingham to the Rev. Doctors Increase Mather and Cotton Mather.*]

[John Davenport was minister of Stamford and Stephen Buckingham was minister of Norwalk.]

Very Reverend Sirs,

We have taken it that yourselves were consulted upon the first erecting a Collegiate School in our colony, nor can we account it improper that yourselves and our reverend fraternity in the principal town of our country [Boston] be apprised of the dark cloud drawn over our collegiate affairs, a representation whereof may already have been made by some of our reverend brethren trustees; but if not, and the case being of general concern, we are willing to make our mournful report, how it hath been matter of surprise to us (as we conclude it hath been or surely will be to you) to find how great a change a few years have made appear among us, and how our fountain, hoped to have been and continued the repository of truth and the reservoir of pure and sound principles, doctrine and education, in case of a change in our mother Harvard, shows itself in so little a time so corrupt. How is the gold become dim! and the silver become dross! and the wine mixt with water! Our school gloried and flourished under its first rector, the Rev. Mr. Pierson, a pattern of piety, a man of modest behaviour, of solid learning and sound principles, free from the least Arminian or Episcopal taint; but it suffered a decay for some years, because of the want of a resident rector. But who could have conjectured, that its name being raised to *Collegium Yalense* from a *Gymnasium Saybrookense*, it should groan out Ichabod, in about three years and a half under its second rector, so unlike the first, by an unhappy election set over it, into whose election or confirmation, or any act relating to him, the senior subscriber hereof (though not for some reason, through malice or mistake bruited) never came. Upon the management of our College three years and a half, how strangely altered is the aspect thereof! That its regents, sc. rector and tutor are become such capable masters of Episcopal leaven, and in such a time how able to cause so many to partake of it!

It appears surprisingly strange that it should diffuse itself into our ministry, and many of them, not of the least note, now appear in the company, viz.: Mr. Hart, of East Guilford, Mr. Whittelsey, of Wallingford, and Mr. Eliot, of Killingworth; these, perhaps, not much short of the rector's years. And two societies, branches of the famous New-Haven, one on the north and the other on the west, are mourning because of their first ministers, in so little a time after their ordination, declaring themselves Episcopal, and their ordination, lately received, of no value, because *a non habentibus potestatem.*

Upon our commencement, September 12, the rector distinguished his performance by the closing words of his prayer, which were these, viz.: "*And let all the people say, amen.*"

On the evening of said day it was rumoured there, that on the next day the gentlemen become Episcopal designed to propound to the trustees three questions: 1. Whether ordination from such ministers, whose ordination was from the leather jackets, be valid? 2. Whether ordination from ministers, who are only Presbyters, be valid? 3. Whether an uninterrupted succession from the apostles' days be not absolutely necessary to the validity of a minister's ordination? But these were not so propounded.

But the day following the commencement, after dinner, these gentlemen appeared in the library before the trustees, where many other ministers were present, and first declared themselves *viva voce*, but after that, on the direction of the trustees, declared themselves in writing, a copy whereof is not with us. But the substance thereof is this:

Some of us doubting the validity of Presbyterial ordination in opposition to Episcopal ordination, and others of us fully persuaded of the invalidity of said ordination, shall be thankful to God or man helping us, if in an errour. Signed, *Timothy Cutler*, *John Hart*, *Samuel Whittelsey*, *Jared Eliot*, *James Wetmore*, *Samuel Johnson*, *Daniel Brown*. The persons doubting were Mr. Hart and Mr. Whittelsey.

Consequent to this declaration, the trustees advised that the doubters continue in the administration of the ministry, word and sacraments, but that the fully persuaded forbear sacramental ministration until the meeting of the trustees, which was appointed on the Tuesday evening at New-Haven, following the opening of our General Assembly there, the said Tuesday being the 16th of the next month. The trustees also advised that the said ministers would freely declare themselves to their respective congregations.

It may be added, that Mr. C. then declared to the trustees that he had for many years been of this persuasion, (his wife is reported to have said that to her knowledge he had for eleven or twelve years been so persuaded,) and that therefore he was the more uneasy in performing the acts of his ministry at Stratford, and the more readily accepted the call to a College improvement at New-Haven. But then if he knew the College was erected for the education of such as dissented from the Church of England, (and how could he not know it,) and knew himself not one; with what good faith could he accept said call, and the considerable encouragement he had, and the rather, if he disseminated his persuasion so contrary to the very design of its erection, and the confidence of those that called him? Indeed, he hath said, that he hath laboured only with one to be of his persuasion; were it so, there would, in one instance, be a foul frustration of the confidence reposed in him; but what a number above one of the students have been leavened by him, who can be assured, but coming time may discover the unhappy instances of it.

Further, Mr. C. then also declared it his firm persuasion, that out of the Church of England, ordinarily, there was no salvation.

To the last we only say Μὴ γένοιτό; for we dare not so offend the generation of the righteous, nor disturb the ashes of the myriads that have slept in Jesus, of the Catholick professors of the orthodox faith in the three kingdoms, yea, and all reformed Christendom, and in New-England particularly, who have not been of the communion of the Church of England.

It must be acknowledged to the Divine goodness, that all the trustees then present, (and of the whole number wanted only three, sc. of Lime, N. London, Stamford,) showed themselves constant to our principles and [well] affected to the trust committed to them; yet desirous that the meeting of the trustees might (if possible) be fuller, and also their doings might be in the face of the colony, represented in General Assembly, they took care that Mr. C. might have the use of the house they had hired for him until the Wednesday next after the opening of the General Court, viz., October 17.

No wonder that it is said in all our towns on the seaside, and probably in our inland towns likewise, the talk in every one's mouth is the surprising conjuncture, wherein such a number, who are now said, at least for a year past, to have distinguished themselves by their frequent meeting together, the design whereof the late declaration is accounted to open, appear fond of that way, an unembarrassment from which moved our predecessors to so voluntary an exile into a then rude wilderness. And in the vagrant surmises of people, others of our principal men are by way of question or affirmation talked of, to belong to this set of deserters; of whom, until time show otherwise, better things are hoped.

One of us subscribing, who was then absent, could have the above account only by report, when the other, being present, bore a part with the trustees at N. H.

Reverend Sirs, having thus bemoaned the dark providence over us, we may not doubt of your Christian sympathy, nor of your prayers, which yet we earnestly ask, unto Him, that holdeth the stars in his right hand, and walketh in the midst of the golden candlesticks. We ask also your assistance, what you may think proper, in a conjoined testimony in the cause of Christ to our government and people, and the encouragement of the trustees, and the recovery (if possible) of those that are gone from us. And with sincere prayers, that how grievous soever our sins have been, and how much his anger hath been kindled against us, it may please the Lord, who is God and not man, yea, the God of pardon, not to give us up, cast us off, forsake us, nor call our name לא רהטה but that his gracious-blessing-presence may be, and continue in your and our churches.

We subscribe ourselves,
Reverend Sirs,
Your unworthy fellow-partners
In the ministry of the Gospel,
JOHN DAVENPORT,
S. BUCKINGHAM.

The very Reverend
INCREASE MATHER, D. D.
COTTON MATHER, D. D.
Stamford, *Sept*. 25, 1722.

[*A Faithful Relation of a Late Occurrence in the Churches of New-England.*]

Of this production, a New-England Editor has remarked, "not very candid or temperate, if faithful."

New-England has lately had in it an occurrence, that has been a matter of some surprise and much discourse unto the country.

The colony of Connecticut being willing to have their Churches well supplied, from an education on the principles which moved their predecessors to settle in those parts of the world, erected not long ago a college at New-Haven. This little college, or collegiate school, which wears the name of Yale College, was lately so unhappy as to borrow a pastor of a Church at Stratford, whose name is Mr. Timothy Cutler, for a rector. This man was a secret Episcopalian, of such high flights that he looks upon his Presbyterian ordination as a nullity, and the acts of his ministry as invalid; and his invitation to the rectorate of that collegiate school was the more agreeable to him, for its delivering him from a ministry which he took to be a cheat; it also gave him an opportunity privately to destroy the principal intention of the academy, and blow up the Churches which he appeared a friend unto. He privately for some time carried on a conversation with several young ministers of the neighbouring Churches, whose frequent meetings at his house were what the people knew not what interpretation to put upon. At last, by a strange coincidence of several circumstances, the plot broke out sooner than it is thought they would have had it; for on September 13th, the day after their commencement, these men appeared in the public library, before the trustees of the College, and many other ministers, and there exhibited a short instrument, wherein they declared that some of them doubted the validity, and others of them were fully persuaded of the invalidity of their Presbyterian ordination; signed by Cutler, the rector, and Brown, a tutor of the school, and five more that were young ordained pastors of Churches in the neighbourhood. The trustees were very much distressed on an occasion so unexpected, and so likely to be attended with a train of unhappy consequences; but they treated the men with all the charity, and lenity, and forbearance that the case would possibly admit of. Nevertheless, the action and apostacy of these men had caused a considerable commotion in the minds of the people, not only in the Churches more immediately betrayed, but also through all the country.

It has appeared marvellous unto them, that a little knot of young men that had read very little of the controversy, but only a few Episcopalian things which their library at New-Haven had been unhappily stocked withal, with little or nothing of the antidote, (and indeed the most that the poor children have to subsist upon is the pretended Epistles of Ignatius, which yet, if they were not impostures, would be of no service to them,) that these young men should have the temerity and presumption to declare for an usurpation in the Church of God, so clearly condemned in the holy Scriptures, which it is the profession and endeavour of those Churches to keep close unto; yea, and thereupon to deny the ministry, and renounce the communion of all the Protestant Churches in the world, except that little party that submits to the English Episcopacy! It has amazed them to see the sons of New-England strengthen and assist the common enemy, by coming into the great and almost the last clamour with which the papists are trying to weaken and perplex the reformed Churches, and that, when it is notorious that the whole body of our first reformers, at their coming out of Babylon, decried the necessity of an Episcopal ordination, and found that they could not shake off the mother of harlots without their doing so; they should in such a country go back from what the very dawn of the reformation arrived unto!

It has caused some indignation in them to see the vile indignity cast by these *Cudweeds* upon those excellent servants of God, who were the leaders of the flock that followed our Saviour into this wilderness; and upon the ministry of them, and their successors, in which there has been seen for more than fourscore years altogether, the power and blessing of God for the salvation of many thousands in the successive generations, with a success beyond what any of them, which set such an high value on the Episcopal ordination, could ever boast of; to vilify this as an invalid ministry; for a degenerate offspring to declare those men of God, and those burning and shining lights, to be no true ministers of Christ; but invaders and intruders upon a sacred office; and robbers that have not entered in by the door; they cry out upon it Good God, unto what times hast thou reserved us!

That which very much adds to the concern on the minds of the good people, is that such highflyers as these who derive their ordinations from Rome, do generally discover themselves too well affected unto a popish pretender, and enemies to the happy revolution; and though of late several conversions to High Church have been made among their children, wherein, to their honour, the great converter has been a foolish and sorry toy-man, who is a professed Jacobite, and printed a pamphlet to maintain that the God whom King William and the Churches there prayed unto, is the devil! (*horresco referens!*) yet they commonly lament it that the Church rarely gains a proselyte but King George loses a subject.

It is a sensible addition unto their honour to see the horrid character of more than one or two, who have got themselves qualified with Episcopal ordination, to fortify little and wretched parties, in disturbing the Churches of New-England, and come over as missionaries, perhaps to serve scarce twenty families of such people, in a town of several hundred families of Christians, better instructed than the very missionaries; to think that they must have no other ministers but such as are ordained and ordered by them, who have sent over such tippling sots unto them; instead of those pious, and painful, and faithful instructors which they are now blessed withal! The Churches treat these new invaders with much civility, and such as can go on in their ministry, they allow to do so. But the spirit of the country, and their zeal for the pure and undefiled religion and profession of their fathers, has been so conspicuous on this occasion, and the folly of the deserters has been so manifest unto all men, (and unto some of themselves,) that they will proceed no further. The apostacy will stop here; and what has happened will strongly serve to the establishment of the Churches; and the abettors of these disorders may spare any further pains for the furnishing of the country with such missionaries. Nor will they be received there by any but a few people of such a character as will be no great honour either to Christianity or to the Church of England.

Since the writing of this faithful relation, a letter from a very eminent person in the government of Connecticut, dated November 9, 1722, has these passages:

"The endeavours of the trustees of the College have been "so far succeeded as to remove the scruples of those ministers who had entertained some, about their ordinations; so "that we have a prospect of peace in the Churches they "were set over, and that they may go on in the work of the "ministry with hope of success. We are not without hopes, "that what has so fearful a tendency to the prejudice of that "Gospel order, which the Churches here have from the beginning observed, may rather tend to their confirmation "therein."

[*From a MS. in the handwriting of Rev. Cotton Mather, D. D., and supposed to have been sent to his Brethren in Connecticut.*]

The sentiments of several ministers in Boston, concerning the duty of the distressed Churches with relation to their pastors, who, in an instrument under their hands, have publickly declared, that they, some of them, *doubt the validity*, others of them *are fully persuaded of the invalidity* of the Presbyterian ordination.

It plainly appears:

I. These new Episcopalians have declared their desire to introduce an usurpation and a superstition into the Church of God, clearly condemned in the Sacred Scriptures, which our loyalty and chastity to our Saviour obliges us to keep close unto; and a tyranny from which the whole Church, which desires to be reformed, has groaned, that it may be delivered.

II. They have had the temerity and presumption to deny

the ministry and renounce the communion of all the Protestant Churches in the whole world, except that little party which submits to the English Episcopacy. Such a schism do they run into.

III. The scandalous conjunction of these unhappy men with the papists is, perhaps, more than what they have themselves duly considered. For first, the great and almost the last clamour with which the papists try to perplex and weaken the reformed Churches, is, that their ministry is invalid for want of Episcopal ordination.

These men strengthen the common enemy in the boundless mischief attempted by this foolish cavil. Secondly, even those defectively and imperfectly reformed Churches in England and Ireland found it necessary to decry the necessity of Episcopal ordination, at their first coming out of Babylon. They did it generally, notoriously, authentically, or they could not have shaken off the mother of harlots. God forbid that we should be such grievous revolters as to go back from what the very dawn of the reformation arrived unto! Thirdly, to maintain their Episcopal ordination, they set up that vile, senseless, wretched whimsey of an uninterrupted succession, which our glorious Lord has confuted with such matter of fact that it is amazing the builders of Babel are not ashamed of it; and they will have none owned for ministers of Christ in the world but such as anti-Christ has ordained for him; such as the paw of the beast hath been laid upon them that they pretend a succession from. Do not those men worship the beast, who allow no worship in the Church but by them who have their consecration legitimated by a derivation through the hands of the beast unto them? Finally, it is well known that at this day the men who are well-willers to the claims of a popish pretender, are the main assertors of the Episcopal ordination being essential to their Christian priesthood; and the most violent and signalized assertors of this paradox are such as decry the happy revolution, which every sincere Protestant, and honest and sober Englishman, must be a friend unto. Will these men unite with such adversaries: To their assembly, O my soul, be not thou united!

IV. They have cast a vile indignity upon those burning and shining lights, the excellent servants of God, who were the leaders of the flocks that followed our Lord Jesus into this wilderness, and upon the ministry of them and their successors in which there has been seen the power and blessing of God for the salvation of many thousands in the successive generations, with a success beyond what any of them, who set such an high value upon their Episcopal ordination, could ever boast of. A degenerate offspring have declared these men of God, than whom the world has rarely been illuminated with brighter stars, to be not true ministers of Christ, but usurpers of the ministry and invaders of a sacred office, robbers that have not entered in by the door.

They have also treated with the utmost contempt the glorious cause and work of God, by which the Churches of the Lord in this country have been so remarkably distinguished, and encouraged the posterity of our faithful predecessors to shake off the faith and order of the Gospel, which was the main end that the country was planted for.

V. They have done what is likely to throw the Churches of the country into disturbance and confusion, beyond anything they have ever yet met withal, and animate an ungodly generation to set up a lifeless religion, and an irreligious life, in the room of that which has hitherto been our glory.

VI. They have rashly done all this, before they have used the most proper means to attain the light which they pretend they are looking for. They have not read many of the most enlightening treatises, and they have not once addressed, so much as by writing to them, those persons, for their satisfaction, who are, of all, the most capable of enlightening them.

VII. It may be, some of the Churches are not satisfied what these gentlemen intend by waiting for further light.

VIII. In the meantime, it is to be doubted how they can lawfully and honestly go on with their pastoral administrations, and keep on good terms with the last words in the fourteenth chapter to the Romans: Inasmuch as it is affirmed, that those of them whose doubts had made the least impression on them, yet professed, that if the doubts which they now have should continue unremoved, they could not go on with the exercise of their ministry.

IX. The offence which those backsliders have given to all the Churches has been such, that the particular Churches to which they belong may, and should, make them sensible that they are greatly offended at them; and we see not why the flocks may not as much decline the owning of them for their ministers, as they themselves question the validity of their ministry. The Churches, by continuing to acknowledge the pastoral relations and oversight of those men, may give them greater opportunities to produce and increase [insidious] parties among them, than they may be at first well aware of.

X. Nevertheless, and after all, we have not heard all that these gentlemen have to say for themselves. And we ought to do nothing rashly; the peace of God, also, in the utmost expressions of reasonable charity, should rule on such occasions; and we cannot watch too much against the wrath of man insinuating on such occasions, which will not work the righteousness of God. It is likewise to be remembered, that none of these men were ordained without a council of Churches to countenance their introduction into the ministry. It seems therefore necessary that the Churches, which withdrew from the ministry of the men that have so disappointed them, and disobliged them, should have some countenance and assistance and instruction from a council of Churches for what they have to do in this lamentable affair. But the council ought to be so chosen, that the Churches may reasonably expect impartial proceedings in them: and therefore the choice had not best be limited by such prudential rules of vicinity, as might be agreed when there was no such extraordinary occasion to be imagined. Perhaps the general court may see cause, upon these awful and grievous and threatening occurrences, to nominate a very large council of Churches, to consider what may be the duty of the day, especially for those Churches that are more immediately now encumbered.

May the glorious head of the Church, whose name is the Counsellor, graciously grant his counsel to his people, that they may let no men take away their crown; but may faithfully preserve his institutions.

[*Mr. Orem to the Secretary.*]

New Bristol in New-England, Oct. 30*th*, 1722.

Sir,

I presume by this to recommend to your friendship and favor three very worthy gentlemen, Mr. Cutler, Mr. Brown and Mr. Johnson, who have lately declared themselves for the Church, though they have been brought up in the dissenting way, and have acted for some time past as Presbyterian or Independent ministers. Mr. Cutler was Rector of the College of Connecticut, the most creditable and profitable employment of any in this country, but has lately been dismissed from that post for declaring in favour of the Church; the other two who joined with him have undergone the same hard fate, the one having been turned out of his living, and the other out of his fellowship in the College. I can scarce express the hardships they have undergone, and the indignities that have been put upon them, by the worst sort of dissenters who bear sway here, and several honest gentlemen who declared for the Church with them; who, by reason of the unhappy circumstances of their families, can't go to England, but lie now under all the hardships and pressures that the malice and rage of the implacable enemies of our excellent Church and Constitution can subject them to; but I hope their suffering condition will be taken into consideration at home. These gentlemen intend to take orders and return in the Society's service. I hope, Sir, your good offices in recommending them to some of the members of that Honourable body won't be wanting; they will depend entirely on your directions how to apply themselves to them; what friendship you are pleased to show them will, I persuade myself, always be readily and thankfully acknowledged by them, and will add to the number of the many good offices you have done to, and the obligations you have laid on,

Sir,

Your most humble and most
obliged servant,

James Orem.

[*Mr. Brown's Memorial.*]

That which I humbly request of the Honourable Society is, that the petition exhibited in the letter of the Churchwardens and Vestry of the Church in New Bristol to the Society, may find a gracious reception, and that I may be permitted, according to their desire, therein expressed, to succeed the Reverend Mr. Orem, by whose removal a vacancy is made in that place, if I may be thought, in a tolerable measure, capable of answering the ends of the Society's mission into those parts. DANIEL BROWN.

[*Mr. Cutler's representation of the state of the Church of England in some parts of the Colony of Connecticut, in New-England.*]

Since I, with sundry others, did appear to favour Episcopacy in the town of New-Haven, in the colony aforesaid, which is a place considerable for the multitude of its inhabitants, and the great resort of people there, as also for a society for ingenious learning there established, the zeal of some dissenting teachers there, and in the parts adjacent to that town, hath signalized itself to perpetuate the interests of schism and depress the Church of England, and the people there have but very little advantage to defend themselves against those uncharitable and undutiful representations which are made of the Church of England, in her doctrine, discipline and worship, though many appear to have a sincerity of mind and honest willingness to receive and cherish the impressions that religion, reason and truth make on them. I therefore, looking on myself to retain some share in the affections of many of the people and scholars there, do humbly offer my service in making a visit to that deluded people, for promoting the interest of the Church of England there, so zealously and rudely opposed, in case the state of the particular Church to which I am sent, and my own personal affairs may allow it, desirous of the encouragement and acceptance of the Honourable Society in so doing.

TIMOTHY CUTLER.

[*Members of the Church of England at Ripton, in Connecticut, to the Secretary.*]

All Saints' Day, 1722.

Rev. and Honourable Sir,

We, the inhabitants of Ripton, in the colony of Connecticut, in New-England, being professors of the Church of England, as by law established, do earnestly request your truly Christian compassion for us who are destitute of a minister to officiate unto us as often as we could wish. It is true Mr. Pigot is solicitous of our welfare, and visits us as often as his extraordinary industry (in common with our neighbours) will permit; but we know not how long his ministrations will continue among us, and therefore are desirous of enjoying a pastor of our own, if so be it will suit your accustomed goodness and bounty to allow it. If you, in your wisdom, shall determine otherwise, we entreat that the ministers settled at Stratford and Newton, between which places we are conveniently situated, may receive your instructions to administer to us, each of them, every third Sunday. We are emboldened to hope this, both because we design to set apart a glebe for our spiritual guide when he comes, and also, because we suffer great persecution, for the Church's sake, from those who have, to our misfortune and oppression, the civil power here, and have made that a handle to usurp the ecclesiastical.

We commit this, our request, to the direction of the great God to touch your hearts with compassion for us, and to the candid generosity of your illustrious Society, and are, honoured Sirs, your very humble servants and petitioners,

Chas. Lane,
Daniel Shelton,
Richard Blacklach, Jr.,
Martin Longworth,
Chas. Lane, Jr.,
Alexander Lane,
Nathaniel Cogswell,
John Gilbert,
Thomas Lattin,
George Black, of Derby,
Abraham Trelford,
James Wakle, Jr.,
Benj. Lattin,
John Beardslee, Jr.,
Joseph Shelton,
Benjamin Mallery.

[*Mr. Pigot to the Secretary.*]

Stratford, Nov. 6, 1722.

Sir,

I have herewith sent you petitions to the honourable Society, from two towns in this neighbourhood, whose inhabitants are above half come over to our Church. I also expect to visit you with another from Fairfield in a short time, after, if not in company with these. The subscribers of Ripton have been, of long standing, inclined to the Church, yet even among them there are some lately brought over. But those of Newtown, to a man, have been induced by my means to embrace our profession. I believe two missionaries might serve all four towns; that is, might attend on Stratford and Fairfield, and the other on Newtown and Ripton, alternately, for the two former are at eight, and the latter at twelve miles distance. I likewise also present you here with an account of the progress of my ministry in relation to my administration of the Sacraments since my last *notitia parochialis*, which you will find in the enclosed list. We are, Sir, in great want of Prayer-Books and Catechisms, indeed in so great, that it is almost impossible ———; therefore I once more heartily beg that some may be sent by the first opportunity. I have a request also to the honourable Society in behalf of a worthy French gentleman, born at Cardillac, in Quercy, and now residing at Fairfield. His name is James Labarie, who having been politely educated, left his native country, and was ordained by Dr. Antonius Clinglet, Antistes of Zurich, in 1688; afterwards coming into England, he procured Bishop Compton's license for teaching grammar, but being invited by my Lord Bellamont, he passed over to America in 1699, and the year following, as successor to Mons. Bondet, was appointed by his lordship to instruct the Keehamoochuck (or new Oxford) Indians, which employment he pursued with great success, till they were cut off by their enemies. This service he underwent three years, having [in that time] capacitated a certain Indian to that degree as to be able to instruct the rest. Ever since he has lived in this colony at Fairfield; but, by reason of his attachment to the Church of England principles, has never been permitted by the Independents to put his license in practice, and more especially has been maligned by the deputy Governor, an inveterate, and, indeed, most implacable enemy to the established Church. This gentleman, having obtained the Indian language, with the honourable Society's good leave, is heartily willing to do the office of a Catechist here, and therefore begs from that auspicious body their orders, books, protection, and benevolence.

Messrs. Cutler, Johnson and Brown are set out toward Boston, in order to their transportation to Great Britain, whom I presume to be arrived ere this comes to salute you, from

Sir,

The Honourable Society's

And your very humble servant,

GEO. PIGOT.

[*Mr. Labarie to the Secretary.*]

Fairfield, *New-England*, *March 5th*, 1722-23.

Mr. Pigot hath acquainted the honourable Society with my circumstances, therefore, I shall not be tedious in giving you an account of them. After that I left my own country by reason of the persecution raging there; I went to Zurich and was ordained by Mr. Clinglet, Antistes of that Canton, as you may see certified by the enclosed copy. I arrived in England at the time of King William's coronation, and there obtained a license from the Lord Bishop of London for teaching grammar and catechising in the parish of Stepney. Some time afterwards I was persuaded by my Lord Bellamont to come into America, where he settled me for the work of the ministry in a town called New Oxford, where Mr. Bondet had been before, and gave me a commission to instruct the Indians there; the original whereof I herewith transmit to your honourable Society. That office I was diligent to perform, and, by the blessing of God, having obtained the lingua of that nation, had so considerable a success that I brought some of them to the capacity of teaching others; but the town being cut off by the Indian enemies, we were forced to forsake the settlement for the security of our lives, and since my abode in this Colony and County of Fairfield, where are many Indians, I have concluded it my duty to continue my labours, though without any prospect of any encouragement or salary, for which purpose applying myself to Governor Saltonstall, whose original letter of approbation attends upon you, and receiving his encouragement, I began by the enclosed introductory discourse, to prepare both the English and native inhabitants; but, having declared myself a member of the Church of England, I was immediately interrupted by the Lieutenant-Governor Nathan Gold, a mortal enemy to that Church, and violently compelled to surcease my endeavours. My commission extending no further than Boston Colony, since Mr. Pigot's arrival in this colony, I have joined with him, and done my endeavours to assist him. He hath the care of four Churches considerably distant from each other, and though no missionary before ever took half the pains that he takes for the propagation of the Church of England, yet the members of his Church are scattered, and the enemies thereof so busy to hinder those who are already communicants, and others who are willing to join us, that it is impossible for one man to entertain them all, and to keep them in the bosom of the Church. Therefore, making use of that license I received from Bishop Compton, I visit the well-disposed people to instruct them in the principles of the established Church, and, on the Lord's day, while Mr. Pigot is at Stratford or some other place, I teach at my own house, which I have destinated for the service of the Church of England. I suppose Mr. Pigot will acquaint your honourable body with the persecutions and threatenings we are exposed to, having in this town of Fairfield the Lieutenant-Governor against us, and the pretended ministers of Independency continually declaiming against the Church, terming her service Popery, the way to hell, and themselves Bishops as regular as the Bishop of London, with many other extravagant expressions. Therefore if your honourable Society would favour me with a larger power than I have, I should be very glad to employ the rest of my days for the propagation of the Gospel among the heathen, and instruction of the remoter members of the Church of England, not doubting but that, under the blessing of God, the Church of Fairfield would be in a short time in a flourishing condition, there being many that desire to be frequently instructed in the principles thereof. We are here under great disadvantages by reason of the scarcity of Catechisms, Common Prayer Books, Psalters, and many other books which are needed for instruction and comfort. We humbly beg the honourable Society to procure some, (for this town particularly,) and shall ever continue to pray for the prosperity of your glorious body, as at present, he cordially does, who is with the utmost submission,

Your very humble servant and well-wisher,

James Labarie.

[*Mr. Pigot to the Secretary.*]

Stratford, June 3d and 7th, 1723.

Sir,

Having completed my first year, and knowing myself under obligation to notify the honourable Society of the procedure of affairs in this Colony, I once more visit you with this my acknowledgment of their indulgence towards me, and do return them thanks for their order for my removal to Providence; not that I propose any other advantage to myself than being nearer the inspection of some land of mine there about.

This is the sixth letter I have sent you without the satisfaction of one in return, so that I am to seek whether Fairfield, Ripton, or Newtown petitions have reached you or not; we are forthwith transmitting a duplicate of each, for fear of miscarriage. Our cause flourishes mightily in this country, indeed so much, that our neighbours look on with astonishment. The Mathers are diligent in sending circular letters to all places, exhorting them to trace the pious steps of their forefathers; and whereas that popular plea has been detected to carry fraud with it, by a printed letter of Governour Winthrop and company to the ministers of Old England, they have been compelled to take refuge in another more notorious untruth, namely, that there are *two* Churches of England, the high and the low; with the low, they pretend to hold full communion, but the high are rank *Papists ;* they terming us no less. This notion, and some books with which every town is glutted, such as [illegible] many thousands of which have been printed off at Boston. An anonymous answer to the Bishop of Derry and Jameson the Scott, are our greatest obstructions by way of controversy, as the Deputy Governour is by way of authority, in this quarter of the world. This last mentioned gentleman has been so weak as to propound to the General Court a law to prohibit me the practice of my function, in all the towns of this Colony besides [except] Stratford. I enclosed an account of my baptized and communicants; since my last, of the former, I have added forty-eight to the Church, of the latter, sixty-seven during the past year's ministry. I had forty-three of these on Easterday and thirty-eight on Whit-Sunday, notwithstanding they live at great distances asunder. I have been once to Norwalk, once to North-Haven, six times to Fairfield, Ripton and Newtown, each; at which last places I have administered both sacraments once already, and do intend it once more before my departure. Our church will be raised on the first of next month, being forty-five feet long, thirty broad, and twenty studd. I understand from Boston that Mr. Whetmore is sailed, so that, in all likelihood, he will pay his respects before this can arrive, from the honourable Society's, and Sir, &c.

George Pigot.

[*Mr. Pigot to the Secretary.*]

Providence, January 13*th*, 1723–24.

Reverend Sir,

Mr. Johnson, my successor at Stratford, having brought me the honourable Society's order for my removal to Providence, I have accordingly been arrived at my charge about two months, and do humbly acknowledge their favour with grateful respect. I left him seventy-nine in communion, having baptized six adults and fifty-seven infants the first eighteen months' ministry, and of whom I have enclosed a list of those not mentioned before. As to the new church at

Stratford, it proceeds but heavily, by reason of the poverty of its professors, who are too closely fleeced by the adverse party to carry it on with despatch; and as to the out-towns, it is my humble opinion, that Newtown merits the preference in the honourable Society's regard; both as it is more remote from Stratford, and also, as its inhabitants are above half come over already, in so much that Mr. Johnson may expect thirty communicants there. Fairfield, also, is well enclosed, and will have as large a communion as Newtown; but Dr. Labarie's industry there takes off the present necessity of a missionary in that town. This last gentleman is an excellent preacher, but by reason of his attachment to our principles, is unimproved by the dissenters, as to his practice in physic, unless upon the greatest emergency. In Ripton (which is a very small place) the Independents have never yet been able to settle a minister of their profession, but at present they are aspiring, (by a sort of association,) with a salary of £40 per annum, and some land, hoping thereby to keep out the Church. Mr. Johnson will find it a most difficult task to answer the expectations of the towns around him, there being work enough for Sunday labourers in the Lord's harvest; however, if Newtown were supplied with one, he might take care of Ripton, as Mr. Johnson might of Fairfield and West Haven. I now pass to you some account of my new mission. The inhabitants here are generally well inclined to the Church of England, but not so much out of principle as out of opposition to the Massachusetts profession. For these Providence people, by bordering upon them, having formerly felt the lash of their resentments, are now utterly estranged to their persuasion;* who, notwithstanding, are thrusting themselves among us, and building a meeting-house, which they never attempted before the honourable Society had resolved to appoint a missionary for this place. The towns of Warwick and Greenwich, (my near neighbours,) are importunate with me to perform Divine Service among them once in a month, which, with the honourable Society's approbation, I shall comply with; because Warwick is the place where the

* This statement is fully verified in the first volume of Mr. Samuel Green Arnold's History of Rhode Island, published in 1859.

Gortonians (a wild crew) first prevailed, and together with Greenwich has always been destitute of a minister of *any* profession whatsoever. I am afraid any minister here will not be so successful as at Stratford, it being much easier to bring over those Schismatics to our communion, than these outrageous and stubborn enthusiasts. I beg the favour of the usual number of small tracts for this town, there being greater occasion for them than ordinary; but I look upon it as my duty to remind you, sir, that these people, (if of any profession,) are chiefly Quakers and Anabaptists. I have nothing more to add, but that I am, with the sincerest attachment, the honourable Society's obliged and humble servant, GEORGE PIGOT.

Not having sealed this for want of an opportunity to transmit it, I have hereunto added something that has since happened respecting the honourable Society. One Mr. Richard Sackett settled at Dover, an up town in the Province of New-York, has taken the pains to give me a visit on purpose to bestow a handsome gift on the Church. This gentleman has a claim of upwards of thirteen hundred acres of land in the township of Stratford, but has been debarred of his right by government there, who thought fit to dispose of it otherwise, though his title be two years older than their charter; the aforesaid tract of land having been purchased of the Indian Sachems in 1661. He has given me an irrevocable power of attorney, and a grant of four hundred acres to the missionary of Stratford for a perpetual glebe, and two hundred acres to finish the church. This glebe, valued at £1,800 paper money, has occasioned great speculation and heart-aching, because Mr. Sackett's title is confessedly as good as any man can have in this country, and also because there is no one legal instance of the disposal of lands here by *charter*, in contradiction to Indian title. It has been Judge ———'s opinion, and is that of the most knowing here, that Mr. Sackett's title is sure, and therefore I expect the honourable Society's order what to do in this affair, and they may confide in,

Sir, &c.,

GEORGE PIGOT.

[*Members of the Church of England, at Newton, in Connecticut, to the Secretary.*]

October 19*th*, 1722.

Honourable Gentlemen,

We, the subscribers, inhabitants of the town of Newton, [Newtown,] in the province of Connecticut, being cordially inclined to embrace the articles and liturgy of the Church of England, and to approach her communion, do humbly and earnestly request your honourable Society to send us a lawfully ordained minister. We are heads of families and, with our dependants, shall appear the major party here; therefore, we intend to set apart for our Episcopal teacher, whensoever it shall please God to inspire your venerable body to appoint us one, at least two hundred acres of glebe for the support of a Church minister for ever. And this we are emboldened to hope, because our town is at so great a distance from Stratford as twenty-two miles, and also situated in the centre of all this country, being surrounded with more than ten other towns at no vast distance. We do likewise return our most hearty thanks for those ministrations Mr. Pigot has introduced among us, who has inclined us to declare boldly for the Church, and thereby to be exposed to the resentments of the Independents, to his and our no small disadvantage and reproach; indeed, we are placed in the midst of an insidious people, but should quietly enjoy our persuasion without the intervention of others, if an Episcopal minister were once settled among us, which we beg of Almighty God to induce the honourable Society to nominate; and in the mean time we remain their very humble servants and well-wishers,

JOHN GLOVER, JAMES HARD, STEPHEN PARMELEE,
SAMUEL HENRIX, ROBERT SEELY DANIEL JACKSON,
JOHN SEALY, JOHN GRIFFIN, JEREMIAH TURNER,
ELIDIA SHARP, *Widow*, SAMUEL MOSHER,
EBENEZER BOOTH, THOMAS WHEELER, of Woodbury,
MOSES KNAPP, at Chestnut Ridge.

[*The Church Wardens and Vestry of Newport, in Rhode-Island, to the Secretary.*]

At a Vestry held at Trinity Church,

October 29th, 1722.

Sir,

'Tis with the greatest pleasure we have this happy opportunity of expressing the grateful sense we have of the honourable Society's compassionate care of, and kindness to, this place, in the generous encouragement they give for the support of religion in it; for which we return our sincere acknowledgments, attended with our earnest desires for the best blessings of heaven upon them; we also think we should be wanting to our duty, if by the occasion of these worthy gentlemen, Messrs. Cutler, Johnson and Brown, who have renounced their schismatical principles wherein they were educated and voluntarily joined our communion, we should not heartily recommend them to the special regard and countenance of the Rev. Fathers of our Church and the patrons of religion. Their coming over to us is justly looked upon here, not only as a very surprising, but a very considerable advantage to the interests of the Church in these parts; their motives and their conversion, they are now going to account for before our Right Reverend Diocesan and the honourable Society, from whom it is humbly hoped they will meet with all possible encouragement. It is plain, these gentlemen have, in this important affair, acted like Christians and men of virtue and honour, without any sordid views of interest or advancement; for, as they were not dismissed their posts and offices for any vice and immorality, they being universally acknowledged, and that even by our Church's greatest enemies, to be persons of unspotted character and the nicest virtue, so neither were they compelled to a conformity by any other necessity than that of pursuing the dictates of a good conscience; and for the sake of that, indeed, they have forsaken their dearest interests and valuable settlements. Though we don't in the least presume to prescribe to our superiors, yet we can't but entertain some humble hopes and wishes that the famous Universities of England will treat Mr. Cutler with distinguished marks of esteem, he having been himself head of a College, which station he adorned, as well as discharged the duties of it with great applause; and could it be obtained by the favour and authority of the Crown that he should be re-established in it, and return in holy orders, it is more than probable that his influence over the youth, and distilling good principles in them, would be of great service to religion and the Church in this country. Nor can we be so injurious to the merits of Mr. Johnson and Mr. Brown as to omit assuring the honourable Society, that the one, viz., Mr. Johnson, having been for some time an ordained minister in the dissenting way, and the other, Mr. Brown, a tutor in Mr. Cutler's College, were extremely beloved and esteemed by their people; and 'tis not doubted, but in proportion to the favours of the communion they have left, they will be favoured by that they have espoused. Upon the whole, it seems highly probable that upon these gentlemen's fate, we mean their reception and encouragement, depends a grand revolution, if not a general revolt, from schism in these parts; and that their example will be followed by many, if not the most considerable men amongst them, whereof we have already an instance in one Mr. Wetmore, a man of learning and piety, who is now become zealous for the service and interest of the Church, but whose circumstances won't, at present, allow him to apply for Episcopal ordination; and his case being that of many, we hope will also be allowed as an argument for the necessity of a Bishop in this country. Conversions from schism, as well as from infidelity and heresy, we humbly conceive to be one of the honourable Society's just designs, and here now presents a happy opportunity of bringing it to some perfection; and, should there not be remarkable notice taken of these gentlemen, the neglect would not only dishearten others, who are in a manner ready to follow their laudable example, but give our enemies the greatest occasion to insult us, and glory in the disappointment. We hope our honourable patrons will excuse the freedom whereby we become faithful witnesses of great truths, and earnestly entreat they will be pleased to continue their compassion and regard for us, who are, with all possible veneration their's, as we are with great esteem, Sir, your most obedient humble servants,

JAMES HONEYMAN, *Minister.*

ADAM POWELL, WILLIAM CODDINGTON, *Churchwardens.*

JOHN BROWN,	NATH'L NEWDIGATE,	*Vestrymen.*
R. GARDNER,	EDWARD NEARGREASSE,	
JOHN FREEBODY,	DANIEL AYRAULT,	
GEO. GOLDING,	JNO. CHACE,	

[*Rev. Mr. Johnson to the Bishop of London.*

Stratford in Connecticut, New-England,
January 18*th*. 1723–4.

May it please your Lordship,

Being, by the favourable providence of God, arrived in New-England, in obedience to your Lordship's commands, when I had the honour of being in your presence, I make bold, in all humility, to lay before your Lordship the state of the colony of Connecticut, to which your Lordship has licensed me. The people here are generally rigid Independents, and have an inveterate enmity against the established Church, but of late the eyes of great multitudes are opened to the great error of such an uncharitable and therefore unchristian spirit.

This is come to pass chiefly in six or seven towns, whereof this of Stratford, where I reside, is the principal, and though I am unworthy and unmeet to be intrusted with such a charge, yet there is not one clergyman of the Church of England, besides myself, in this whole colony, and I am obliged, in a great measure, to neglect my cure at Stratford, (where yet there is business enough for one minister,) to ride about to the other towns, (some ten, some twenty miles off,) where in each of them there is as much need of a resident minister as there is at Stratford, especially at Newtown and Fairfield, so that the case of these destitute places, as well as of myself, who has this excess of business, is extremely unhappy and compassionable

Now at the same time, my Lord, there are a considerable number of very promising young gentlemen, five or six I am sure of, and these the best that are educated among us, who might be instrumental to do a great deal of good to the souls of men, were they ordained; but, for want of Episcopal ordination, decline the ministry, and go into secular business, being, partly from themselves, and partly through the influence of their friends, unwilling to expose themselves to the danger of the seas and distempers, so terrifying has been the unhappy fate of Mr. Brown; so that the fountain of all our misery is the want of a Bishop, for whom there are many thousands of souls in this country that do impatiently long and pray, and for want of whom do extremely suffer.

My Lord, permit me to remember the concern your Lordship was pleased to express, for sending a suffragan into this country, when we were before your Lordship, which gave me the greater pleasure, because I have the satisfaction to know, that so great is your Lordship's deserved interest with his most sacred majesty King George, (whom God long preserve,) that you might very probably be the first, under God and the King, in effecting for us so great a blessing.

And suffer me further, my Lord, to say that there is not one Jacobite or disaffected person in this colony, nor above two or three (that I know of) in America; but for want of a loyal and orthodox Bishop to inspect us, we lie open to be misled into the wretched maxims of that abandoned set of men, as well as a great many other perverse principles.

May God, therefore, direct your Lordship's thoughts, and succeed your pious endeavours for effecting this, or any other good work, that may contribute to the advancement or enlargement of his Church, and may I have an interest in your Lordship's compassion, prayers and benediction in the great task that lies upon me. I am,

May it please your Lordship, your Lordship's

Humble and obedient servant,

SAMUEL JOHNSON.

[*Rev. Mr. Johnson to the Bishop of London.*]

Stratford in Connecticut, New-England,
June, 23*d*, 1724.

May it please your Lordship,

The pious concern which your Lordship hath expressed for the advancement of religion, in your most excellent letter to your clergy here, fills us with a great deal of joy and gratitude, and encourageth us to hope that the representation which, by that wise expedient, will be made to your Lordship of the necessitous state of English America, will, in your Lordship's hands, be a prevalent inducement to move the pious compassion of his most sacred Majesty, and of his wise ministers, to furnish this destitute and unhappy country with Bishops, or at least Suffragans. Your Lordship will find, by the account I shall give, that this town, and indeed the whole colony, is destitute of any Episcopal school, by which means our youth are trained up in prejudice against the established Church; and since your Lordship hath expressed so pious a care, as to inquire concerning the state of our schools, I have been encouraged to recommend this honest gentleman, the bearer hereof, Mr. Thomas Salmon, (whose affairs obliged him to voyage for England,) to your Lordship and the honourable Society; he is one of our churchwardens, and is well qualified for an English schoolmaster, and hath kept the school for several years in this town, to the universal satisfaction of both the Church people and Dissenters; insomuch that, if he was continued our schoolmaster, sundry even of the Dissenters would continue their children under his care, which would very much take off their prejudices against the Church. My humble request, therefore, to your Lordship is, that you would be graciously pleased to favour his address to the honourable Society to be sent over, with a small annuity, their schoolmaster to this town; and I doubt not but that he will approve himself both a loyal subject to his most sacred majesty King George, (to whose person and government he hath always appeared heartily well affected,) and likewise a faithful instrument to promote all useful English learning and serious piety among our children. My Lord, the poor people here are very much discouraged on account of the unreasonable demands of the government in exacting taxes from them to the support of the Independent teachers, for which sundry people, and those of both sexes, have been unmercifully imprisoned, contrary to the indulgence granted to them in government, by their charter, which forbid them to do any thing contrary to the laws of England, and we humbly beg your Lordship's protection. I have complained of this grievance to the governor here, but can get no relief; and unless it can be removed, the Church can never flourish, but the pious design of the honourable Society will be utterly defeated. If your Lordship should write to our Governor, as I am informed you have done to the Governor of Boston colony, I believe it would answer the ends; but I humbly submit to your Lordship's wisdom in that matter. One thing more I beg leave to trouble your Lordship with, and that is this: the late Queen (of blessed memory) gave sundry sets of Communion furniture to the Churches here, and among the rest, one supernumerary set, which happened first to be lodged and used at Narragansett; but upon the breaking up of the Church there, for the want of a minister, the late Bishop Compton, (of pious memory,) ordered them to this Church at Stratford, which hath possessed them these 12 years, and it would cause our adversaries very much to triumph over us if we should be deprived of them. Indeed, the people of Narragansett did lay claim to them, and produced an order from your Lordship's immediate predecessor to return them to that Church; but the Church here being then without a guide, and imagining they had a right to them from Bishop Compton's order, did not deliver them. Now I am informed that Mr. Macsparran hath an order from your Lordship to this Church to deliver them, but we have not received it; we will cheerfully obey it, if your Lordship insists upon it, when it comes. But, in the mean time, I will in all humility submit it to your Lordship, whether we have not a right to this furniture from Bishop Compton's order, whereby the Church at first became possessed of it. And now I humbly ask pardon for this tedious letter, and beg your Lordship's benedictions, presuming to subscribe myself, my Lord,

Your Lordship's
Humble servant,
SAMUEL JOHNSON.

[*The Secretary to the Rev. Mr. Johnson.*]

London, *August* 25*th*, 1724.

Reverend Sir,

The Society have received a petition from the members of the Church of England at Newtown, and another from those at Ripton, in Connecticut, wherein they request the Society to send them a missionary, and promise to settle upon him and his successors some land. The Society are inclined to send a missionary to officiate among them, but have thought proper to write over to them first to know what the value is at present of the land which they offer towards the support of their minister, and what they will contribute further, annually; and, if they find the people are willing to do what they can, the Society will add a salary for the more decent support of a clergyman, to reside in one of these parishes; and by this means, the Society hope your cure will be considerably easier taken care of, and you will have more leisure to attend the Church at Stratford.

I am, &c.,
D. HUMPHREYS.

[*Rev. Mr. Johnson to the Bishop of London.—Extract.*]

Boston, *October* 10*th*, 1724.

My Lord,

There are indeed a number of very worthy clergymen here in New-England, but yet many things occur from time to time which make it very apparent how extremely unhappy we are, for want of an ecclesiastical governor to have an immediate inspection over us. Among other instances of this kind, the conduct of Mr. Harris, of Boston, is a very flagrant one. The malice wherewith he hath all along persecuted good Dr. Cutler is very extraordinary, and for no other reason but because the good people of Boston were desirous, and are so happy as to obtain, that the Doctor should be the incumbent of their new Church, which, it seems, Mr. Harris had an expectation of. Your Lordship will, I believe, be sufficiently sensible by looking into the Doctor's sermon, how far it is from the least favourable aspect upon Popery, and yet this gentleman would persuade people that the Doctor is a Papist, and that sermon, at the same time, is all he pretends for a foundation for it. It is from the same fountain of envy and malice that the false report was originally derived, which represented us to your Lordship as disaffected, when we had the honour to be in your presence; but we should be glad of an opportunity to submit all our conduct to your Lordship's immediate inspection, if the thing were possible.

Another instance, my Lord, of what I was mentioning, is the injuries which our people suffer from the governments here. Since my last letter to your Lordship, notwithstanding my humble addresses to the government of the Colony of Connecticut, yet sundry of my people have been persecuted for their taxes to the Independent teachers; and that, notwithstanding that the honourable Society have obliged them to pay to the support of the established Church. One man has had above £50, first and last, thus injuriously taken away from him; and have, as yet, no mitigation, so that many people are almost discouraged. I beg, my Lord, if possible, we may have some relief; for all their conduct towards the Church has been a direct abuse of their charter privileges.

I am, my Lord,

Your Lordship's most dutiful son and servant,

SAMUEL JOHNSON.

[*Mr. Browne to the Bishop of London.*]

New-Haven in New-England, March 15*th*, 1724–5.

My Lord,

I humbly ask pardon for giving your Lordship this trouble from one, not only a perfect stranger to your Lordship, (having never been out of this country,) but also a plain man, and therefore unworthy to presume so far, which I never should have done, were it not that I humbly conceive what I venture into your Lordship's presence, were an affair of very great consequence. Your Lordship very well knows how much it concerns the weal of his most sacred Majesty's dominions here, as well as in England, that a good affection to his Majesty be preserved among his people, and, therefore, we shall be very unhappy if any measures are taken to propagate disaffection among us.

Now, my Lord, though there are none of your Lordship's clergy here that ever have expressed the least disaffection to King George's person or government, but always the contrary, yet it is certain that the non-jurors have sent over two Bishops into America, and one of them has travelled through the country upon a design, as I am well assured, to promote that cause.* I had, accidentally, a little acquaintance with him, and though I hope I had considered the matter too well to be wrought upon by them, yet I am sensible that many well-meaning people, otherwise well enough affected, will be in great danger of being imposed on and led aside, for I am sensible that their powers of insinuation are very considerable. Your Lordship sees from hence, how miserable the case of this country is from want of Bishops of the established Church, and such as are well affected to our rightful Sovereign, to preserve the flock of Christ from wan-

* The two here referred to were the Rev. Dr. Welton, and the Rev. John Talbot, who were consecrated by the non-juring Bishops of Scotland, and of whom more will appear in the Documents of New-Jersey, Pennsylvania and Maryland.

dering out of one schism into another, and with all, into disaffection to the King.

I pray God preserve his Majesty, and inspire the government with compassion towards this country, that if possible so great a part of the Christian Church, daily languishing for want of Bishops and longing for a supply, may at length be provided for, to the taking away our reproach among the adversaries of our glorious Church. I speak, my Lord, the wish of great multitudes of souls in this land, and the necessities of a vast many more who perish for lack of vision. I pray God bless your Lordship, and presume to subscribe myself, (though unknown,)

Your Lordship's most dutiful Son,

And humble servant,

JOSEPH BROWNE.

[*Rev. Mr. Johnson to the Secretary.*]

Stratford, Connecticut, January 10th, 1724.

Reverend Sir,

I have received yours of Aug. 25th, with the letters to Newton and Ripton inclosed, which I have delivered, and am desired by them to offer their humble thanks to the honourable Society for their kind and generous notice of them. When they made those addresses to the honourable Society, and so for some considerable time since I came into these parts, there was a much more promising disposition among them to the Church than there is now. For last summer, upon the dismission of their teacher, the Independent ministers of this country, taking the advantage of the want of a Bishop to supply them immediately, (which they upbraided the poor people with, telling them that if the Church of England were a true Church, and thought Bishops necessary, they would have sent one before now,) prevailed upon a very popular, insinuating young man to go among them, who pleaseth them so well, that many of them, impatient for want of the ministrations of religion, and thinking him well affected toward the Church, because he takes some of the prayers out of our Liturgy, &c., are disposed to have him settled with Presbyterian ordination. There are yet at Newton 10 families, and 6 or 7 at Ripton, that still cleave to the Church, and they hope they should be able to give £10 to £15 per annum and 100 acres of glebe, but their land has yet never been cultivated at all, and, therefore, can't be of any profit for sundry years; and if the honourable Society, under these disadvantages, will be pleased to send them a missionary, they will be very thankful to them. The interest of the Church gains ground daily at Fairfield, where they are vigourously going forward in building a Church, and fix their expectations on a young gentleman here whom I am preparing for the service of the Church, but his age will not admit of his being ordained this 2 or 3 years, but he promiseth well against that time. This last half year I have baptised 18 and admitted 12 to the Communion. On Christmas we opened our new Church; it is a very pleasant and comfortable building, and many new proselytes are upon this come over to the Church, and more there are whose hearts are with us, but are deterred from appearing by the spirit of bitterness and falsehood which is gone out amongst us upon this occasion. I pray God prosper the honourable Society. I am, reverend sir,

Your most humble servant,
SAMUEL JOHNSON.

[*Rev. Mr. Johnson to the Secretary.*]

Stratford in Connecticut, June 11th, 1724.

Reverend Sir,

I hope you have received my former letter, wherein I offered my most humble thanks to the honourable Society for their kind notice of me, when I had the honour to offer my service to them, and my people's thanks for their continual care for them in supplying them upon Mr. Pigot's departure, and wherein I represented the necessitous estate of the Church here for want of a Bishop and minister, and its oppressed estate in people being barbarously imprisoned for taxes to Dissenting ministers; all which necessities and grievances are daily increasing upon us as the Church increases, which I thank God it does daily, though not so fast in any measure as it would if we could have any relief. Besides Newton and Fairfield, (whose case I recommended to them,) I have since preached at New-London, where I had 60 hearers, and where there is a good prospect of increase if they had a minister. Newton is distressed for a minister, their teacher being quite beat out; and the whole town would, I believe, embrace the Church if they had a good minister at Fairfield. I have a vast assembly every time I visit them, but though I have made all proper and modest applications to the government, both privately and publicly, we have yet no abatement of persecution and imprisonment for taxes, which sundry people, and those of both sexes, have unreasonably suffered since my last, and I fear, that if we can't have some relief from the honourable Society, people will grow quite discouraged. I now humbly presume to recommend to the honourable Society this honest gentleman, the bearer hereof, Mr. Thomas Salmon, whom I humbly desire may be admitted schoolmaster for this place, who is (as is attested in his certificate) well qualified to keep an English school, and will be content with a small annuity of £10 or £15 per annum, if he may be admitted. And I am the rather encouraged, because our Right Reverend Diocesan hath been pleased to inquire, among other things, into the state of the schools here, which is very unhappy, there being not one in all this colony which is Episcopal. If the honourable Society can add this to their former favours, it will much contribute to the advancement of the Church here, for this gentleman having been schoolmaster sundry years in the town, the Dissenters have much approved of him, and sundry of them will yet continue their children under his care.

I am, &c.,

SAMUEL JOHNSON.

[*Rev. Mr. Johnson to the Bishop of London.*]

Stratford in Connecticut, New-England,
November 4th, 1725.

May it please your Lordship,

I had the honour of your Lordship's letter of June 23d, full of a great deal of kindness and condescension, for which I now return your Lordship my most humble thanks, and particularly for your prayers and good wishes for my preservation and success in my work, which (I thank God) is as great as can be expected, in the midst of the many discouragements and low circumstances which the Church labours under. It is a great satisfaction to us to understand, that one of your Lordship's powerful interest and influence, is engaged in so good a work as that of sending Bishops into America, and that there is nothing you desire more or would be at greater pains to compass. This gives us the greatest hopes, that by your Lordship's pious endeavours, under the blessing of God and the benign influence of our most gracious King, it may, at length, be accomplished. And we humbly hope, that the address and representation of the state of religion here, which we have lately presumed to offer, may, in your Lordship's hands, be of some service in this affair. I pray God give it success.

Your Lordship informs me of Governor Shute's account of the method of Independent ministers settling themselves in particular towns. My Lord, I never took this to be the case in any part of New-England, for I never understood that there were any ministers maintained by subscriptions of each particulár parishioner. Indeed, I cannot be positive how it is in Boston Government, though I am apt to think that it is, at least, far from being a general practice there, and I am well assured that there is no such thing here. Your Lordship desires to know exactly how it is, and promise to do us what service you can, for which we are very thankful

That your Lordship may not wholly depend on my representation of it, but may have an exact knowledge of the state of this government from themselves, I have presumed to trouble your Lordship with all the public transactions of this colony about the affairs of religion; and because all their authority depends on the charter granted to them by King Charles the 2d, I have laid before your Lordship a printed copy of that charter, by which it does not appear, that ever it was the King's design to give them *any* authority about *ecclesiastical* affairs, or in any manner to enable them to establish any way of religion different from, much less in opposition to, the Church of England, by law established in all his Majesty's dominions For which reason I cannot understand how it came to pass that they ever undertook to establish any religion, as your Lordship will observe, by their laws, they have done; which, therefore, seems to me to be repugnant to the laws of England Your Lordship has here likewise, for the more full understanding of the laws here transcribed, the Articles of Faith and Church Government, which are what they call the established religion of this country, though they fall very much short of acting up to them, and greatly disagree among themselves about them. But as to settling ministers and supporting them, the general practice of the colony is according to these laws, which is not by *subscription*, but by a major vote, both for the person chosen and the annual support he is to have. But as for the Church people of this colony, I know not of any of them that were ever concerned in voting for any of these ministers, or for their support; and I know that many have entered their protests, and desired to be excused from being in any way concerned, because of their belonging to and being obliged to pay to the support of the Church of England. And, as for others that may at any time come over to us, from their side, I would submit it to your Lordship whether it be not hard and unreasonable that they should be obliged to continue to pay to them, merely because they are overruled by a majority, when at the same time they are persuaded in their consciences that it is safer to retire into the unity of the Church, than to live and die in a state of schism and separation from her. I beg leave further to let your Lordship know that the Government here, putting a very wrong construction on your Lordship's letter, are rather encouraged to go on in persecuting people for their taxes, than to desist, because, they say, your Lordship begs pardon, if you have desired any thing inconsistent with the laws of this government. As to the plate, books, &c., your Lordship offers certain questions, and desires me and the people of Stratford to be clear upon these subjects. My Lord, had it been possible to be clear upon those heads, we should never have offered to trouble your Lordship about them. As to myself, it is impossible for me to be clear either one way or the other, having been a stranger to the whole affair. I hear the account the Narragansett people give of it, and that may be right for aught I know. Stratford people give another account of it, but neither side produces any evidence where the original property was lodged. All the papers relating to this matter were lost. I have impartially inquired of the people of Stratford, and cannot satisfy them that ever the things controverted were appropriated to any place, till Bishop Compton's order fixed them here. I have inquired also of all the clergy in Boston, Rhode Island and New-York; and can find nobody that can give any light in the matter, unless it be Col. Nicholson, who undoubtedly knows the true state of it, and my people are willing to resign them, if it appears from his account of it that they were, in the design of the donor, appropriated to Narragansett. If your Lordship shall think fit to inform yourself from him concerning this matter, and give us the least hint of your pleasure, we shall submit.

In the mean time, things lying, as they do, in the dark, we have as an expedient for peace yielded to a division, and above a year ago sent all the books thither, in hopes that our so doing may satisfy our brethren at Narragansett, unless it should plainly appear from Col. Nicholson that they were originally given to that Church. However, I earnestly desire, with your Lordship, that no religious offices may by any means be maintained at the expense of plain justice and equity. Forgive, my Lord, this tediousness, and impute it to my earnest desire and endeavour that your Lordship may have a satisfactory answer to your letter, which I could not contrive in a less compass; and permit me still to have an interest in your Lordship's favourable thoughts and benediction.

I am, my Lord, your Lordship's humble servant,

SAMUEL JOHNSON.

[*Rev. Mr. Johnson to the Secretary.*]

Stratford, August 14th, 1725.

Reverend Sir,

I have not much to inform the honourable Society of, besides what is contained in the general representation of our case, which we jointly offered at our last meeting, and which, I conclude, will come to your hands before this arrives. My congregations, especially at Stratford, Fairfield and New-London increase, but not so fast, by a great deal, as they would if it were not that all worldly motives are against the Church. I can observe, however, that a good opinion of her doctrines, government and liturgy gains greatly in the minds of people, and especially those of the soberer and better sort; a serious sense of religion visibly increases among my own people, and juster notions of religion daily propagate among others, who are kept back by their teachers and friends from appearing for the Church. Sundry of the young candidates for the ministry repair to me frequently for books and conversation upon religious subjects, and many, I hope in time, especially if there were a Bishop here, may enter into the Church's service. I have baptised within the last half-year twenty-eight, whereof five are adults, and one of them a negro man, and admitted thirteen to the Holy Communion. But those who come to Church are generally of the poorer sort, and unable to contribute any thing worth mentioning to my support; some are unable to buy any books, and would therefore be exceeding thankful to the honourable Society for a few prayer-books, if it were but ten or a dozen, with a few sheets of catechisms, with Lewis' or Sing's Exposition. Ostervald's Catechism is a book likewise which poor people thirst after very much; and, indeed, these books are not to be had in this country, even if they had money to purchase them.

I am, Reverend Sir, the Society's much obliged,
And your most humble servant,
SAMUEL JOHNSON.

P. S.—The Church at Fairfield goes on a-pace, and New-London people are likewise going to build with all expedition. I have got considerable subscriptions, and a piece of land to set it on.

[*Governor Talcott to the Bishop of London.*]

Hartford, July 27th, 1726.

Right Reverend Sir,

I had the favour and honour of your Lordship's letter of June 3d, 1725, with the copy of the former sent to Boston. I readily embrace the opportunity to let your Lordship know the true state of the Church in this, his Majesty's government in this colony of Connecticut, and that by letter dated December 1st, 1725;* but being now informed the ship that letter went in was lost, with all, save the lives of the persons, I held myself obliged to inform your Lordship by this second letter, that† there is but one Church of England minister in this colony, and the Church with him have the same protection as the rest of our Churches, and are under no constraint to contribute to the support of any other minister. There are some few persons in another town or two, that have stipulated with the present ministers now living in said towns, (which persons cannot be much recommended for

* A copy of this letter (December 1st, 1725,) is among the MSS. of the Connecticut Historical Society, (No. 102, Talcott MSS.,) and we have been favoured with a copy of it. As we learn from the letter we here print, which we obtained from the *Fulham* MSS., that of December 1st never reached its destination. On a comparison of the Connecticut copy with our own, we find that, with the addition of a single explanatory fact, the two copies agree. Ours is a duplicate, sent because the ship that took the first was lost.

† From this point the letters agree almost *verbatim.*

their zeal for religion or morality,) who cannot well be judged to act from any other motive than to appear singular, or to be freed from a small tax, and have declared themselves to be of the Church of England; and some of them that live 30 or 40 miles from where the Church of England's minister lives; these have made some objections against their customary contribution to their proper minister, under whose administration they have equal privileges with their neighbours.

The law of this colony is such, that the major part of the householders in every town shall determine their minister's maintenance, and all within the precincts of the town shall be obliged to pay their parts in an equal proportion to their estates in said towns or societies; and so in the precincts of each ecclesiastical society. Under this security, all our towns and ecclesiastical societies are supplied with orthodox ministers. We have no vacancies at present. When the death of the incumbent happens, they are quickly supplied by persons of our own communion, educated in our public schools of learning; which, through the Divine blessing afforded us, we have a sufficiency of those that are both learned and exemplary in their lives. I beg your Lordship's pardon, and am with great observance,

Your Lordship's most humble servant,

JOSEPH TALCOTT.

NOTE.—Of course, it will not be forgotten that the governor was a Congregationalist, and naturally viewed the Church with distrust and suspicion, not to say dislike.

[*Rev. Mr. Johnson to the Bishop of London.*]

Stratford, New-England, Feb'y 10th, 1726-7.

May it please your Lordship,

I must confess that I am ashamed thus to tire your Lordship's patience with complaints of this nature; neither should I have given you this trouble, but at the importunity of the distressed people whose names (some of them) you behold at the foot of the inclosed address to your Lordship. It was their own contrivance to fall into this method. The complaint was drawn up, and some of the persons were in prison before I was sent for. Upon their request I came to the prison, and found it full of them, and an insulting mob about them. I administered what comfort I could to them, but I wish your Lordship, or some of your sacred character, could have been by to behold the contempt and indignity which our holy religion here suffers among an ungrateful people. It could not fail to excite your utmost zeal and compassion; and I assure your Lordship, the Church here is in a gasping condition, though, indeed, our people bear it with as much meekness and patience as can be expected. I venture so far upon my hopes of the success of your Lordship's concern and endeavour for us, as to promise them before our enemies that they should find relief; and if after all this we fail, there will remain no more hope, or good to be done here. Your Lordship required me in one of your letters to let you know particularly the state of things in the country. Accordingly, besides what I have formerly informed you of, I would further observe to your Lordship, that some of the errors which, in the course of my ministry, I have to encounter, are the same with many of the principles of the book called "The Rights of the Christian Church;" errors so great and so subversive of all religion, that I make no doubt but that your Lordship, (whatever may be suggested to you to the contrary,) will not only justify my faithful and honest endeavours, made with a temper becoming Christianity, to undeceive the unhappy people; but likewise think it to very good purpose, that I, or some body of better capacity, (and I hope, ere long, more than one,) should be supported in these parts to guard what little flock we have against such dissolute principles. Absolute lay ordination is the avowed principle of some of the chief of their ministers, and has been frequently practiced in the country, and even in this town, though now, of late, their ministers generally ordain; but the people claim a share of authority with their ministers in all public acts of discipline.

One thing more I beg leave to observe to your Lordship, and that is this: our government, I understand, imagine that if their laws are confirmed in England, they shall then be an establishment as much as the Church of England. And, accordingly, I am certified, that they have lately sent home their laws, with the colony's seal, to get them confirmed to that purpose. Among the rest are those I sent copies of to your Lordship; if, therefore, those laws, with the rest, should get confirmed, we shall then be more effectually borne down under their pretended establishment. My Lord, I am obliged to pass along through the world, but hardly among my poor oppressed people, from whom I can have nothing for my support worth mentioning. I should be very thankful if the honourable Society could augment the salary that belongs to Stratford, which is, and I fear always will be, extremely poor, perhaps the poorest place of any to which their charity is extended.

I am, &c., &c.,

SAMUEL JOHNSON.

[*Rev. Mr. Johnson at Stratford to the Secretary.*]

Sept. 16*th*, 1726.

Reverend Sir,

I have received the honourable Society's letter to me of March 15th, in which I have an account of some books which they have been so kind as to send, and which I have since received I return the most humble thanks, both of me and of my people, for their kind notice of us, and continual care of our souls; and the joy and gratitude my poor people express on this occasion will, I doubt not, be attended with making such a religious use of these good books as will abundantly answer the pious designs of the honourable Society in bestowing of them; and they do in some measure comfort them, under the hardships and difficulties which are not yet removed, and upon the account of which the Church gains ground but very slowly. At Fairfield, however, the number daily increases, and they have erected a small Church, which I opened last fall, and we call it Trinity Church. And Mr. Caner takes a great deal of pains to very good purpose, and will, I don't doubt, prove a very worthy man, but he has a very slender support from the people. He designs, about two years hence, to wait on the honourable Society for orders and a mission, unless they see cause to forbid it. In the mean time, as he stands in very great need of it, so he and the people would be very thankful if the honourable Society would be pleased to grant him a small encouragement for the pains he takes in instructing that people and their children in the principles of religion, which he now performs in the quality of a sort of Catechist, omitting every thing that is properly sacerdotal. But not only he, but sundry other very worthy young gentlemen, dreading the thoughts of so tedious a voyage, wait with great impatience in hopes that, possibly, Providence may send us a Bishop, for want of which the Church in these parts is derided and laughed to scorn, while our enemies can take the advantage of immediately fixing teachers wherever they please, in opposition to the Church, and defy us to our faces.

These things make us mourn and go on heavily, and indeed it would make any serious person's heart ache to behold the contempt and dishonour cast on religion, and especially on our Holy Church, on this account, and the grief of our poor people, who know not how to answer the reproaches they are hereby forced to lie under. It is very much lamented by the Rye people, that they are in danger of being denied the good services of Mr. Wetmore, for whom they have a great esteem, and who might have been much more serviceable than a perfect stranger. And I would humbly presume to suggest to the honourable Society that it might be much more for the interest of religion in general, and for the satisfaction of Rye people of New-York or Westchester, if the honourable Society would be so kind to order it, that Mr. Wetmore might yet be appointed for Rye, and Mr. Colgan, either to succeed him at New-York, or to be at Westchester. But this I do with the greatest submission and deference. I have admitted 11 to the Communion and baptised 9 within this half year. But while the Church in the country continues under the present oppressions, little or nothing can be expected from Newtown or Ripton to encourage the Society to send them a missionary. In the mean time, my burthen is very great, and I would humbly hope the honourable Society will consider me with compassion, who have a more troublesome and less profitable province than any one missionary I know of; for I have nothing to depend on but the bounty of the Society. I am entirely alone in a large colony.

I am, Sir,

Your and their most humble

And most obedient servant,

SAMUEL JOHNSON.

[*Rev. Mr. Johnson to the Bishop of London.*]

Stratford in New-England, September 26, 1726.

May it please your Lordship,

I have received your Lordship's kind letter of June 28th, d take this opportunity to return my most humble thanks to your Lordship for the honour you have done me therein, and I am exceeding glad that I could in any wise contribute to your Lordship's satisfaction upon the subject you wrote to me about. I hope the issue of it will be that we shall at length find better quarter in the country than we have done; though at present things remain just as they were, and we are oppressed and despised as the filth of the world and the offscouring of all things, unto this day. They all boast themselves an establishment, and look down upon the poor Church of England with contempt, as a despicable, schismatical and popish communion; and their charter is, indeed, the foundation of all their insolence. Happy would it be for the Church of England if it were taken away, and unless they could be made sensible (as the truth is) that they have no warrant from it to despise the Church, or to do any thing to her disadvantage. I am not, my Lord, for any severity towards the Dissenters, and I always treat them with all the tenderness that becomes our common Christianity; but with submission

I cannot but think it very hard, that that Church, of which our most gracious King is the nursing father, should not, in any part of his Majesty's dominions, be at least upon a level with the Dissenters, and free from any oppression from them.

There is another instance I will presume to trouble your Lordship with, and that is this: Your Lordship observes that all persons that shall come to inhabit this colony, or are born here, have, by the charter, all the liberties and immunities of free and natural subjects, as if they were born within the realm of England. Notwithstanding which, they have made laws to prevent strangers from settling among them. As soon as any stranger, though an Englishman, comes into the town, he is, according to their laws, immediately warned to go out, which they always do if he is a Churchman; and it is in the breast of the selectmen of the town whether they will accept of any bondsmen for him. Neither can he purchase any lands without their leave; and unless they see cause to allow him to stay, they can, by their laws, *whip* him out of town, if he otherwise refuses to depart. By this means several professors of our Church, for no other crime but their profession, have been prevented from settling here. A very worthy man, who had not before been of any religion, but was, by God's blessing on my endeavours, induced to become a very serious conformist to our Church, came here to set up a considerable trade; but, for want of men to carry on his business, (occasioned by the fore-mentioned practices,) and by reason of the discouragements he everywhere meets with from them, he is forced to break up and depart, to his unspeakable damage, and the Church has lost a very worthy friend and benefactor. I intended to have given your Lordship some further and more particular account of the state of religion in the country; but I dare not, at this time, trespass further upon your Lordship's patience, but leave that to another opportunity

I am, my Lord,

Your Lordship's most obedient servant,

SAMUEL JOHNSON.

[*Rev. Mr. Johnson to the Secretary.*]

Stratford, *February* 10*th*, 1727.

Reverend Sir,

I have just come from Fairfield, where I have been to visit a considerable number of my people, in prison for their rates to the dissenting minister, to comfort and encourage them under their sufferings. But, verily, unless we can have relief, and be delivered from this unreasonable treatment, I fear I must give up the cause, and our Church must sink and come to nothing. There are thirty-five heads of families in Fairfield, who, all of them, expect what these have suffered; and though I have endeavoured to gain the compassion and favour of the government, yet I can avail nothing; and both I and my people grow weary of our lives under our poverty and oppression. Some few, however, do now and then come over to us. I have baptised thirty this year, whereof five were adults, and three of them were negroes, and admitted about a dozen to the communion, and reclaimed two from very disorderly lives. A very worthy young gentleman lives with me in my house, who is a scholar, having lately been graduated in a neighbouring College, whom I have reconciled to our Church, and, indeed, (I may say,) to Christianity, for he never was baptised, not even by any of the lecturers which the country swarms everywhere with. Him, therefore, I have baptised and admitted to the communion; and he is a very religious, sober, studious and sensible man, and will, I doubt not, be an ornament to our Church. He designs, with Mr. Caner, in due time, to offer himself to the honourable Society's service, to whom, I hope, they will both appear very acceptable.

I am, Reverend Sir,

Your most humble and obedient servant,

SAMUEL JOHNSON.

[*Rev. Mr. Johnson to the Secretary.*

Stratford, *April* 28*th*, 1727.

Reverend Sir,

This comes to recommend to the honourable Society's notice and acceptance the young gentleman who is the bearer hereof, Mr. Henry Caner, who was bred up in one of our Colleges, and has, for the time of three years, lived under my eye, and made considerable proficiency in the study of Divinity, and other parts of learning, necessary to qualify him for the ministry, and has all along proved himself a sober, studious and religious young man; and I don't doubt but he will prove a very worthy missionary, if the honourable Society will make use of his services, to the advancement of whose pious concerns he is willing to devote himself. He has already done a great deal of good service at Fairfield for the time he has been among them, in the quality of a catechist and schoolmaster, and will be very acceptable to them as a missionary, as appears by their address inclosed; and will be likewise a great comfort to me, in my solitary neighbourhood, in conspiring with me to forward the interests of religion in this country, and thereby relieving me of a great part of that burthen that lies upon me, who, besides Fairfield, have five places which I am obliged to visit and administer to as often as conveniently I can. I wish, for the encouragement of the young gentlemen who go from hence, that the honourable Society would be pleased to defray the expenses of their voyages thither, according to a declaration made in their account of the Society, printed by their order in 1706, page 74, and that Mr. Caner might have the benefit of it. I should be very thankful if that charitable order of the Society might look back, with a favourable aspect, upon us, who first undertook this difficult and dangerous expedition.

I am their, and, Sir, your most humble

And most obedient servant,

SAMUEL JOHNSON.

[*Rev. Mr. Caner to the Secretary.*]

Fairfield, March 15th, 1727-8.

Reverend Sir,

My arrival in New-England was so late in the fall that I had not opportunity to give the honourable Society any account thereof, nor yet to lay before them the state of the Church when I came to Fairfield. I would now, therefore, supply that defect by presenting the honourable Society with the following account.

At my first coming to Fairfield, the professors of the Church expressed their thanks, in a just sense of the noble charity to their souls, which the honourable Society had bestowed in granting their request for a missionary, but were very sorry their abilities could not by any means answer their expectations from them ; the heavy taxes levied for the support of dissenting ministers, joined with a small and voluntary offering to the Church, rendering them almost incapable of carrying on the Church, which is not yet finished, nor in any way likely to be so presently. The truth is, the people are heartily ready and willing to do their utmost to be as little burthensome to the honourable Society as possible, but being generally poor, and Fairfield being the chief seat of the Dissenters' opposition, they are able to contribute but very little to the support of that worship which their consciences urge them to maintain.

Besides Fairfield, which I constantly serve, and the villages contiguous which belong to that town, as Poquannuck, Greens Farms and Greenfield, I have several times preached this winter at Norwalk, a town 12 miles distant from Fairfield, and at Stamford, which is about 20 miles, and at Greenwich, about 27 miles distant from Fairfield, and which is the utmost town within the borders of this government westward. Besides these, there is a village northward of Fairfield, about 18 miles, containing near 20 families, where there is no minister at all of any denomination whatsoever ; the name of it is Chesnut

Ridge, and where I usually preach or lecture once in three weeks. Newtown, which is about 22 miles northwest of Fairfield, Mr. Johnson and I supply between us, it being equally distant from us. There are still two other towns which I serve as often as my occasions will allow, both still to the northward of Fairfield, viz., Ridgefield and Danbury, the one 17 and the other 23 miles distant from Fairfield. In most of the above mentioned places there are, 7, 10 or 15 families professing the Church of England, from which places, joined with Fairfield, the taxes strained from members of the Church for the support of dissenting teachers amount to £100, which is about £40 sterling, of which Fairfield pays about half. The taking away of these sums very much hinders the building they are carrying on, as well as of contributions to the support of a minister, for which latter use they are not able to raise above £10 sterling per annum.

Notwithstanding this discouragement, the Church grows and increases very much, four families being added since my coming, one whereof was a Jew, whose wife only was before a Christian. This person, besides his excellent skill in Hebrew and Greek and other Eastern languages, is very well studied in the Rabbinical learning, and is a very accomplished person upon all accounts; neither is his conversion balanced with any views of interest or friendship, as I can learn, but upon very good and serious principles he embraced the Christian faith, being baptised with his family very lately. Besides these, since December last, I have baptised one adult and 17 infants, one whereof was an Indian, and have eight new communicants, the whole number of which is now 49.

I have further prospect, likewise, of baptising two other Indians, in a short time, of about 30 years of age, who are very seriously disposed, and attend Divine worship with some constancy.

Thus I have laid before the honourable Society a just account of the state of the Church at Fairfield, and humbly hope, therefore, upon the whole, they will not think the charity they have bestowed lost, but pray continually that they may see the happy effects of these, as well as all their other pious labours for the good of souls. I am the honourable Society's most dutiful and obedient, as well as, Sir,

Your most humble servant,

HENRY CANER.

[*Rev. Mr. Johnson to the Secretary.*]

Stratford, New-England, September 20th, 1727.

Reverend Sir,

I have received from the honourable Society two letters, one dated May 23d, the other June 16, for which I take this opportunity to return my humblest thanks, and particularly for their kind notice of my low and difficult circumstances, and the addition they have made to my salary, which I shall ever gratefully consider as a fresh motive and obligation upon me to exert myself, with the greatest zeal and industry I am capable of, in endeavouring to answer their expectations from me, and their pious designs in supporting the mission in this place, where there is a great deal of good to be done, but little to be expected of the poor people. Five pounds sterling per annum is more than I have ever received or can expect, while the government continues as it is.

I likewise thank the honourable Society for the regard they have expressed to my recommendation of Mr. Caner, who has, I conclude, before now, paid his duty to them in person. The afflicted condition of his people, and no prospect of a redress, was the occasion of his waiting on the honourable Society sooner than he would otherwise have done. I hope, however, he will be found in some measure acceptable to them; but I should be very glad that the same salary, which was allowed to him as schoolmaster at Fairfield, might be allowed for a school in this town, where there is a great need of one; and it might be of good service, not only for forming the minds of children to a sense of religion, but likewise for a resort for such young gentlemen successively as from time to time leave the College here, and are rejected from all business by the Dissenters, on the account of their being reconciled to the Church of England. Under the eye of the missionary here, they might, while they keep school, improve themselves in the study of Divinity till they are qualified for higher business. There is one Mr. Bennett now in town, who very well deserves to be recommended as an instance of what I now speak of, and might do good service in such a school.

I now proceed to answer the queries of the honourable Society which are contained in their last letter; and to the first:

1. Christ Church, in Stratford, was founded in the year 1723, partly at the charge of the members of the Church of England here, who, by subscriptions, raised what money they could for the erecting of it, and partly by the liberal contributions of several pious and generous gentlemen of the neighbouring provinces, and sometimes of travellers who occasionally passed through the town. It is a neat, small wooden building, forty-five feet and a half long, thirty and a half wide, and twenty-two between joints, or up to the roof; but there is no house or glebe belonging to it, nor is it at all endowed, nor has it any settled salary besides the honourable Society's bounty; only the poor people are as liberal in small presents as can be expected of them.

2. To the second: The first beginning of the Church of England in this town was by about ten or fifteen families, most of them tradesmen, some husbandmen, who were born and bred up in England, and came and settled here; some of them were born here, and by means of the rest were reconciled to the Church. It is nigh twenty years since they first endeavoured to have the worship of God in the method of the Church among them, but were disappointed till about five years ago; ever since which, the numbers have been considerably increasing, so that now there are about fifty families within the compass of about fifty miles square of ground, (which is the extent of this town,) who pretty steadily frequent the Church; and besides them, there are a considerable number of people scattered up and down in the neighbouring towns, some five, some ten, twenty and thirty miles off, who

come to Church as often as can be expected; for there is no Church westward within forty miles, only Fairfield, which is eight miles off, where there is a small wooden Church built, and about forty families, who hope for Mr. Caner to be sent them from the Society; and there is no Church eastward within one hundred miles, only at New-London, about seventy miles off, where I sometimes preach to a good number of people, and they are building a wooden Church something larger than ours, and hope for a missionary, and have desired me to recommend their case to the honourable Society, that they may be supplied as soon as may be, and there is there a good prospect of a large increase. There is no Church northward of us at all. We lie upon the sea; [*i. e.*, Sound;] and directly over against us, southward on Long Island, lies Brook Haven, about twenty miles over the water, where I have often preached, both before Mr. Standard was there and since he left there, to a considerable congregation, who are building a handsome Church, and have also desired me to intercede for their speedy supply. They stand in great need of a minister, and much good might be done among them. The towns in this country are pretty thick, scarce any above ten, some not five miles asunder; some of them have sundry little villages belonging to them, and most of them consist of two, three or four hundred families, which, though scarce any of them are contiguous, yet the main body of them live in very near neighbourhoods; the roads are generally well cleared and much used, so that travelling is for the most part indifferent good, and it is a fruitful and thriving country; but the people of our Church are mostly of the poorer sort.

3. As to the third: It must be confessed that our number is very small in comparison with the Dissenters, who are very numerous, perhaps three hundred and fifty families to fifty of us, and they are generally of the Independent or Congregational persuasion, though the principles they support themselves upon are but little different from those of the book falsely called the "Rights of the Christian Church." They have a large meeting-house in the body of the town, within a few rods of the Church, and two small ones besides in the villages. The way of supporting their ministers is by a rate

levied in proportion to their estates, according to law, which the government hath enacted for that purpose, by which they have, as I humbly conceive, without any warrant from their charter, *established* their way of worship and discipline in opposition to any other, and by means of which establishment they oppose the Church.

4. To the fourth: The Dissenters have two poor schools in this town, but the Church hath none, though there is a considerable number of children among us.

5. To the fifth: We have no donations made to our Church, save what have been mentioned, no benefactions to the minister or schoolmaster, no library belonging to the parish, save what the honourable Society have bestowed.

6. To the sixth: The Dissenters in this town have perhaps one hundred and fifty or one hundred and sixty negro slaves among them, who are, some of them, instructed, and a few baptised in their way; but we have but six or seven come to Church, four of which I have baptised.

This is the substance of what account I have to give of the rise, progress and present state of the Church here.

I am, Reverend Sir,

Your most humble and most obedient servant,

SAMUEL JOHNSON.

[*Rev. Mr. Johnson to the Secretary.*]

Stratford, N. E., October 23d, 1727.

Reverend Sir,

I have very lately written to the honourable Society in obedience to their commands, yet I humbly hope they will forgive me, though I trouble them so soon again with relation to the necessity of a school in this town. In the last I informed the Society of what service it might be to the interest of religion to have a school here, and that Mr. Bennett (who has for above half a year kept school among the Dissenters here, and been rejected by the greatest number of them upon conformity to our Church) would be very serviceable and acceptable in a school upon the honourable Society's foundation. Since which time I have endeavoured to gain subscriptions, and have been very successful, not only among the Church people, but with a considerable number of Dissenters, who seem at present, many of them, to be in a good temper, especially for Mr. Bennett's sake, not only in contributing to the support of such a school, but in allowing that their children be taught and regulated according to the Society's rules, provided he might be continued, whom they find to be the best schoolmaster they ever had among them; and I believe the greatest part of what subscriptions we shall make will be from among them, for their number and ability are beyond ours. We have already raised nigh thirty pounds per annum, equal to about ten pounds sterling, and hope if we might have the Society's usual salary to schoolmasters, we might make so good a support as would be some encouragement and relief for such young men of the College from time to time as are neglected in the country, by reason of their adherence to our communion. I beg, therefore, if the honourable Society can find themselves able, they would be pleased at so happy a juncture to allow us their charitable assistance in this affair, for nothing could so happily contribute to the enlargement of our Church, by begetting in the tender minds of children a sense of the excellency of our holy religion.

I am, Reverend Sir,
Your most humble and obedient servant,
SAMUEL JOHNSON.

[*Anonymous Letter to the Bishop of London.*]

Stratford, N. E., October 30th, 1727.

My Lord,

Right Reverend Sir,

May it please your Lordship, these lines wait upon your Grace from a true sense of duty to yourself and of justice to the great work and purpose of promoting religion in these ends of the Earth, which your Lordship hath so much at heart, and that which moves me to write at this time, is a jealousy that you may be imposed upon by kindnesses received for this place. I think we can never be thankful enough for your Lordship's benignity, under heaven's favour, that one minister is freely maintained among us with so very little charge as ours; and truly our depending in this matter is wholly on the Society's bounty, for, whenever this fails, we shall surely no longer have a minister, because we have no prospect of our ever being able to afford him any thing like a maintenance; for our whole company in this great town consists of about ten or a dozen families, and that of the meaner and poorer sort. I am obliged to say, notwithstanding the relation I bear to them, there is no view of our increasing; there comes now and then a disaffected person to us, and when his passion is over, he returns from whence he came; for the ministry of the town is somewhat of a Presbyterian humour, having shaken off the old Independent notions that were so disgustful, so that the people are under no temptation to change their pastor, and very few have yet done so in this place, except those that were unwilling to pay rates; and we find them as unwilling to be at any public charge now as before. We could not have built our Church had not travellers and strangers bestowed their favours upon us; and truly, our brethren of the Church of England in this colony in the neighbouring towns are none of them persons of any note that were famed for religion; and what more might be said I leave, lest I might discourage your Lordship's further care about us. And now, our Reverend Father, that our brethren may not grow intolerable to you, may these lines be a happy preventive.

The addition of our [prosperity] will not be in asking a salary for our schoolmaster, a project that is now on foot among us; and though our Reverend Pastor may lead or encourage the matter, I cannot but think it is more from oversight than notice, to say that we shall have more interest or benefit in the schools of the town than we now enjoy. I am persuaded this will prove a mistake, for we have the same privileges in either of them as any of the Dissenters have; the houses are within sight of each other and well supported, which bespeaks the ability of the town, so that if any thing be allowed from home, it will be some ease to the town in general, but of no particular advantage to us, but I much rather think, a prejudice and a wrong to us; for now, there is such a friendship between us and the committee of the schools, as that we have in times past and at present a man of our own persuasion in one of them, and with the general allowance. If by encouragement from your Lordship's benignity to us, we should make a division in this matter, we can expect no such favour for the future. Most of the people of the town are ready to think we have some ill-design in asking a pension for their school, which they are so well able to support of themselves, so that if it be granted we shall hazard their greater dislike to us, and thereby wrong ourselves, rather than reap any advantage by the means, whatever may be pretended by the petitioners. And now, not willing to be further troublesome, I conclude with humbly asking pardon for my boldness in writing, and especially in concealing my name, which I must beg leave to do, lest my brethren become displeased with me. I heartily wish your Lordship length of days, riches and honour; that all your endeavours for the propagating of the Gospel and advancing the interest of our great Lord and Redeemer may be crowned with happy success; and your rewards in glory, when you shall cease from your painful labours, may be very great.

I remain, with submission,

Your Lordship's

Humble servant to command.

Note.—It is by no means certain that this letter was not written by a *Congregationalist*, in the assumed character of a Churchman, to defeat Mr. Johnson's application for a school under the patronage of the Church. It may well be doubted whether any one of the congregation of the Stratford missionary either could or would have written the letter.

[*Petition of the Churchwardens and Vestry of Fairfield to the Connecticut Legislature.*]

[This document has been kindly furnished to the Editor from the original among the State Archives at Hartford.—*Ecclesiastical*, VOL. III., DOC. 188.]

To the honourable the Governor, Assistants and Representatives in General Court assembled, this 15th of May, 1727, the request of sundry members of the Church of England in Fairfield, humbly sheweth, that—

Whereas we are, by the Honourable Society in England and the Bishop of London, laid under obligation to pay to the support of the said established Church, and have accordingly constantly paid to it, and been at great charge in building a Church for the worship of God, we pray this Assembly would, by some act or otherwise, as your wisdom shall think fit, excuse us hereafter from paying to any dissenting minister, or to the building of any dissenting meeting-house. And whereas we were, ten of us, lately imprisoned for our taxes, and had considerable sums of money taken from us by distraint, contrary to his Honour the Governor's advice, and notwithstanding solemn promises before given to sit down and be concluded thereby in this affair, we pray that those sums of money taken from us may be restored to us again. If these grievances may be redressed, we shall aim at nothing but to live peaceably and as becometh Christians among our dissenting brethren; and your petitioners, as in duty bound, shall ever pray, &c.

MOSES WARD,
SAMUEL LYON, } *Churchwardens.*

DOUGAL MCKENZIE,
JOHN LOCKWOOD,
NATHAN ADAMS,
BEN. STURGIS, &c., } *Vestry.*

In the name and behalf of all the rest of our brethren.

[Upon this petition, the General Assembly enacted, that all persons who were of the Church of England, and those who were of the churches established by the law of the colony, living in the bounds of any allowed parish, should be taxed by the same rule and in the same proportion for the support of the ministry; but where it happened that there was a society of the Church of England, having a clergyman so near any person who had declared himself to be of that Church, that he could and did attend public worship there, then the collector was to deliver the tax collected of such person to the minister of the Church of England to whom he lived near, who was also authorized to receive and recover the same; and if such proportion of taxes was not sufficient in any society of the Church of England to support the incumbent, such society was authorized to levy and collect of those who professed and attended that Church greater taxes at their discretion. The parishioners of the Church of England were also excused from paying any taxes for building meeting-houses for the established Churches of the colony.]*

[*Rev. Mr. Caner to the Bishop of London.*]

Fairfield, March 15*th*, 1727-8.

My Lord,

I take this opportunity to wait upon your Lordship, (the winter season preventing my doing it sooner,) with my humble duty, as well as to inform your Lordship of the state of the Church, since my arrival in this place, where your Lordship, with the honourable Society, have been pleased to appoint me. My Lord, I find it to my very great satisfaction; the people to whom I am sent are, however, low and poor in fortune, yet are very serious and well-minded, and ready to entertain any instructions that may forward them in the paths of virtue and truth and godliness. I have presumed to lay before the honourable Society an account of the hardships they labour under, in being obliged to pay taxes to dissenting ministers; and shall depend upon your Lordship's usual goodness, to forward that matter, if any thing may be done for our relief from such a burthen; for beside, my Lord, that it hinders the finishing the Church they have begun to build, it is utterly inconsistent with what your Lordship and

* See the Statute on p. 340 of the Law Book of the Colony, edition of 1715.

the honourable Society have been pleased to enjoin me; for although the Dissenters in this government have lately passed an act to exempt all professors of the Church from paying taxes to the support of their ministers, yet they take the liberty to determine themselves who may be called Churchmen, and interpret that act to comprehend none that live a mile from the Church minister; by which means, not only two-thirds of the Church, but of its revenues likewise, we are entirely deprived of the benefit of; and the favour which they would seem to do us proves, in reality, but a shadow. These difficulties, your Lordship will easily be persuaded, very much hinder the growth and weaken the hands of the Church; however, amidst all this, your Lordship will find, by the representation I have made to the honourable Society, there are daily added to the Church such as, by the blessing of God, added to their own honest endeavours, will finally be saved. To this end suffer us, my Lord, to assure ourselves of your Lordship's continued prayers and blessing, which will always be justly valued by one, who is,

With the greatest respect, my Lord,

Your Lordship's humble servant,

HENRY CANER.

[*Rev. Mr. Johnson to the Bishop of London.*]

Stratford, in New-England, April 2d, 1728.

May it please your Lordship,

I am thankful to your Lordship for despatching Mr. Caner so soon to his parish, for I find great advantage to the interests of the Church, from his neighbourhood, and assistance, and I hope the Society will enlarge his salary, as soon as their ability will admit of it. The government here have pretended to make a law in favour of the Church, whereby all that live near our parish Churches are exempted from paying to the dissenting ministers, and it is of some service to such; but those that live scattering in the country are yet persecuted as bad as ever; and in this law they still call themselves the established Churches, and treat us as Dissenters. I have lately been preaching at New-Haven, where the College is, and had a considerable congregation, and among them several of the scholars, who are very inquisitive about the principles of our Church, and after sermon ten of the members of the Church there subscribed £100 towards the building a Church in that town, and are zealously engaged about undertaking it; and I hope in a few years there will be a large congregation there.

The Church at Boston has lost a very worthy pastor in Mr. Myles, and I doubt they will break into sad confusion there, unless a very worthy and discreet minister be sent them from England, for I am told above five to one are so greatly disgusted with Mr. Harris, that they will never be content under his ministry. Your Lordship has doubtless been informed of the controversy between Mr. Myles and Dr. Cutler on the one hand, and the overseers of Harvard College on the other, and that the General Court have given judgment for the overseers against the clergy of the Church, whereby they have excluded them from being overseers, after they have for many years been allowed that character, and notwithstanding the plain sense of the charter or act of Assembly which comprehends them; so that this matter must now have a trial in England, and I presume to hope that your Lordship's wisdom and goodness will be engaged in behalf of this affair, which, I humbly conceive, is a matter wherein the interest of the Church in this country is much concerned. I have nothing more to add, but that I am,

May it please your Lordship,

Your Lordship's humble servant,

SAMUEL JOHNSON.

[*Rev. Mr. Johnson to the Secretary.—Extract.*]

Stratford, April 3d, 1728.

Reverend Sir,

Since my last, I find the advantage of Mr. Caner's neighbourhood and assistance, and the growth of the Church in these parts is considerable. The government have made a law pretending favour to the Church, by which all that live near our parish Churches are excused from paying rates to their ministers, and it is of some service to such, but those that live scattering in the country are yet persecuted as bad as ever; and in this law they still call themselves the established Church, and treat us as Dissenters.

I have likewise since preached to a considerable number of people at New-London, where they are vigorously carrying on their Church, and I hope they will meet with the honourable Society's encouragement. At Norwalk, where I preached since I wrote last, there are several families who are reconciled to the Church, to whom Mr. Caner since has preached again. And in that town there is a sober and sensible Jew, considerably acquainted with the writings of their Rabbis, with whom I have had much conversation ; and he seems seriously inclined to embrace Christianity, and I hope before long to persuade him to be baptised, if the enmity of his countrymen do not prevail against his convictions. I have also (besides other neighbouring parishes) lately preached at New-Haven, a large town about fourteen miles eastward, where there is a College. Great pains were taken to hinder people from coming to Church, and many well wishers to it were over-persuaded not to come; however, I had near a hundred hearers, and among them several of the College; after service about ten of the members of our Church there subscribed £100 towards building a Church in that town, and seem very zealously engaged to prosecute the design, and I hope in a few years there will be a large congregation there. Here, in Stratford, I have another family added to the Church, and I have a sober, ingenuous Indian, one of the natives, a young man whom I have brought over to the belief of Christianity, am teaching him to read and write, and make a business of catechising and instructing him now in the season of Lent, and design to baptise him at Easter, and with him, a little girl about six years old, of the same tribe; both of them are bound to me by indenture from their parents.

[The following petition, upon which nothing was granted, was presented in May, 1728, and is procured from the State Archives at Hartford.—"*Ecclesiastical*," Vol. III., Doc. 138. *Vide ante.*]

To the Honourable General Assembly, now sitting at Hartford, May the ninth, A. Dom. 1728 :

The Memorial of Isaac Brown and the rest of the Churchwardens, Vestrymen and brethren of the Church of England, humbly sheweth :

That sometime in May, 1727, the Churchwardens, Vestrymen and some of the brethren of the Church of England did exhibit a prayer to the honourable Assembly, complaining of some hardship and injury done them by having money forced from them, and some of them imprisoned, on the account or for the support of the dissenting ministry in the County of Fairfield, and for building meeting-houses and settling of ministers ; and forasmuch as the prayer of the distressed was by this honourable Assembly heard, and they in their great wisdom, as well as Christian compassion, was pleased to provide a remedy for the relief of the professors of said Church, that they should no more be oppressed by contributing to the support of the Dissenters ; and forasmuch as in the act of the honourable Assembly it is not fully understood what part of the professors of the Church of England are exempted, all being within the district of the Reverend Mr. Johnson and Mr. Caner's ministry, within the County of Fairfield, assigned to them by the ministry at home.

We, the subscribers, in behalf of the rest, humbly move to this Assembly, that an explanation of the Assembly's Act in May last, relating to the premises, may be given by them ; and also, that for the future the affairs of the Church may be wholly managed by the book of canons relating to gathering taxes for the support of the ministry, that is established by law according to the rubrick of the Church of England ; and that for the future, so long as there remain missionaries among us, we may gather all needful taxes by said book of canons and not by your collectors. Great contentions have already arisen, and many lawsuits, as well as great hardship imposed upon us, who are but small and at great expense in building of Churches, and to help us, the honourable Society in England designs, by their contributing to our missionaries for their subsistence, as sometimes this honourable Assembly have done to small places; but as the act now stands, no donations will be of any advantage to the body of the people, which we humbly conceive is not agreeable to that rule given by our blessed Saviour, Do as you would, &c. We humbly conceive that this honourable Assembly doth not design to oppress us, but make people honest and religious; (not Churchmen for ease, as sometimes they have chapels;) and we humbly hope that 'tis our unfeigned desire that all men were so, and then we should not have these animosities amongst us. We do assure this Assembly, that we are bound in our consciences to adhere to said Church in doctrine and discipline, let our difficulties be ever so great. We humbly ask the Assembly's act for our relief in these things we have prayed for, and in so doing this honourable Assembly will engage us both to duty and respect, and we shall ever pray, as in duty bound.

Dated May 9th, 1728.

ISAAC BROWN,
BENJA. BURTT, } *Vestrymen.*

MOSES WARD,
SAM'EL LION, } *Churchwardens.*

HENRY JAMES,
MOSES KNAPP,
NATHAN ADAMS,
JNO. LOCKWOOD, } *Vestrymen.*

[*Rev. Mr. Johnson to the Secretary.*]

Stratford, New-England, September 21*st*, 1728.

Reverend Sir,

Though so considerable a number of my former hearers are gone off to make up Mr. Caner's parish, and notwithstanding that three families are removed this year from this town, out of the government, yet my Church has been considerably fuller this summer than ever it was before. Seven entire families are reconciled to the Church; and though such a number of communicants are gone off to Fairfield parish, yet I have fourscore here and in the neighbouring town, who constantly, and as frequently as may be, attend the communion at Stratford. Beside two of the native Indians I have brought within the pale of the Church, (of whom I made mention in my last,) there is one large family of English, who have heretofore lived like heathens, but are now become serious Christians, and I have baptised them; it consists, beside the two parents, of seven children, of which five are adults. And beside the Jew I mentioned before, who is a sincere good Christian, and has since been baptised, here is another Jew, a very sober sensible young gentleman, whom I have been instrumental in bringing over to the Christian faith, and who is preparing himself, in a short time, to be baptised.

I continue to preach with success at New-Haven, and I hope there will be a Church there in time; though they labour under great opposition and discouragements from the people of the town, who will neither give nor sell them a piece of land for them to build a church on.

The people of Brook-Haven, on Long Island, have earnestly [asked] my intercession with the honourable Society that they may again be supplied with a minister. They are under great necessity of one.

The difficulties and oppressions that the people of our Church have met with under this Independent government have been, and are, so great, that no less than seven families have removed hence into New-York government since I came hither, of which three removed this year. At present, indeed, we have a little better quarters with them, by reason of the terror they are under from Mr. Winthrop's complaints against the government; and I wish they may be taught a better temper towards the Church.

This is all at present from, Reverend Sir,

Yours, &c.,

SAMUEL JOHNSON.

[*Rev. Mr. Caner to the Secretary.—Extract.*]

Fairfield, October 10th, 1728.

Sir,

It seems proper to observe to the honourable Society that the Province of Connecticut is divided into four counties, whose denominations arise from their first towns, Fairfield, New-London, Hartford and New-Haven. That of Fairfield being the westernmost in the province, borders on New-York, and contains the towns of Fairfield, Stratford, Norwalk, Stamford, Greenwich, Ripton, New Town, Danbury, Ridgefield and Woodbury, beside their several villages, as four about Fairfield; Green Farms, Greenfield, Poquanuck and Chesnut Ridge, three of them about four miles distant, the last about sixteen; one belonging to Stratford, called Unity, one to Norwalk, one to Greenwich; each of these villages contain 50 or 60 families; the towns, one with another, have twice that number; the sum of whose inhabitants, though difficult to come at, by reason of some of them not having kept any register of births, and very few of baptisms, I have, at length, pretty justly attained, and find them as set down in my Notitia Parochialis, herein inclosed; where, likewise, the honourable Society will find I have collected out of these the number of the baptised, as also the number of infants and adults baptised by me this half year. In my account of the number of inhabitants, I have left out Stratford, with its village; also New Town and Ripton, which places are under the care of the Rev. Mr. Johnson; all the other towns and villages in the county I serve to the best of my power, preaching to those on week days whom I cannot attend on Sunday, there being several, families as well communicants as professors of the Church of England, in every one of these towns and villages.

As to the Indians in this county, their number is now become very small, by reason of distempers brought among them by the English, together with the excessive drinking which destroys them apace; and of those few that remain, to the eternal shame of the English in these parts, it must be said, that, although I constantly labour with them, as I find them in my way, yet very seldom conceive hopes of doing them any good, who have taken up an inveterate prejudice against Christianity, grounded on the shamefully wicked lives of us, its professors.

The difficulties which chiefly affect both me and my people are what have been often complained of, the heavy taxes by the government imposed on those who profess the Church of England, for the support of dissenting teachers, which very much hinders the finishing our Church, and providing decent ornaments for its service, as well as discourages others from joining with us in so good a work, when they observe how we are slighted and despised, and imposed upon, accounted as the filth and dross of the earth, and the off-scouring of all things.

To the rectifying of which, in some measure, for the future, I would, in most humble manner, lay before the honourable Society the following scheme.

The government has lately passed an act, that all professors of the Church of England, living so near any place where there is an Episcopal minister settled, as that they can conveniently, and do constantly attend upon his preaching, they shall be excused from fees to the Dissenters, and shall pay them to the Church minister; by which means all the professors aforesaid, who live within a mile or two of our Church, are excused, while others are obliged to pay, and some are deprived of two-thirds of its revenues. Now, I humbly conceive that if the honourable Society, instead of appointing me their missionary at Fairfield, would, by a like instrument, under their common seal, appoint me their missionary, to serve from Fairfield to Byram River, or the borders of the government westward, then by an order of the honourable Society, in their Instructions to Missionaries, (page 25, parag. XI.,) I should be under obligation to reside sometimes at one of these places and sometimes at another, as the necessities of either should require; by this means shall the objection of our people, living too remote, be taken off, seeing they will all be equally near to me, and therefore shall the Church gain all her revenues, and be able to go forward with business.

[*Minute of the Society relating to Mr. Caner's being appointed Missionary to two or threeplaces, and Mr. Ketelby's opinion thereon.*]

Read the 18*th of July*, 1729.

The Rev. Mr. Caner, missionary from the Society for the Propagation of the Gospel in Foreign Parts, to Fairfield, in Connecticut government, in New-England, in his letter dated 10th Oct., 1728, writes as follows:

"The government has lately passed an act, that all professors of the Church of England, living so near any place where there is an Episcopal minister settled, as that they can conveniently, and do constantly, attend upon his preaching, they shall be excused from taxes to the Dissenters, and shall pay them to the Church minister. By which means, all the professors aforesaid, that live within a mile or two of our Church, are excused, while others are obliged to pay, and some are deprived of two-thirds of its revenues. Now, I humbly conceive that if the Society, instead of appointing me missionary at Fairfield, would, by a like instrument, under their common seal, appoint me their missionary to serve from Fairfield to Byram River, or the borders of this government westward, then, as I should be under an obligation to reside sometimes at one of these places and sometimes at another, as the necessities of either should require, the objection of people living too remote would be taken off, seeing that they will all be equally near to me, and thereby shall the Church gain her revenues, and be able to go forward with business."

At a meeting of the Society, 16th May, 1729, agreed, that this matter be laid before Mr. Ketelby, and his opinion desired whether the Society's appointment of their missionaries to two or three places will exempt the Church there from paythe Independent teachers. Though at first reading this case, I was clear in my own opinion, yet, it appearing to be a matter in which the interest of the Church ministers and the honour of the Society were, in some measure, concerned, I have conferred with other gentlemen, of undoubted probity and judgment, and we all agree that the Society ought not to grant what is proposed by Mr. Caner; that their appointment of their missionary to two or three places will not exempt the Church people from paying to the Independent teachers; that it is neither within the intention nor the letter of the Act, which, as it requires a constant attendance upon the minister's preaching, so it must necessarily suppose his constant residence in one place; this may be construed as an attempt to evade the Act, only with a view to the secular advantages of particular persons, and may, perhaps, involve the Church ministers there in greater trouble, and more to their detriment, than any benefit they hope for from the compliance of the Society in this particular.

ABEL KETELBY.

[*Rev. Mr. Johnson to the Secretary.*]

Stratford, May 26th, 1729.

Reverend Sir,

We yet labour under so much uneasiness in our government, that several people have moved out of it into New-York government, of which no less than four families since my last; and I think I have gained but three new families to be steady upon the services of the Church, though there are many, and those daily increasing, who are really, in their minds, reconciled to the Church, but are kept back from declaring themselves for fear of the displeasure of the government; and yet I think a more charitable and friendly temper towards the Church is, from time to time, visibly increasing among the people in these parts. I have baptised the Jew, Mr. Mordecai Marks, concerning whom I wrote in my last, who is a very worthy proselyte and steady communicant, as also two native Indians, both adults, two adult negroes and two negro children, all this last half year, so that the state of my parish at present is this:

		Families.
1st.	Number of inhabitants in this town,..............	260
	" " " of the Church,............	53
2d.	Number of baptised,..........................	223
	Of which this half year,........................	23
3d.	Number of adults baptised this half year,.........	6
4th.	Number of actual communicants in Stratford and places adjacent, excepting Fairfield parish,.....	86
	Of which admitted this half year,................	6
5th.	Number of professors of the Church, about.......	200

I am, Rev. Sir,

Your most obedient and humble servant,

SAMUEL JOHNSON.

[*Rev. Mr. Johnson to the Secretary.*]

Stratford, November 20th, 1729.

Reverend Sir,

I am very thankful to the honourable Society for admitting Mr. Dwight into their service, though I could have been glad had he been fixed somewhere else in New-England, particularly since Brook-Haven was supplied before, (and I hope to their content.) We are all sorry that he had not been placed at Providence, where it is to be feared not only the interest of the Church, but even all sense of religion, (what little there was of it,) will in a manner be lost, by means of the bad character and vile behaviour of the person who is missionary in that place, and upon whose account the Church is sadly dishonoured and we are all filled with shame and confusion of face.

I find in the abstract of the proceedings of the Society last year, mention made of a salary for a school at Stratford, but have never received any letter, or otherwise any intimation from the honourable Society about it; which makes me fear there was some mistake about the matter. However, though I should be very thankful if there was a salary appointed for that purpose, and there is great need of it, yet since we want ministers more, of the two, than schoolmasters, I would not desire that the providing for a school should stand in the way of providing for missionaries, and particularly, not only Mr. Caner stands in need of an augmentation of his salary, but there is New-London, in this colony, and Westerly, in the Narragansetts, (in both which places they have built and are finishing very handsome small Churches,) that are in great necessity of ministers, and I have this summer visited them, and find a good prospect of great increase to the Church.

Besides which places, I have not long since visited the people on Connecticut River, and find a considerable number who are subscribing towards a Church at a town called Wethersfield, where there is likely to be a flourishing colony, and will need the honourable Society's assistance. I likewise still continue frequently to preach at New-Haven, Ripton and Newtown with success; though, at the last of these places, it must be confessed that the Dissenters have of late got the advantage of us, partly by the craft and assiduity of their teachers, and partly by means of the removing of a considerable man of our Church, (whose influence used to be great in that town,) from thence into New-York government.

The Church here at Stratford has of late been unhappy by means of a foolish contention, that has sprung up among my people, to the great hindrance of the growth of the Church, and has given me a great deal of trouble. However, I have had some success, having baptised one adult and twelve infants, one of which was native, and admitted six to the Holy Communion since last April, otherwise my *notitia parochialis* stands much as it did in my last.

Sir, yours, &c., &c.,

SAMUEL JOHNSON.

[*The Churchwardens, &c., of Wallingford to the Bishop of London.*]

May it please your Lordship,

We, the Churchwardens and parishioners of Wallingford and the adjacent parts in the Colony of Connecticut, in New-England, beg leave to offer our humble duty to your Lordship.

We are a Church but newly planted, and however content we are at present to have the service of the Church only once a quarter by a minister, on every Lord's day besides we perform the service as far as is proper for laymen; but in that part we are something deficient for want of sermon books, &c., which we cannot easily procure in this country. We are sensible the Reverend Theodore Morris cannot leave his other parishes oftener, yet we hope God, in his providence, will so order it, that we may at last be oftener attended; there are many ready to join in our communion, and have nothing to object to it, but our having service so seldom by a minister. We greatly rejoice that we are assisted in learning to know which is the true Church of Christ, and the manner how we ought worship. But with melancholy hearts we crave your Lordship's patience, while we recite that divers of us have been imprisoned, and our goods from year to year distrained from us for taxes, levied for the building and supporting meeting-houses; and divers actions are now depending in our courts of law in the like cases. And when we have petitioned our governor for redress, notifying to him the repugnance of such actions to the laws England, he hath proved a strong opponent to us; but when the other party hath applied to him for advice how to proceed against us, he hath lately given his sentence "to enlarge the goal and fill it with them," (that is, the Church.) But we supplicate both God and man that our persecutors may not always prevail against us.

And now, that God may bless your Lordship, and the charitable endeavours of the honourable Society, and enable them to send more labourers to a harvest truly plentiful, is the sincere prayer of

Your Lordship's

Most dutiful and obedient servants,

THOMAS IVES,
NORTH INGHAM, } *Churchwardens.*

EBENEZER WAINWRIGHT,
SHADRACK SEAGAR,
JOHN BELLAMY,
THOMAS DEWLITTLE,
WAITSTILL ABINATHER,
AARON TUTTLE,
PHINEAS IVES,
MATTHEW BELLAMY,
EBENEZER BLAKESLEE,
ENOS SMITH,
JOHN MEKY,
THOMAS WILLIAMS,
GEORGE FISHER.

[*Inhabitants of New-London to the Secretary.*]

April 13*th*, 1730.

Reverend Sir,

We, the underwritten inhabitants of New-London, Groton, and other places adjacent, having once and again petitioned the Society for the Propagation of the Gospel in Foreign Parts for a missionary, beg leave, by you, to renew that, our most earnest request.

We have, at a very great expense, erected us a Church, which (unless when Mr. McSparran visits us) continues shut up, to the derision of its enemies, but to our great grief and discomfort, with this only abatement, that it stands a monument and witness for us, how earnestly we desire the blessing we now pray for.

Mr. Samuel Seabury, a gentleman born and bred in this country, goes home recommended to the notice of the Bishop of London and the Society, by the clergy here; therefore, he may be sure of a welcome reception in what vacancy soever he is sent to fill in New-England, where he is known, so we beg (with all the importunity, the utmost necessity, and most earnest desire of a Gospel minister among us is able to inspire) our destitute condition may come in remembrance at the Board, when that gentleman applies for a mission.

We are, Reverend Sir, &c.

[*Rev. Mr. Johnson to the Secretary.*]

Stratford, New-England, May 5*th*, 1730.

Reverend Sir,

This comes to the honourable Board by Mr. Samuel Seabury, who has been educated and graduated in the colleges in this country, and has led a sober, virtuous and studious life, and now heartily embraces the principles of the Church of England, and is sincerely well affected to the present government, and desirous to devote himself to the service of the honourable Society; and, I doubt not, but if they shall see cause to employ him, they will find him faithful in the discharge of his duty wherever they shall please to send him. There are several places here, in New-England, that much need to be supplied, particularly Providence, Westerly and New-London, in either of which he is well known, and will be very acceptable.

I have visited several places in the government, since my last, and find a growing disposition toward the Church, particularly at Greenwich, where the Rev'd Mr. Canes hath laboured with good success; and there seems to be a good prospect that the whole parish, which never have had any minister of any denomination settled among them there, will come into the Church.

Nothing remarkable has happened in my parish since my last; one family has been added to our number, and one, likewise, has removed from us into New-York government. I have reason to fear that my last letter, of November 15th, miscarried, and therefore I have set down my Notitia Parochialis.

1st.	No. of inhabitants in this town,................	270
	Families of which belong to the Church,........	53
	Beside those that belong to the neighbouring villages.	
2d.	No. of the baptised since the mission here,.......	250
	Of which, this year, were baptised,.............	20
	Of which one only was adult.	
3d.	No. of communicants here in the neighbourhood,.	89
	Of which were admitted this year,.............	9
4th.	No. of professors of the Church, about..........	200
	Beside many in the neighbouring towns.	
5th.	No. of heathens uncertain, because of their frequent changing their habitations.	

I am, Reverend Sir, &c.,

Samuel Johnson.

[*Rev. Mr. McSparran to the Secretary.*]

Narragansett, May 20, 1730.

Rev. Sir,

Mr. Samuel Seabury, at whose hands you will receive this, was educated at the seminaries of learning here, and did, for some time, preach to the Dissenters, by whom he is well reported of for a virtuous conversation. He has, for some time past, conformed to our Church, and, manifesting a desire of going upon the Society's mission, I thought it became me to encourage a person of his merit by recommending him to the Society's notice. The place of his birth and most intimate acquaintance is Groton, in the neighbourhood of New-London, which I thought proper to observe, in hopes that it might prove an inducement to determine his mission to that place, where a minister is exceedingly wanted. Your letter of the 19th November last came too late to my hands to be communicated to the gentlemen of New-London in time to have their answers transmitted by this conveyance. I am but a few days returned from that place, where I preached, and saw them renew an address for a minister; but shall do my endeavours, when I go again, (if not before,) to bring them together, in order more fully to answer the Society's expectations. In the mean time I beg leave to observe, that beside the forty odd pounds they have subscribed, there will arise upon these subscribers a ministerial rate, due to the established Presbyterian minister, of at least twenty pounds per annum, but which, by a particular act of the Colony of Connecticut, is transferred upon the Episcopal minister, where one resides, which quota of sixty pounds is triple the sum their neighbours pay, and is in a much greater disproportion to what is paid by the members of the Church of England in this government, (numbers and abilities considered.)

I thank God my Church thrives, and those that attend the established worship are, with a few exceptions, persons of good conversation. But I cannot give a better instance of the success God has given me, than to take notice to the Society that, since my incumbency, I have baptised one hundred and seventy-six persons, whereof sixty are adults, and that the communicants are still increasing.

I am, Reverend Sir, &c.,

JAMES MCSPARRAN.

[*Rev. Mr. Caner to the Secretary.*]

Fairfield, New-England, Sept. 18*th*, 1730.

Sir,

In my last letter, dated on Easter Monday, I laid before the honourable Society my own as well as my people's hearty thanks for their care and bounty relating to the increase of my salary. The churchwardens and vestry, I there informed the honourable Society, desired some time to try the purses as well as the readiness of the people to advance the sum expected of them. Their accounts they have now brought in, and do find the utmost willingness in the people to comply with any proposals consistent with their abilities, which the churchwardens find to be very slender, and not answerable to the honourable Society's expectation from them.

The truth is, there doth appear in the people a great forwardness to hearken to instruction, and they seem really willing to contribute the utmost they are able to the support of those means whereby they receive it. But the number of those who have actually reconciled themselves to our constitution is yet but small; there are greater numbers come to us as Nicodemus to our blessed Saviour, and whom, therefore, the others are not willing to discourage, by representing the great difficulties that will ensue upon their joining with us, but are rather willing to bear a greater burden themselves than fright them back by severe proposals.

The utmost they do declare themselves able to raise, is fifteen pounds sterling per annum; though, to balance this, they have set on foot a design which I am confident in some years will enable them to maintain a missionary themselves. It is this, that every professor do, in his will, make over a certain sum (what he sees fit) to the support of this particular Church, to be paid at his decease, which sum being secured, the churchwardens have power to use the interest of it to any purposes the Church shall think fit to order. There have deceased two members of our Church since this design hath been laid, each of which hath left one hundred pounds to the advancement of it, and two others, supposed at the point of death, have ordered, the one an hundred, and the other fifty pounds, in their wills, though both of them are since re-recovered.

Now, I presume it is easy to see that this thing, having due encouragement, will, in the compass of some years, enable them to maintain their own ministers, and do therefore declare that they will, from time to time, as they prove able, give notice of it to the honourable Society, that the salary which may be now afforded, may gradually be transferred to others who may then be in their present circumstances; that is, unable to help themselves.

The particular state of my parish the honourable Society will best be informed of from my *Notitia Parochialis*, herein enclosed, from which the honourable Society will, I hope, see encouragement sufficient to induce them to continue, if not add, further favours to my people. I believe, in our present circumstances, they could not be more acceptable to them and the honourable Society's most dutiful and obedient servant, as well as, Sir, &c.,

Henry Caner.

Notitia Parochialis.

1. Number of inhabitants, upwards of 8,000. 2. Number of baptised, about 7,140. 3. Number baptised by me this half year, 30; adults 10—blacks 2, Indian 1, whites 7; infants 20—whites 18, Indians 2. 4. Number of actual communicants of the Church of England, 65. 5. Number of those who profess themselves of the Church of England, about 500 in all the parishes. 6. Number of heathens and infidels, about 40. 7. Number of converts from a profane life, 4.

[*Rev. Mr. Johnson to the Secretary.*]

Stratford, in Connecticut, October 25th, 1730.

Reverend Sir,

I have but little to write in respect to my charge since my last, though I think my Church is more frequented by Dissenters, who, many of them, come once in a while to Church, yet I cannot say there have been any throughly reclaimed within this half year; however, a good temper toward the Church still very sensibly increases, and upon Connecticut River they are contriving to build a Church. One thing I have particularly to rejoice in, and that is, that I have a very considerable influence in the College in my neighbourhood; and that a love to the Church gains ground greatly in it. Several young men that are graduates, and some young ministers, I have prevailed with to read and consider the matter so far, that they are very uneasy out of the communion of the Church, and some seem much disposed to come into her service; and those that are best affected to the Church are the brightest and most studious of any that are educated in the country.

Many poor people complain of the want of Prayer-Books and Expositions of the Church Catechism; I should, therefore, be very thankful if the honourable Society would be pleased to order a few of them to be sent to me, and if, with them, I had a few Ostervald's Catechisms and Whole Duties of Man, I could make them very useful. I desire that if any Prayer-Books are sent, that they may have Tate and Brady's Psalms bound up with them; they only are used among us.

I am, Reverend Sir, &c.,

SAMUEL JOHNSON.

[*Rev. Mr. Johnson to the Secretary.—Extract.*]

Stratford, 2*d* *June*, 1731.

Reverend Sir,

Since my last there has happened an unfortunate alteration in my parish, by the loss of a worthy parishioner, Mr. Loring, who was the most considerable person of any influence we had among us; the most able and the most forward in promoting the interests of the Church, and always at the head of every good design; for want of whom, I doubt the Church here will greatly suffer and languish, for his example and influence had the greatest hand in its advancement, the rest being generally poor tradesmen, and, consequently, apt to be despised and dispirited.

However, I have had one or two new converts, and especially one, from a loose irregular way of living, to a life of virtue and industry; and our Church is not less, if any thing, more frequented, and, in the villages, it remains much as it was.

New-London I think well provided for in Mr. Seabury, and I hope the Church will flourish in that town. I have laboured much to promote the Church at Westerly Narragansett, as I have occasionally passed that way; but for the want of a resident minister, I doubt, through the multitude of sectaries that abound in those parts, and a prevailing spirit of irreligion and profaneness, the Church's interest will decay among them, where the means of religion, of any sort, are so much wanted, that they are truly the objects of the greatest compassion.

I have visited Brook-Haven, on Long Island, since the departure of Mr. Campbell, and find them almost sinking under the wounds they have received by the frequent changes of ministers, and the non-good conduct of some that have been among them. However, I preached to a considerable congregation, and afterwards called their vestry together, who desired me to express their humblest gratitude to the honourable Society, that they have been allowed an interest in their charity, and earnestly desire that it may be continued, and that they may be still reckoned among the Society's dependents. But, for fear of being disappointed, as they were before of Mr. Dwight, they humbly desire the Society not to send them another missionary till they shall find some young gentleman to send from these parts, whom they have known before and he them, that they may have a future prospect of mutual liking, and so not be under any temptation of parting again suddenly, as the case has been.

They desire me to look out a young man to reside awhile among them. I mentioned a virtuous and discreet young man and of good abilities, whose name is Brown, (brother to that excellent person who went home for orders with Dr. Cutler and myself, and died of the small-pox,) who has ever since been steadily following his learning under my direction, and has already taken one degree in the College, and is within about a year and a half of age for orders. They were desirous I would send him to them upon probation, to read prayers and sermons and catechise their youth, and he is accordingly gone among them, and, I believe, will be very acceptable to them; they promised to subscribe toward his support, and purpose, if he and they shall be on both sides suited, to recommend him to the honourable Society, and beg he may be their missionary.

In the mean time, they would be very humbly thankful to the honourable Society, if he may be allowed £10 or £15 toward his better support, or, at least, some assistance to defray his expenses when he shall go home for orders, for he has laid out almost all his estate upon his education.

I am, Reverend Sir, &c.,

SAMUEL JOHNSON.

[*Rev. Mr. Johnson to the Bishop of London.*]

Stratford, in New-England, June 14th, 1731.

May it please your Lordship,

My Lord, there are two things which have occasioned some dispute among the clergy and people in these parts, about which I humbly presume to beg your Lordship's directions. One is relating to the exhortation after baptism to the godfathers to bring the child to the Bishop to be confirmed. Some wholly omit this exhortation, because it is impracticable; others insert the words, (if there be opportunity,) because our adversaries object to it as a mere jest, to order the godfathers to bring the child to the Bishop, when there is none within a thousand leagues of us, which is a reproach that we cannot answer.

The other dispute is about employing young scholars, that are candidates for the ministry, in villages and destitute places, in reading sermons and prayers, (omitting everything that is proper to the priest's office.) This, I own, is what I and some others have earnestly recommended as excusable, by reason of the necessities of the country, and have, in several instances, found it highly useful in keeping up a sense of religion, and propagating it, when resident ministers cannot be had; and though I have always let the honourable Society know of my proceedings herein, they have never intimated the least disapprobation of this method, but, on the other hand, have practically approved of it, in receiving once and again those who have been so employed. Notwithstanding this, there are some of our brethren who, with great zeal and importunity, cry out against this practice as a betraying of the Church, and giving up the necessity of ordination, &c., to the great mortification of those poor destitute people who have no other way of keeping up the worship of God among them.

My Lord, I humbly submit to your Lordship's correction, if in this or any other instance my conduct has been faulty, and earnestly beg your direction and benediction, who am, with the greatest veneration,

May it please your Lordship, your Lordship's

Humble servant,

SAMUEL JOHNSON.

[*Petition of several members of the Church of England, in Reading and Newtown, in Connecticut.*]

New-England, March 20th, 1732.

May it please the honourable Society,

We, the subscribers, members of the Church of England, in Reading and Newtown, within the County of Fairfield and Colony of Connecticut, in New-England, being under very great difficulty to come at the worship of God according to that excellent establishment, by reason of our distance from the honourable Society's missionaries, the Rev. Mr. Johnson and Mr. Caner, which is about twenty miles, and being indeed, some of us, at a great distance from any publick worship at all, whereby not only we ourselves, but our poor children, also extremely suffer, and are like to be trained up in very great ignorance of the knowledge of the Gospel, do beg leave to lay this our calamitous state before your venerable board, and become very humble petitioners for a share in that charity which is conspicuous even in this dark corner of the earth.

To this we are the rather encouraged by a favourable letter to some of our number from the honourable Society, obtained about two years after the Rev. Mr. Johnson's first coming among us, wherein the honourable Society were pleased to offer us a missionary upon certain conditions, which, at that time, we were not able to come upon, by reason of the settlement of the bearer hereof, Mr. John Beach, a gentleman, at that time, of a different persuasion; but now, more and further encouraged by the said gentleman's being reconciled to the established Church of England, especially in that being now bound home to receive holy orders from the Lord Bishop of London, he is willing to return to this place of his former settlement and abode, if his Lordship and the honourable Society shall think proper.

The good opinion that persons of all persuasions have of him here, where he has been known for several years past, and accounted a gentleman of a remarkable sober and regular conduct, and of learning and good ability to discharge the ministerial office, gives us reason to promise ourselves a great deal of happiness and comfort from his future ministration, if the honourable Society shall think fit to return him to us.

Though we are poor, the unavoidable consequence of settling an uncultivated country, and so cannot possibly, without assistance, provide a suitable support for the abovesaid gentleman, yet what we are able we are very ready to engage, and have affixed to our respective names underwritten; and we do humbly hope and pray that the honourable Society, out of their great charity, will supply wherein we are wanting towards the said gentleman's support; as we flatter ourselves with hopes of success in this affair from the former goodness and great charity of your venerable board, so we would humbly hope that the consideration of several towns lying about us, at a distance of about seven miles, as Danbury, Ridgefield, Woodbury and New-Milford, and numbers of Indians, would be of some further inducement toward some suitable relief to our truly deplorable state; for, indeed, we are not so selfish as to expect Mr. Beach's service should be wholly confined to ourselves, but that he may be capable of propagating Christian knowledge in those other towns likewise.

Thus, the Reverend Mr. Johnson and Mr. Caner, though settled at Stratford and Fairfield, have been and are still very ready to assist us, so far as is consistent with the distance between them and ourselves, for whose service, as flowing from the Society's charity, we are truly thankful, wishing withal there may never be wanting pious men in these parts to promote the Church's interest.

Fearing we have been already too tedious, we only add our hearty and fervent prayers to Almighty God for success in your truly charitable designs to the souls of men.

We are, &c., &c.,

LEMUEL MOREHOUSE and others.

[*Rev. Mr. Johnson to the Bishop of London.*]

Stratford, in New-England,
April 5th, 1732.

My Lord,

I humbly thank your Lordship for your kind letter of September 30th, and am, as to myself, perfectly well satisfied with the answers you give to the difficulties I presumed to lay before you. Only, I imagined there might be some difference between the case of those who are immediately under an establishment, as it is in England, and those who are situated, as we are here, where the attorney and solicitor-general have declared there is no establishment of religion at all, and, therefore, not even of the Church of England, and, consequently, the obligations to an exact conformity seem not altogether the same as there. I write not this, my Lord, on my own account, as though I desired the least abatement of any thing established in England; I heartily wish to God every thing established there was admitted and established here, nor did I ever vary from the establishment in the least instance, unless where there was an evident necessity for it; but my solicitous concern for the weal of my dear country makes me willing, if it could consist with my duty to the best of Churches, and be indulged by the authority to whom I owe subjection, to abate, in some circumstantial matters, of what is wisely established at home, that I might have less occasion to spend my time and pains and pleading, and with so little success, because of things confessedly in their own nature indifferent and circumstantial, which I would much rather, and could, with greater success, devote to the advancing of the great essentials and vitals of religion, for which it seems as if there would be the more occasion, inasmuch as (besides many other gross errors) the pernicious books and notions, which your Lordship found it so necessary to guard your Diocese against, are coming in upon the plantations like a flood, and will I [fear] take the more effect, by how much the less there is of the face of an establishment among us, or of Bishops to preside over us. And, indeed, I doubt, unless the Church be beforehand with them, these things, together with their wretched broken condition in the way they are at present in, will, 'ere long, induce those of the Congregational and Presbyterian persuasion to endeavour (and they may possibly succeed) to get themselves formed into an establishment, after the manner as it is in Scotland. These considerations, my Lord, induced me, upon a conversation with, and even at the desire of several ingenious men among the Dissenters in these parts, to draw up the enclosed proposals, which I humbly submit, with an entire resignation to your Lordship's wisdom, and which I hope, of your wonted goodness, you will pardon, and impute the vanity of my presumption to an earnest desire, if I could, to be doing something wherein I might be some way serviceable to my poor, confused and divided country. My Lord, as the Church here has been very unfortunate in the defeat of the noble design of the Reverend the Dean of Londonderry, which, especially, if it had been executed on the Continent, would have been of vast advantage to the interest of religion and learning in America, so it has, on the other hand, been happy since in the conversion, (besides a number of other good people,) of the worthy persons who have all had a publick education in the neighbouring College, and two of them have been dissenting teachers; two of them will go into other business, and one of them is Mr. Beach, the bearer hereof, whom I know, by long experience of him, (he having been heretofore my pupil, and ever since my neighbour,) to be a very ingenuous and studious person, and a truly serious and conscientious Christian; but I forbear to say any thing further of his case, and refer your Lordship to our joint recommendation of him,

And remain, &c., &c.,

Samuel Johnson.

Proposals relating to some method for the more successful reformation and propagation of religion in America, humbly submitted to the Right Reverend the Lord Bishop of London.

(1.) INASMUCH as the Attorney and Solicitor-General have declared that there is no establishment of religion in these countries, it is humbly suggested whether some practicable method might not be devised and carried into execution for the establishment of religion in these English Dominions. (2.) For seeing there are many parts of the English plantations that are in a manner destitute of any publick instruction at all, and where they are (generally, but very poorly) provided with teachers in the Independent or Congregational way, they are, according to the natural tendency of those opinions, miserably broken to pieces with divisions and contentions among themselves, insomuch, that they seem hastening on a-pace toward an utter dissolution, and some very corrupt doctrines are propagated without control, so that most people of sense and consideration among them are even sick and weary of their present situation, and long to come into some more effectual method for promoting the ends of government, religion, peace and order; it is therefore thought very likely that some establishment, even under an Episcopal form of government, would, in a little time, be generally submitted to. And yet, (3.) it will perhaps be impossible to procure a general reconciliation, especially among the populace, to all the ceremonies and constitutions of our Church, and much time and pains spent in pleading about them might be employed, and with better success, in promoting the great essentials and vitals of religion; it is, therefore, humbly submitted, whether it would be necessary or expedient to insist or be much intent upon the external and confessedly circumstantial matters, if any establishment were to be promoted; for, (4.) as the truly excellent rules which our most venerable reformers proposed to themselves, carried them into such a method of publick worship and discipline as is happily established in England, as being in the best manner suited to the times and circumstances, that there had been, were and are, so it is with the humblest deference suggested, whether considering the vastly different circumstances of these places and times, the same rules would not lead to methods in several things differing as to circumstantial matters, if the reformation and propagation of religion were to be carried into an establishment in these countries? And, therefore, (5.) might there not be projected some such a comprehension suited to these countries, as was endeavoured by many in England in King William's time; according to which, many things as they now stand might be enjoined, viz., such as are of the greatest importance in themselves, and will be the most easily admitted, and some things a little altered to suit the present circumstances, and other things, which are of less importance and most objected against, only recommended? And (6.) lastly, is it impossible for the English Dominions in America to be provided for with one or two Bishops, and those subject to the Lord Bishop of London as Archbishop of the Plantations abroad; and is there no way to provide revenues, (though they were but small,) compared with those in England? Would not £400 or £500 sterling per annum a-piece, or, rather than fail, £300, enable them, in some good measure, to answer the ends of their sacred functions; and is it impossible that such a provision might be made without breaking in upon the interest of the governors and governments as they now stand? Though, indeed, it would be much happier for the Church, especially unless we had a Bishop, if the charters were taken away; and most people begin to think, since they have got into such a wretched, mobbish way of management, that it would be best for the people themselves.

If some such things as these could be accomplished, as the present situation of things here renders it now a very suitable juncture for something to be done, so it would be a truly great charity to the souls of men, and it is hard indeed if we must forever despair of such happiness.

[*Rev. Mr. Caner to the Secretary.—Extract.*]

Fairfield, New-England, Sept. 18*th*, 1733.

Sir,

I hope it will be some satisfaction to the honourable Society to be informed that the spirit and temper of the people, formerly so hot against us, very much abates, and that they begin to treat us in a much more friendly manner than they were wont; this good disposition, I hope, by God's assistance, to cultivate and improve to beneficial effects. I have the half year past baptised ten infants and one adult, and received seven new communicants, the whole number of which is now seventy-eight. The state of my Church in general is indeed much more promising than in time past; some difficulties, it is true, we still labour under, but which time and industry will in great measure remove.

I beg leave to subscribe myself, &c.,

H. Caner.

[*Rev. Mr. Johnson to the Bishop of London.*]

Stratford, in New-England,
December 10*th*, 1733.

My Lord,

Your Lordship remembers that, in the year 1725, upon a representation made by the ministers of the Church in Boston, of a design then on foot in that government of a council of their ministers, to meet by appointment of the General Assembly there, the Lords Justices were pleased, in a letter to the Lieutenant-Governor of that colony, to express their disapprobation of any such proceedings, as implying an invasion of his Majesty's prerogative, and ordered him to forbid any such council of ministers to meet, and declare that it is not lawful for the clergy to meet as in a Synod, without authority from his Majesty. Now, my Lord, how far the case of this government differs from that, your Lordship will judge; but I presumed you would not take it ill of me if I should lay before your Lordship any case of that nature that should occur here, and humbly submit it to your Lordship, whether it should deserve your notice; and I am desired by several even of the dissenting ministers here to submit the vote and order of the Assembly, enclosed to your Lordship's perusal.

I humbly thank your Lordship for your interest with the honourable Society for settling a school in this place, and likewise in behalf of Mr. Pierson and Mr. Brown, who are returned back to their native country, full of a grateful sense of your Lordship's and the Society's goodness to them; and, I doubt not but they will be very useful in promoting the ends of the Society in the places for which they are appointed.

I beg leave, also, to inform your Lordship, that the growing confusion among the Dissenters in these parts very much tends, among other means, to put thinking and serious persons upon coming over to the Church. Among others there are two or three very worthy young ministers in this colony who, I have reason to believe, from no other reason than the love of truth and order, and a sense of duty, will, in a little time, declare for us, and two of them especially have hopes that the most of their congregations will conform with them. One of them is one Mr. Arnold, who succeeded me at West-Haven, near the College, where I preach once a quarter.

If they can't be admitted to the Society's service in holy orders, which they would earnestly desire, they will do what good they can in a lay capacity; but as they would be glad to be employed by the Society, if it be practicable to have new missions, so I have written to the Secretary to know whether any encouragement could be had for them to go over with such a view. Indeed, there are daily growing and pressing occasions in many parts of these plantations for new missions and missionaries, and I wish to God the Society's abilities to provide for them might increase in proportion as they do.

I am, may it please your Lordship, your Lordship's most obedient, most dutiful son and servant,

SAMUEL JOHNSON.

[*The Clergy of Connecticut to the Bishop of London.*]

Fairfield, in Connecticut,
March 14*th*, 1733–4.

May it please your Lordship,

It is with great pleasure that we see the success of our labours in the frequent conversions of dissenting teachers in this country, and the good disposition toward the excellent constitution of our Church, growing up among the people wherever the honourable Society have established their missions. Sundry other of their teachers are likely to appear for the Church, and two very honest and ingenuous men have declared themselves this winter, one of which is Mr. Ebenezer Punderson, the bearer hereof, who being bound to England with design to apply himself to your Lordship and the honourable Society for holy orders and a mission, we humbly beg leave to lay before your Lordship our recommendation of this worthy gentleman. He has been for above four years a settled minister in the dissenting way to a parish near New-London, called New-Groton; and as he has a good prospect that a considerable number of that parish will conform to the Church with him, he has a solicitous desire to return back in holy orders to that people with whom he has so long dwelt, and among whom he is greatly respected.

As to the circumstances of his people, our distance from them renders us incapable of saying any thing further of them; but as to the gentleman himself, we have well known him for at least seven years, are able, with truth, to assure your Lordship, that he has always been remarked for a person of good parts, earnestly inquisitive after truth, and indefatigably studious in the pursuit of it; that he has read many of the best of our English divines; and has made as great a proficiency in learning as can be expected from his age and circumstances, and that he has ever been esteemed a sober, virtuous and devout person, and remarkable for his contempt of the world; and we are persuaded that it is from a serious and impartial examination of things, and the sincere love of truth and sense of duty, that he has declared himself for our excellent Church and come over to our communion; and he is sincerely well affected to the present government; we humbly, therefore, beseech your Lordship he may be admitted to holy orders, and added to the number of our brethren, and remain,

May it please your Lordship,

Your Lordship's servants,

SAMUEL JOHNSON,
J. WETMORE,
H. CANER,
ISAAC BROWNE.

[*Rev. Mr. Seabury to the Secretary.—Extract.*]

New-London, March 30th, 1734.

Reverend Sir,

These wait upon the honourable Society by the hands of Mr. Ebenezer Punderson, who comes to make his application to my Lord Bishop of London and the Society for Propagation of the Gospel in foreign parts, for orders and a mission. He hath been educated in Yale College, Connecticut, where I had a particular acquaintance with him, and where he always had the character of a sober person. About five years ago he was called to preach in the Presbyterian or Independent way, at Groton, near New-London, where he soon received ordination; but falling under doubts and scruples concerning their power of ordination and method of Church government, and, at the same time, acquainting himself with the Church of England, he found himself obliged, upon true and regular conviction, to embrace her communion, and thereupon he laid down his ministry in which he was settled to good advantage; but a considerable number of the people of that place being also convinced of the reasonableness and necessity of Church Communion, and having strong affection for the person of Mr. Punderson, on account of his abilities and pious, exemplary life, have been very solicitous with him to make his application to the honourable Society for Propagation of the Gospel in foreign parts for a mission to that place. In testimony of which, they have signed a desire or petition to the honourable Society, with the promise of contributing a certain sum considerably to his support and maintenance, and it is most probable that many more will conform to the Church of England upon better knowledge of it and acquaintance with it.

[*Rev. Mr. Beach to the Secretary.*]

Newtown, in Connecticut,
August 7th, 1735.

Reverend Sir,

I think it my duty to acquaint the venerable Society with the present state of my parish, although the alteration since my last has not been very considerable. I have baptised twenty-nine children and admitted twenty-five persons more to the communion, so that the number of our communion now at Newtown, Reading, and the places adjacent, is ninety-five. I preach frequently and administer the Sacrament at Ridgefield, being about eighteen miles distance from the place where I dwell, where there are about fourteen or eighteen families of very serious and religious people, who have a just esteem of the Church of England, and are very desirous to have the opportunity of worshipping God in that way. I have constantly preached, one Sunday at Newtown, and the other at Reading; and after I have preached at Reading in the day-time, I perform divine service and preach at Newtown in the evening; and although I have not that success I could wish for, yet I do, and hope I always shall, faithfully endeavour (as far as my poor ability will allow) to promote that good work, that the venerable Society sent and maintained me for.

I am, Reverend Sir,

Your most humble servant,

JOHN BEACH.

[*Rev. Mr. Seabury to the Secretary.*]

New-London, *August* 22*d*, 1735.

Reverend Sir,

By this opportunity, for which I have long waited, (otherwise my accounts of the year past would have come much earlier,) I have the satisfaction of informing the honourable Society that my congregation increaseth; that there are one hundred people commonly attending divine service in the summer season, which is double the number that attended constantly at my first coming; that I have had seven new communicants, and baptised thirteen infants the year past; and beside my attendance of the Church at New-London, I have always, from the beginning of my mission, preached at Norwich, a town about fourteen miles from New-London, three times a year, until it was put under the care of the Rev. Mr. Punderson; and sundry times have preached lectures at North Groton; and during the absence of the Rev. Mr. Punderson, in his voyage to England for orders and a mission, I preached there once a month on Sundays, by consent of the Church at New-London, and in this instant, August, I preached at Windham, a place about twenty-six miles from New-London, to a congregation of eighty people, of whom some stayed sundry hours with me after sermon was over, and were desircus to be informed concerning the Church of England; and upon my conversing with them they confessed that the Church had been sadly misrepresented, and that they should have a more favourable opinion of it for the future, and desired that I would come again; and in justice to the members of the Church of England, in New-London, I am obliged to observe that they treat me with great respect and affection, and are very just in paying me the value of their promised subscriptions, which I receive by way of contribution every Sunday after evening service, and I must own further, that the dissenting party also are very civil and obliging to me.

But though the Church at New-London hath increased, yet it hath met with great losses and disadvantages, of which the honourable Society will be sensible when I assure them that there is not one man of any considerable estate or circumstances remaining in the Church at New-London, who first requested the Society for a minister. The worthy Mr. Stackmaple, who laboured with abundance of zeal, and freely contributed his estate to the erecting of the Church, is since dead; he was a gentleman of great charity and virtue, and was the collector of his Majesty's customs in this colony. The honourable Major Merritt, who hath subscribed £50 toward the building of the Church, is since dead. The honourable Major Pryor, who gave £100 to the building of the Church, is since removed, and of the common people, who were the first petitioners to the Society, Mr. Jarrard Peel, Mr. Daniel Apley, Mr. Samuel Fairbank, are dead; and Mr. Thomas Mumford, Mr. James Packer, Mr. Giles Goddard, Mr. Thomas Eldridge, Mr. Joseph Latham, who are all men of good estates, dwelling in South Groton, are put into the Rev. Mr. Punderson's parish in North Groton, though they ever looked on themselves to belong to the Church at New-London, as is evident from there being three of them always chosen of the vestry of New-London; and they have always been at equal charges with those living at New-London Church, and not at North Groton, and are much nearer to Church at New-London, South Groton being parted from New-London only by a river half a mile wide; and the honourable Society, I humbly conceive, were moved to place South Groton in Mr. Punderson's mission at his request and representation of the case only, for the people never requested it nor expected it, and still attend oftenest at the Church at New-London.

But notwithstanding these losses and disadvantages, the Church at New-London grows, and I trust will grow and increase, by the blessing of Divine Providence and the countenance and charity of your honourable Corporation. And I can assure the honourable Society, that my utmost diligence is employed in their service, and that I shall always embrace every opportunity of enlarging the influence of their extensive Church.

I am, Reverend Sir,
Yours and the honourable Society's
Most obedient and most humble servant,
SAM'L SEABURY.

[*Rev. Mr. Seabury to the Secretary.*]

New-London, in New-England,
August 11*th*, 1736.

Reverend Sir,

You will receive the trouble of this to acquaint the honourable Society of my success in promoting their designs, which hath been something remarkable at Hebron, an inland town in this colony, about thirty miles distance from New-London. Some of the inhabitants of that place, about the 20th of January last, desired me to preach among them, which I did to a numerous congregation, who attended the service of the common prayers with great seriousness; and when the service was concluded, there stayed of the company about thirty or forty persons, inquiring concerning the Church of England, and proposing the vulgar objections against it, beside many others which were raised entirely from falsehoods, and had no shadow of truth to support them; to all which I answered them with truth, and the best reasons and arguments that my understanding and knowledge could suggest, and in this manner I conversed with them at least four hours, who, in fine, appeared very much surprised to find that they had always been very prejudiced with so many false notions about the Church; wondering how men could leave its pious and holy communion, and, most of all, that any could have the conscience to load the established Church with so many odious and injurious slanders.

They earnestly desired me to come again, and at their importunity I have visited them six times, twice of which hath been on Sundays. More than twenty families there and in some neighbouring places do embrace the Church; and when I was last there, which was on the first day of this instant, August, I administered the Sacrament to fourteen communicants.

They are very desirous of a missionary, but defer offering any petition to the Society for Propagating the Gospel, having been informed that the Society are not in a condition at present to establish any new missions; but they have importuned me to visit them, and administer the Sacrament among them, four times a year, to which I have given them encouragement, till I could inform the honourable Society and receive their commands.

As to the Church in New-London, it continueth in nearly the same state as when I wrote last, which is about last September, since which I have baptised nine, of whom one was adult, and the communicants are seventeen.

The people here continue to treat me in a very handsome manner, and annually do something more than make good their obligations in contributing to my support.

Reverend Sir, your,

And the honourable Society's most dutiful

And most obedient servant,

SAM'L SEABURY.

[*Rev. Mr. Beach to the Secretary.—Extract.*]

Newtown, in New-England,
September 8th, 1736.

Reverend Sir,

Since my last I have baptised twenty-five children and five adults, and have admitted to the communion two persons more; the whole number of my communicants is now one hundred and five; but by reason of our people living very distant from each other, I seldom have more than fifty communicants together at once, and for that reason I administer that Sacrament every other Sunday. I have lately, upon the repeated invitations of the people of Newark, in New-Jersey, visited them. I performed divine service two Sundays, and had about three or four hundred hearers; they appeared very desirous of having a minister of the Church of England settled among them, and are now about sending a memorial to the venerable Society for that end, and have earnestly desired me to certify that honourable Board of my willingness to be removed, if they see fit to erect a mission, and remove me thither.

Thereupon, I thought it my duty to acquaint that honourable body that I am perfectly contented with my present condition, and should have no inclination to remove if I did not think that I could do much more good there than I can in this parish; and that within a little time there will be, it is probable, at Newark, the largest congregation within two hundred miles; and it is very likely they will soon be able to maintain a minister without any assistance, though at present they cannot well do it; but in this I entirely submit to the wisdom of the venerable Society,

And am, Reverend Sir,
Your most humble servant,
JOHN BEACH.

[*Rev. Mr. Caner to the Secretary.*]

Fairfield, in New-England,
13th September, 1736.

Reverend Sir,

In a letter by the Rev. Mr. McSparran, I acquainted the honourable Society of my safe arrival in New-England; since then I have so good a state of health as to be capable of serving my parish in a constant way. The professors of the Church of England here increase in numbers and seriousness.

The Dissenters among us are busily employed in examining into the conduct of the missionaries in order to have whereof to accuse us; some instances, misinterpreted, I understand they pitch upon. I trust they will not find any instance in my conduct to make the foundation of a complaint. I am not conscious that I have laid myself open to misinterpretation, and as to real misconduct, I defy them; however, as they seem resolved to make thorough work, if any complaint of this nature should come before the honourable Society, I beg I may have notice of it, and an opportunity to vindicate myself from any such aspersions. I hope, when we are sufficiently sifted and tried, we shall come out purer and less exceptionable.

The particular state of my parish at this time the honourable Society will find expressed in my *notitia parochialis*, underwritten, to which I beg leave to refer.

I am the honourable Society's

Most dutiful and obedient, and, Sir,

Your most humble servant,

Henry Caner.

[*Rev. Mr. Arnold to the Secretary.*]

West Haven, in Connecticut,
September 22d, 1736.

Reverend Sir,

I performed divine service last Sunday at Milford, one of the most considerable towns in Connecticut Colony, where the use of the Lord's Prayer, the Creed, and the Ten Commandments, or the reading the Scripture in divine service, was never before known. There was a very numerous auditory, most attentive and desirous to be instructed in the worship of the Church of England; but these who are looking towards the Church are commonly the poorer sort of people; for the staff of government being in the hands of the Dissenters, who rule the Church with an iron rod, those who receive honour one of another set themselves at a distance, and allow their rage and revenge to increase in proportion to the increase of the Church. That God, in mercy to our land, may continue and prosper that honourable Society, is, and shall be the fervent prayer of their, and your most obliged, devoted, humble servant,

JONATHAN ARNOLD.

[*From the Clergy of New-England to the Secretary.—Extract.*]

Fairfield, in New-England,
March 29th, 1739.

Reverend Sir,

Notwithstanding it has once and again been declared by the Attorney and Solicitor-General, (and approved of by the Lords Justices in their letter to the Lieutenant-Governor of Boston, dated October 7th, 1725,) that there is no establishment of any religion in these colonies, nor can be without his most sacred Majesty's explicit consent; yet this government have taken upon them to make an establishment of the Congregational way, (as they call it,) appears by several acts in their printed law book, and do act as an establishment, and to treat the Church of England as Dissenters. They have, indeed, made a law by which they pretended to exempt the people of the Church of England from paying to the support of their ministers and the building of their meeting-houses, but they have contrived several methods to elude it.

2. Among which, a principal contrivance is to make certain funds in each town to be let out to use for raising the salaries of their ministers, without any tax upon the people. This first began at Fairfield, by the sale of certain lands, sequestered by the proprietors of that town for the support of the ministry, the money arising from which sale they divided to each parish according to their propriety, only excluding the members of the Church of England in each parish from any share or benefit in this sale, though there were many of them as considerable proprietors as any of those who were admitted to enjoy it. And the success with which this unjust action was attended has put them upon much the same measures throughout the colony; and one means of making such funds is by the sale of seven new townships of common lands belonging to this government, wherein (as we apprehend) the people of the Church of England have equally a right, according to their proportion, with the rest of the people of the government; and the money arising from the sale of these lands they have appropriated either to the schools, or to what they call the established ministry of this government, at the election of the several towns, (as will appear by their printed acts to this purpose,) so that, according to their sense of their law, we of the Church of England are excluded from any benefit of that sale.

Another of these devices for raising of the above mentioned funds has been by a bill, (not yet indeed passed into an act, though we have reason to believe the design is not yet laid aside,) to appropriate the loan of their last commission of £50,000 of bills of credit to that purpose.

To prevent these proceedings, the people of our Church

have laid an humble address before the General Assembly, signed by more than six hundred and thirty males above sixteen years old, (and the number could have amounted to above seven hundred if all would have had opportunity to sign,) praying that they might have their proportion of these public moneys toward the support of their ministers; but they have been pleased in their last Assembly to negative that petition, so that our people can expect no favour or justice from our government in this regard, and beg of us to lay their oppressed state before the Society.

3. Another grievance that we have to complain of is, the case of sundry people (to the number of fifty families) in the westernmost parts of this colony, chiefly belonging to Horseneck and Stamford, living so near to the Parish Church of Rye, as that they can and do attend upon the ministrations of the Reverend Mr. Wetmore, who also does frequently officiate among them, to which he was requested by their joint application to him. When, according to the tenor of the abovementioned act, he demanded his due proportion of the tax, viz., what was paid by the professors of the Church of England, payment was refused; upon which he commenced an action against the collector, which went through the courts and was finally lost. The people, perceiving themselves destitute of any hopes of relief in a course of law, applied themselves in an humble address to the General Assembly, praying for a redress of this grievance, which address was set aside, and nothing was done for their relief; so that they, and all others living but a few miles from any Church of England, whatever care and pains the minister may take in visiting and administering to them, shall, notwithstanding the said act, be obliged to pay to the support of dissenting ministers, unless relief can be obtained from home.

4. That we may be as little tedious as possible, we will pass by several other instances whereby they have endeavoured to elude the act they had made in our favour, and proceed lastly to lay before the Society the case of the Rev. Mr. Arnold, which is as follows: William Greyson, of London, Esq., made a donation of a piece of land in New-Haven to him, as trustee for the Church of England, to build a

Church on, and when he went to take possession and make improvement of said land by ploughing the same, he was opposed by a great number of people, being resolute that no Church should be built there, who, in a riotous and tumultuous manner, being (as we have good reason to believe) put upon it by some in authority, and of the chief men in the town, beat his cattle and abused his servants, threatening both his and their lives to that degree, that he was obliged to quit the field. And though he made presentment against sundry of them, for breach of the peace, to the civil authority, yet they refuse to take cognizance of it, and so he could obtain no relief.

We beg leave to subscribe ourselves, Reverend Sir, the venerable Society's and your most humble and most obedient servants,

SAMUEL SEABURY, SAM'L JOHNSON,
EBEN'R PUNDERSON, J. WETMORE,
JONA. ARNOLD, HENRY CANER,
JOHN BEACH.

[*Rev. Mr. Punderson to the Secretary.—Extract.*]

Groton, June 18*th*, 1739.

Reverend Sir,

There is not any more considerable alteration in the parishes under my care than that of the spirit and temper of our dissenting brethren, many of which, from being revilers and haters of our Church, are brought to have a good opinion of it, and occasionally attend our worship. I believe that at the last Christmas, and upon a Lord's day since, there met in our Church upwards of four hundred persons who behaved soberly and devoutly, many of which had been our bitterest enemies, which to me is an unspeakable comfort. Upon the earnest desire of a considerable number, I have made a journey to Middletown, about forty miles from my home, and preached to a sober body of people, near one hundred, two of which have since come and joined themselves to our communion.

Reverend Sir, I am,

Yours, and the Society's most obedient servant,

EBEN'R PUNDERSON.

[*Rev. Mr. Beach to the Secretary.—Extract.*]

Newtown, August 24*th*, 1739.

Reverend Sir,

I have been here almost seven years, and have baptised one hundred and sixty-four, of which thirteen are adults, and have one hundred and twenty-three communicants, but they live so far distant from each other, that commonly I can administer to no more than about fifty at once, which occasions my administering it the more frequently; and, though I meet with many discouragements, yet I have this satisfaction, that all my communicants (one or two excepted) do adorn their profession by a sober, righteous and godly life.

I am, Reverend Sir,

Your very humble servant,

JOHN BEACH.

[*From the Clergy of New-England to the Secretary.—Extract.*]

New-London, May 4*th*, 1740.

Reverend Sir,

We, the Clergy of New-England, convened at New-London, beg leave to represent to the honourable Society the state of a considerable congregation of the Church of England settled at Hopkinston and the parts adjacent. This town has been for some years a place of resort to several creditable families of Conformists, whose inclination or employment has caused them to remove from Boston into the country, to whom many of the old inhabitants, both of the Church and dissenting persuasions, have united themselves in promoting the Episcopal Church, being induced thereto by a monthly lecture preached among them, and some encouragement they received of being recommended to the Society's favour; there is likewise a probability of a large increase by the addition of many others who have purchased farms in the same town, so as to possess near a third part of the township, in order to settle themselves or children thereon, provided they can enjoy a constant public worship of the Church of England, and procure some assistance toward the support of an Episcopal minister to reside with them, which they express an earnest desire of, and a readiness to contribute to the utmost of their ability towards his comfortable subsistence.

We are the honourable Society's,

And, Reverend Sir,

Your most humble servants,

Arth. Browne,
Sam'l Seabury,
John Beach,
Eben'r Punderson,
Sam'l Johnson
John Usher,
Henry Caner,
Roger Price,
James Honeyman,
James MacSparran

[*Rev. Mr. Morris to the Secretary.—Extract.*]

West Haven, September 13th, 1740.

Reverend Sir,

I was received by the Church people with no small pleasure, for, upon Mr. Arnold leaving them, they seemed to despair of having another to succeed him; beside, the Dissenters used to boast and affirm confidently that the Society would never send here another missionary, which was some mortification to them, who are a people indeed not to be despised, and are ready enough to express their gratitude. I must further say of them, that they are the most versed in casuistry of any people I ever met; I mean of those that can only read English. The Archbishop of Canterbury's Treatise on Church Government, and the late Archbishop of Dublin's Collection of Cases, with several other books, have been read here to good purpose, and what they are further to be valued for is, that their conforming to the Church has exposed them to many inconveniences and oppression from the Dissenters. I have two warrants by me, granted before my time, to take up two men in Waterbury for not frequenting their meetings; and when one of them offered to give his reasons why he could not go to their extempore prayers, he was silenced and ordered to prison, or pay his fine; two more in North Haven were some time in jail before my arrival, for not paying their rates to the dissenting teachers, which is contrary to a law made here in our favour, (as I am informed,) at a time when they were apprehensive of losing their charter. The governor of this colony is elected yearly, and one Williams, who was lately rector of the Seminary in New-Haven, quitted that office with a view to be elected governor next year; but if he succeeds, we are likely to have a troublesome neighbour.

Though there be some hot spirits among the Dissenters, especially their teachers and those in power, yet there are many others more moderate, and who seem well affected to our Church, and are apt to frequent it.

Should I give you an account of the geography of my mission, you would find it large enough for a Diocese; but I would not be understood to mean this by way of complaint of the difficulty and length of the roads; and if I may be allowed to complain of any thing, it must be of the wretched fanaticism that runs so high in this country, and a body would be apt to think higher than it did in England in Cromwell's time, which does not so well suit one of my complexion; yet I have been serviceable in the Church, and will endeavour to be more so.

I have been informed since I came here, that the Dissenters

in North Haven have obliged the Church people to contribute towards building a meeting-house, and sent one poor fellow to jail who was not in a capacity to pay his cess; however, this may be contrary to law here, yet it is found, by repeated experience, that a poor Churchman can expect no redress in any court here.

I am, Reverend Sir,

Your most obliged and very obedient servant,

THEO. MORRIS.

October 28th, 1740.

[*Rev. Mr. Johnson to the Secretary.—Extract.*]

Stratford, in N. E., Nov. 10th, 1740.

Reverend Sir,

As to the complaint we designed to lay before the Society about the money arising from the sale of the seven new townships, the event is that, rather than the Church should have any share in it, the last Assembly have repealed the act that vested in the several dissenting ministers their dividends of it, exclusive of the Church, so that now, by a former act, it belongs to the schools, though I imagine they yet have some contrivance to exclude us from any advantage from it; for the increase of the Church in this country is very displeasing to those at the helm, and disposes them to distress us in all the ways they can, and particularly by so explaining the law, in their execution of it, as to oblige many of our people to pay their public dues to the support of their ministers and building their meeting-houses, if they happen to live at such a distance from our Churches as renders a constant attendance impracticable, by which means some of them have been hauled to jail, and there been forced to abide 'till they paid the utmost farthing. This has been the case with some people at a village called Cheshire, who have lately complained to me; and this is threatened and doubtless will be shortly executed upon the people of another village called Scotland, belonging to Simsbury, a town sixty miles northward.

I am, Reverend Sir,

Your most obedient, humble servant,

SAM'L JOHNSON.

[*Rev. Mr. Punderson to the Bishop of London.*]

N. Groton, 12*th Dec.*, 1741.

My Lord,

The duties and labours of my mission are exceedingly increased by the surprising enthusiams that rage among us, the centre of which is the place of my residence, a short account of which I shall trouble your Lordship with. Since Mr. Whitefield has been in this country, there has been a great number of vagrant preachers, the most remarkable of which is Mr. Davenport, of Long Island, who came to New-London in July, pronounced your ministers unconverted, and, by his boisterous behaviour and vehement crying, "Come to Christ," many were *struck*, as the phrase is, and made the most terrible and affecting noise, that was heard a mile from the place. He came to this Society, acted in the same manner five days, was followed by innumerable [people;] some could not endure the house, saying that it seemed to them more like the infernal regions, than the place of worshipping the God of Heaven; many, after the amazing horror and distress that seized them, received comfort, (as they term it,) and five or six of these young men in this Society are continually going about, especially in the night, converting, as they call it, their fellow men; two of these act as their ministers, and they affirm, converted above two hundred in an Irish town about twenty miles back in the country. Their meetings are almost every night in this and the neighbouring parishes, and the most astonishing effects attend them: screechings, faintings, convulsions, visions, apparent death for twenty or thirty hours, actual possession with evil spirits, as they own themselves. The spirit in all is remarkably bitter against the Church of England. Two who were "struck," and proceeded in this way of exhorting and praying, until actually possessed, came to me, asked the same questions: "Are you born again?"—"Have you the witness of the Spirit?" &c., as they all do; used the same texts of Scripture; taught the same doctrines; called me Beelzebub, the prince of devils; and, in their possession, burnt about £1,200. They have since been to me, asked my forgiveness, and bless God that He has restored them to the spirit of a sound mind. There are at least twenty or thirty of these lay holders-forth, within ten miles of my house, who hold their meetings every night in the week in some place or other, excepting Saturday night, and incredible pains are taken to seduce and draw away the members of my Church; but, blessed be God, we still rather increase.

I am, my Lord,

Your obedient servant,

EBEN'R PUNDERSON.

[*Rev. Mr. Morris to the Secretary.*]

Derby, *June* 20*th*, 1741.

Reverend Sir,

Since I wrote before, I made it my business to be further acquainted with the people, especially the Dissenters, many of whom I found, on my travel, well affected to our worship, and ready to conform, had they an opportunity of a Church at a reasonable distance. Others, I have heard since, object to their not being attended as often as they could wish. This proves too strong an objection among weaker people, where dissenting teachers are so numerous. There are others who, in their private conversations, profess a great liking for the Church, will readily own what they cannot be reconciled to in the Dissenters' scheme, especially the sort of ordination first set up in this country; and though they may be brought to approve our liturgy, notwithstanding all the industry of their teachers, yet, as they are men who have little places and employments, or obtain hopes of having them, they will not easily be persuaded to conform. This last difficulty is the greatest I have met with; indeed, the governing party, who are the most violent, seem to be a little more moderate than they have been, but their moderation is owing to their being afraid of England. I have lately been at Simsbury, where I found about thirty females of our communion; they are in hopes of having a minister at last, and have accordingly prepared some timber to build a Church. I remitted their rates, which amount to about fifty pounds of this currency, to help them forward with the building. I do not mention this as an act of generosity, for, however I may have a right to protect them from the Dissenters, I think I ought not to apply their money to my own use, since they are too remote to be visited above twice a year at most, considering how many parishes I have beside to attend, and, indeed, remote enough from one another. I urged upon my brethren at the Convention to assist me in attending Simsbury, which some consented to do, so that they can be served now eight times a year, and this, I hope, will keep them in heart.

I have taken another Church into my care at Wallingford, which consists of twelve families. I engaged to attend them once a quarter, which they seem to be satisfied with, for they know it is as much as I can do for them. I procured Mr. Thomson, whom I mentioned before, to officiate every Sunday in some one parish in my absence, and as his prudence and discretion have rendered him entirely agreeable to the people, he proves very serviceable to me.

I must further acquaint you that, in many places, there are some undivided lands laid out for the use of the ministry; and those of the Church party who are proprietors think it reasonable their proportion should be appropriated to the use of their minister, and are ready enough to engage in a lawsuit if there was hopes of success in England; indeed, if Dr. McSparran gain his cause, it will pave the way to do the

Church a very considerable service.* Since I came to this mission there have been added to our communion eight persons, four of whom conformed lately; six more have conformed, but have not been yet at the Sacrament. This, Sir, is all I have to add to my first letter, dated last September, and which I hope has not miscarried.

I am, Reverend Sir, your most obliged
And very obedient servant,
THEO. MORRIS.

[*Rev. Mr. Punderson to the Secretary.—Extract.*]

N. Groton, 20*th December*, 1741.

Reverend Sir,

I would inform the venerable Society, &c., that enthusiasm exceedingly rages in the parts under my care, but especially in this; the most amazing screechings, screamings, faintings, convulsions and visions attend it, and are made the inseparable marks of conversion and the new birth; and two persons in this parish have been so wonderfully wrought upon in this manner as to become actually possessed by a devil, as all grant; and one of them who, by the good providence of God, is restored to the use of reason, confesses the Spirit, in these demoniacs and enthusiasts, is extremely violent against the established Church; and both I and all under my care are declared both by teacher and people to be unconverted, and going straight down to hell. 'Tis amazing how this wild scene prevails, and how it will end God only knows. It increases my labours to that degree, that I can scarce spend a whole day in my study or family. I have twice been desired to preach to a large congregation of Seventh-day Baptists, in Westerly, and complied with their desires.

I am yours, and the honourable Society's
Real friend and servant,
EBEN'R PUNDERSON.

---

* Dr. McSparran was then engaged in prosecuting a suit he had brought for the recovery of certain lands in Narragansett, which he claimed in behalf of the Church. The Rhode Island Documents will furnish the history of this proceeding.

[*Rev. Mr. Punderson to the Secretary.—Extract.*]

N. Groton, March 30*th*, 1742.

Reverend Sir,

There never was more pressing need of good books among us than in this astonishing season, in which the wildest enthusiasm and superstition prevail; and it is attended with the most bitter fruits of uncharitableness and spiritual pride, an instance or two of which I shall trouble the honourable Society with. Some time since, immediately after I had preached a sermon in Norwich, one of these enthusiasts came to me and demanded my experience; (which is very common;) his request being denied, he pronounced me unconverted, and, not only going myself, but leading all under my charge, down to hell. Soon after, he was attended with a dumb spirit, and uttered nothing for five or six days, except two or three blasphemous expressions, viz., Go tell the brethren I am risen; at another time, Suffer little children to come unto me, &c. There also came another of these exhorters (as they are called here) to my house, attended by many; declared me as upright and as exemplary a person as any he knew in the world, yet he knew I was unconverted, and leading my people down to hell; he affirmed that he was sent with a message from God, and felt the Spirit upon him, &c.; he seemed sincere. Soon after, Mr. Croswell, the dissenting teacher in this parish, with two attendants, came singing to my house, pronounced me unconverted, yet, at the time, declared that he did not know me guilty of any crime. I assured him that, in my opinion, it was a greater crime for him thus to murder my soul, usefulness and reputation in the world, than for me to attempt his natural life; and that he certainly must be a worse man, thus, in cool blood and under a religious pretence, to pronounce damnation against me, than for a common swearer to say to another "God damn you;" since this he is not so fierce as before.

At the first rise of this enchanting delusion, I was under melancholy apprehensions that the infant Church of England, in this and the adjacent places, would be crushed, those being the centre of the religious delirium; some have gone after it, but more been added, and I am more and more convinced of the promise of our blessed Lord, that the gates of hell shall never prevail, &c. My labours abundantly increase, and I have scarce been at home a week together the past winter; sometimes I preach two or three sermons a week, beside constantly on the Lord's-day, and I have good hope that my labour is not in vain.

Your and the honourable Society's

Real friend and servant,

EBEN'R PUNDERSON.

[*Rev. Mr. Seabury to the Secretary.—Extract.*]

New-London, in New-England,

May 3d, 1742.

Reverend Sir,

I observe in the collection of papers aforesaid, page 37, order the 23d, a direction to the several missionaries to send an account of the founding and building the Churches in their respective parishes, and how the same have been supplied with ministers, and also an account of the glebe, &c. In compliance therewith, I state that, from the records of St. James' Church, at New-London, it appears that the said Church was built by subscription; the first bears date June 25th, 1725. That on the 27th of September following, seven of the members of the Church of England did, by an instrument under their hand, form themselves into a committee for the purchasing a convenient place in New-London, and for erecting and building a Church for the service of Almighty God, according to the liturgy of the Church of England as by law established; that at the same meeting the Reverend Mr. McSparran, the Society's missionary at Narragansett, was made treasurer; that on June the 20th, 1726, a carpenter was agreed with for a wood frame; that on the 9th of August following the timber was brought to the ground; on the first of October the frame was raised and completed, and on the 28th of November, 1727, the house was enclosed, glazed, the underfloor laid, a neat desk and pulpit finished, and in this state was the Church at New-London when I arrived there, December 9th, 1730, in the service of the honourable Society.

New-London is a small town, standing by a pleasant river about two miles from the sea, [sound,] the principal port of Connecticut colony, first settled by the Independents and a few Anabaptists and sort of Quaker Baptists.

The first members of the Church of England who founded St. James' Church were either Europeans, not long settled here, or persons brought up in other colonies. The government here makes no provision for the Church, though they commonly grant large tracts of land in every town for the advantage of the Independents; but the Church at New-London has neither glebe nor parsonage-house, and except a weekly contribution of its members for the use of the minister, which amounts to about a crown sterling per week, it is wholly supported by the charity of the honourable Society.

The sectaries here seem crumbling into more parties and divisions daily, branding each other with anathemas. The Church under my care remains steadfast.

Yours, and the honourable Society's
Most humble and most obedient servant,
SAMUEL SEABURY.

[*Rev. Mr. Caner to the Secretary.—Extract.*]

Fairfield, New-England, July 1st, 1742.

Reverend Sir,

Enthusiam has made no progress at Fairfield, and the effects of it at Stamford, Norwalk, Ridgefield, &c., where it has a large spread, has been the reconciling many sober, considerate people to the communion of our Church. In order to prevent as much as possible the spreading of enthusiastic principles, both now and hereafter, among us, I have applied myself closely to the duty of catechizing young and old who do not appear to have sufficiently digested the grounds of our most holy faith; the catechumens, being divided into three classes, are examined and instructed, according to their several improvements, every Lord's-day after sermon, in the afternoon.

The venerable Society's

Most dutiful and obedient, and, Sir,

Your most humble servant,

HENRY CANER.

[*The Clergy of Connecticut to the Bishop of London.*]

Fairfield, in Connecticut,

August 24th, 1742.

May it please your Lordship,

We, your Lordship's clergy of this Colony of Connecticut, humbly beg leave to lay before your Lordship the difficulties which at present affect us. The want of a Bishop to reside among us has been often mentioned as a very great obstruction to the propagation of religion in this remote part of the world; and we take leave upon this occasion to renew our most humble thanks, as for all your Lordship's good offices toward the Church in these plantations, so particularly for your kind attention to the several representations of this nature, which we have formerly made, and your sincere endeavours to obtain this advantage for us, and, since that could not be effected, for the kind provision your Lordship has made for us, as some remedy to this inconvenience, by appointing Commissaries among us under your Lordship's own special direction. But as the number of Clergy within this district is considerably increased, since the appointment of a Commissary at Boston, we humbly hope your Lordship will excuse us if we presume to suggest, with great submission, whether it might not be highly expedient for your Lordship to appoint a Commissary in this colony; our distances from the Commissary at Boston is such as makes it impracticable for us to attend upon the yearly Convention, and, consequently, to receive the benefit of that appointment. There are now fourteen Churches built and building, and seven Clergymen within this colony, and others daily called for; the nearest of us about one hundred and twenty, and the most of us upward of two hundred miles from Boston; and the charge of such a journey, yearly, is too considerable for our circumstances well to admit of. Beside, the absence from our parishes, which such a distance requires, proves oftentimes great prejudice to our people, not only from the want of publick worship, but likewise in regard they are liable to be seduced by the indefatigable endeavours of enthusiastic teachers, who, since Mr. Whitefield's tour through this colony, have made an astonishing progress.

We would not be thought to prescribe, and therefore bespeak your Lordship's candour, when we presume to mention the Reverend Mr. Johnson, of Stratford, as a person from whose ability, virtue and integrity we might hope all the advantages which such an authority would enable him to derive to us, if your Lordship should think proper to bestow this honour upon him. Your Lordship does not need to be informed, and therefore we forbear to mention, the particular advantages to be enjoyed by the residence of a Commissary among us, especially at a time when enthusiasm, in its worst colors, is daily gaining ground. We flatter ourselves with hopes of your Lordship's pardon and indulgence on this point, and beg to assure your Lordship that we are,

May it please your Lordship,

Your Lordship's obedient servants,

Henry Caner, John Beach,
Samuel Seabury, Eben'r Punderson,
Rich'd Caner.

[*Rev. Mr. Johnson to the Bishop of London.—Extract.*]

Stratford, in New-England,
September 5th, 1742.

May it please your Lordship,

This letter accompanies another to your Lordship from my brethren of the Clergy in this colony, wherein they humbly represent the necessity, or, at least, the great advantage of a Commissary to be resident among us, by reason of our great distance from Boston, which, at a medium, is between 150 and 200 miles.

On this occasion I humbly beg leave to join my voice with theirs to the same purpose, (for I do believe, with submission to your Lordship,) that it would be a very considerable means for the promoting the interests of religion and order among us; especially considering how much the Church has increased here within these few years. When I came here there were not one hundred adult persons of the Church in this whole colony, whereas now there are considerably more than two thousand, and at least five or six thousand, young and old; and, since the progress of this strange spirit of enthusiasm, it seems daily very much increasing.

My brethren have, indeed, done me the honour to mention my name to your Lordship. As to this, I beg leave to assure your Lordship that it is from their own motion, and not in the least owing to any influence of mine, that they have so done; and that if your Lordship shall think it fit, at all, to appoint a Commissary in this colony, I shall be very well satisfied to submit to any other person whom your Lordship shall think proper to appoint to preside over us.

May it please your Lordship,
Your Lordship's most dutiful
And most obedient son and servant,
SAMUEL JOHNSON.

[*Rev. Mr. Seabury to the Secretary.—Extract.*]

New-London, in New-England, Nov. 2d, 1742.

Reverend Sir,

At Hebron the Church increaseth. I had forty communicants present the last Sacrament. Mr. Barzillai Dean, whom my brethren of the clergy of Connecticut have desired and advised me to recommend to the Society's notice, has attended the Hebron Church the year past, (when I have not been there,) by reading a form of prayer out of the Liturgy of the Church, and sermons of the Church of England divines, to the great edification of the people. In compassion to them, I beg leave to lament to the honourable Society, that poor people's want of a resident minister, who, I am well sensible, might be far more useful to them than it is in my power to be; and to repeat their desire, that Mr. Dean might be permitted to come home for that charge.

At Simsbury, sixty-two miles from New-London, and eight miles west of Connecticut River, and about fifty miles up said river, there is also a large congregation of the Church of England. I have visited them twice in the year past; the last time there were one hundred and thirty adults, who, I was assured, were either real conformists, or desirous of instruction in the doctrine and worship of the Church. They beg to be recommended to the Society's charity, and I expect they will, in a little time, send the Society a token of their sincerity; a copy of a deed of fifty acres of choice land, which they have purchased for a glebe.

At Middletown, one of the most flourishing towns in Connecticut, and lying upon Connecticut River, thirty-two miles from the mouth, and forty miles from New-London, which I have visited twice the year past, there are thirty families of the Church of England, earnestly desiring to be mentioned to the venerable Society, in hopes of their future favours.

I am, Reverend Sir, yours, and the honourable Society's

Most humble and obedient servant,

SAMUEL SEABURY.

[*Churchwardens of New-London to the Secretary.—Extract.*]

New-London, February 26th, 1742-3.

Reverend Sir,

The very great convulsions occasioned here, and in divers other places in this colony, by the breaking out of what is called the New Light, makes this a melancholy juncture to have our Church empty and unsupplied; and the more, in regard that the present discords having set sundry of the most cool and considering people on thinking and reading, there is a promising prospect of those inquiries into religion, ending in a thorough and well-weighed conformity to our Church; and this again makes it the more necessary that this Church should be made happy in the appointment of a missionary, who, for morals, learning and experimental knowledge in the present state of things, might be equal to the difficulties of the present times.

Reverend Sir,

Your most obedient humble servants,

NATHANIEL GREEN, EDWARD PALMER, } *Churchwardens.*

[*The Secretary to the Rev. Mr. Johnson, Missionary at Stratford.—Extract.*]

April 25th, 1743.

Reverend Sir,

In order to make some provision, as soon as may be, for those young men recommended by you, that have been educated at your neighbouring Colleges, and are desirous of entering into the service of the Society, they [the Society] are come to a resolution, that in all future appointments of catechists and schoolmasters, a principal regard shall be had to such persons as are already in, or intend to offer themselves candidates for holy orders; that, as vacancies happen, they may be filled with these young men after they have been ordained Deacons and Priests, in England; and then, with a small stipend, (but of not less than £20 per annum,) from the Society, it is proposed to fix them at places where the inhabitants are able and willing to give as much more, for their officiating to them in the holy functions; and, as the greater missions become vacant, and they are found worthy, to advance them to them, while other deserving young men may succeed to the lesser.

I am, &c.,

P. B.,

(*i. e.*, Philip Bearcroft

[*Rev. Mr. Johnson to the Secretary*

Stratford, in New-England,

April 6*th*, 1743.

Reverend Sir,

Since my last I have baptised sixteen, whereof five were adults and of them four were negroes, and admitted sixteen to the Holy Communion, of which two were candidates for holy orders, whose names were Watkins and Lamson. The late enthusiasm is now abating, (though the venomous effects of it still prevail,) and has driven a great number into the Church, so that there are five or six places wanting ministers greatly, of which Simsbury the most, being at, by far, the greatest distance; and there are five or six valuable young candidates that would gladly serve the Church, and to very good advantage, if they could be encouraged to go home for orders; and, as the Society may think proper to make New-London vacant by removing Mr. Seabury, we should all be very glad if that place might be kept vacant till one or other of our candidates could go home for it. Mr. Thomson, whom I have several times mentioned as having long served the Church in a lay capacity, and done much good, would be a very suitable and useful person in that place. And I beg the Society to give us leave to recommend two or three in the fall, for new places, if possible, though it were with a view of but small salaries. Indeed, I humbly hope the venerable Board will excuse us if the pressing necessity of the times should prevail upon us to recommend any one for orders, though we should not have opportunity to hear from you. Mr. Dean is said to have done good service at Hebron, and, I conclude, will be recommended by the Convention.

The Church in this town has so increased of late that our house will not hold us, which has obliged us to build a new Church, for which £1,500 of our money has been subscribed, and we have got timber and are going on vigorously. It is to be sixty feet long and forty-five feet wide, and twenty-four feet high to the roof; with a steeple sixteen feet square, to be one hundred and twenty feet high; and eight feet the Chancel, which is to have a library on one side and vestry on the other. And we should be very thankful if any generous benefactors could be found that would contribute books to our library, which are very much wanted, and would be most eagerly read by many of our people, who are very inquisitive after Christian knowledge.

My *Notitia Parochialis* is as follows:

I. No. of families in this town, about............ 400
II. No. of baptised here and places adjacent by the missionary of the town,.................... 617
III. No. of baptised since my last, of which five were adults and of them were four negroes,....... 16
IV. No. of actual communicants here and at Ripton, 166
Of which, were admitted the last half year,.... 16
V. No. of those that profess the Church, families,.. 89
VI. No. of Dissenters from all the rest, Papists, only 1
VII. No. of heathens, beside anabaptised negroes,... 10
VIII. No. of converts, no remarkable instance, they being generally a sober people.

I have drawn on the treasurer for my salary, due to last Lady-day, of the same date with this letter,

And remain, Reverend Sir,

Your most obedient, humble servant,

SAMUEL JOHNSON.

[*From Mr. Stewart to the Secretary.—Extract.*]

New-London, in New-England,
January 14th, 1743.

Reverend Sir,

The unhappy difficulties our Church in this town labours under at present oblige me, in behalf of the congregation and self, to give you the trouble of this. Some time ago the Rev. Mr. Seabury obtained the consent of the venerable Society to remove to Hempstead; the Rev. Mr. Morris was appointed to fill the vacancy, which (for some reasons) was not pleasing to the people, who made application to the Rev. Mr. Commissary Price, who, together with the Rev. Dr. McSparran, came hither, and after strict and impartial examination of both parties, the Rev. Mr. Morris resigned his claim to the Church. Now we have certain intelligence that some underhand endeavours are used here to fill our Church without our privity, with one of their own creatures, in particularly with one Mr. Dean, a person of no other attainments than what are usually acquired by the low education of some men in this country. We beg leave by you, Reverend Sir, humbly and with the deepest submission, to represent to our wise, charitable and truly provident patrons, the Society, that New-London, being the seat of his Majesty's custom-house and so the port of greatest note in the colony, and, in many other respects, as a city set on a hill which cannot be hid, a missionary of mean and ordinary abilities, who might, perhaps, discharge the duties of his function with advantage in the more enclosed, remote and obscure settlements, where defects and inconformity to rubric and canon might pass with less observation, would have a direct tendency to bring the Church here into contempt, and the more so, as the Independent minister of this town has a well established character, and is in every respect the most superior person of his order in this colony. Permit us, therefore, to implore the compassion of the venerable Board to a Church like to be left in a tottering and ticklish condition; and as none of the worthy gentlemen on the mission already in New-England have mentioned their desire of being removed to us, and as he that was appointed could not make us happy, we earnestly entreat that none may be sent that goes from this country but such as the Reverend Mr. Commissary Price will recommend to the venerable Society to be appointed to this Church. We have a good character of one Mr. Cleverty [?]* from some worthy gentlemen of the Clergy, and as he has been bred up in the Church, if we can prevail on him to go home for orders, doubtless he will make us happy and all easy; but if we fail of him, and that no other to the Commissary's liking offers before he writes, then we humbly beg leave to rely on the choice of the venerable Board, and earnestly entreat that a gentleman regularly educated at home, and always bred up in the Church of England, may be singled out for the service of the Church here, which will be very unlikely to keep it's ground, much less to thrive, under the ministry of a man of incompetent capacity, tinctured with Independency, or, in the least, addicted to any kind of inconformity or vice.

[*Rev. Mr. Seabury to the Secretary.*]

Reverend Sir,

The last half year has produced nothing remarkable with regard to the Church, which continueth steadfast in the midst of the wildest enthusiasms; a most extraordinary instance of which happened here, in the sixth day of this instant, being the Lord's-day, when a large congregation gathered in the street, made a fire, and, in the sight of the sun, burned a great number of books of divinity, and, among others, Bishop Beveridge's Thoughts on Religion; and, on the next day, in a public assembly, threw down of wearing apparel to be burned to the value of one hundred pounds sterling, but by some means they were restrained from executing this last attempt.

---

* We think the name intended is Cleveland—Ed.

The Society will observe by the *Not. Paroch.*, here enclosed, that the communicants at New-London have increased, three of whom are late conformists from the Independents.

I have, since my last, beside my visit to Hebron, where the Church still prospers, visited Simsbury, sixty-two miles from New-London, where there is a great prospect of a flourishing Church.

For my last quarter's salary, due me the day of the date hereof, I have drawn in favour of Daniel Lothrop, which I hope the Society's treasurer will honour.

I am, Reverend Sir,

Yours, and the honourable Society's

Most obedient and most humble servant,

SAMUEL SEABURY.

New-London, March 25th, 1743.

[*Rev. Mr. Beach to the Secretary.*]

Reading, in New-England,
April 20th, 1743.

Reverend Sir,

The enclosed is the state of my parish, which is very little altered in this last half year. My people are not at all shaken, but rather confirmed in their principles by the spirit of enthusiasm that rages among the Independents round about us, and many of the Dissenters, observing how steadfast our people are in their faith and practice, while those of their own denomination are easily carried away with every kind of doctrine, and are now sunk into the utmost confusion and disorder, have conceived a much better opinion of our Church than they formerly had, and a considerable number in this colony have lately conformed, and several Churches are now building where they have no minister. Indeed, there is scarce a town in which there is not a considerable number professing themselves of the Church of England, and very desirous to have it settled among them; but God only knows when and how they can be provided for. Were there in this country but one of the Episcopal order, to whom young men might apply for ordination without the expense and danger of a voyage to England, many of our towns might be supplied which now must remain destitute. To express this opinion to the venerable Society (I am sensible) may be deemed impertinent, but I am moved to it by hearing so frequently numbers of serious people of our Church lamenting their unhappiness, that they can rarely enjoy that worship which they hunger and thirst after, there being so small a number of Clergymen in this country; while Presbyterians, Independents, and all sects are here perfect in their kind. But, although we have not the utmost that we could wish for, yet I bless God for the pious care and charity of the venerable Society, to which it is owing that so many hundreds of souls are provided for in this government; and had it not been for that, we have reason to think there would not have been at this day as much as one congregation in this colony worshipping God according to the Church of England.

I have this day drawn upon the treasurer for my half year's salary.

I am, Reverend Sir, yours,

And the venerable Society's

Obliged and obedient servant,

John Beach.

[*Rev. Mr. Johnson to the Secretary.*]

Stratfora, in New-Englana,

May 16th, 1743.

Reverend Sir,

We humbly presume upon the letter you wrote to the Rev. Mr. Morris, relating to Mr. Ebenezer Thomson, the bearer hereof, to recommend him to the honourable Society for holy orders, and a mission to one part of Mr. Morris' charge, which has grown too extensive and burthensome for him; for, although your letter mentions him only with a view to his being appointed a schoolmaster, yet, considering how much greater necessity there is for ministers than schoolmasters, especially in these times of the great prevalence of enthusiasm and confusion in this country, we humbly hope the Society will be prevailed to admit that he be sent back in holy orders, with a mission, upon such a security as can at present be obtained of £20 sterling per annum by the people of Derby and Oxford; which, although it be not directly a land security, (which they are providing as soon as may be,) yet it may be equally depended upon as though it were so; since we can assure the Society that the men who have undertaken for it are sufficiently responsible, and that every parishioner is, in like manner, obligated to them as they are to the Society, and that they are a people that do truly deserve the Society's favours.

As to Mr. Thomson, we beg leave to give this testimony concerning him, that he has been bred up and received both the degrees of Bachelor and Master of Arts at Yale College, New-Haven, of nine years' standing; and ever since he left the College he has been very laborious, both in suffering much hardship and doing all the good offices he possibly could for promoting the interests of religion and the advancement of the Church of England in these parts, while at the same time he has had a family of his own to provide for, which now consists of a wife and four children, being above thirty years of age, and he has always proved himself a person of a very serious and virtuous life, an orthodox and faithful son of the Church as by law established, and entirely well affected to the present government. We do, therefore, humbly hope the Society will be pleased to admit him into their service, and beg they would inform us by him, when he returns, whether we may not, upon the same foot, recommend two or three more, there being as great a necessity for providing for Simsbury, Waterbury and Ridgefield, not to mention Hebron, which we conclude will be recommended by our brethren in the eastward part of this government; and there are three other valuable candidates that beg leave to be employed as soon as may be, viz., Messrs. Watkins, Cole and Lamson, beside others that might be mentioned. We humbly take leave to subscribe ourselves,

The Society's, and, Reverend Sir,

Your most faithful and obedient humble servants.

[This letter, though written by Mr. Johnson, was in the name of and signed by all the Clergy.]

[*Rev. Mr. Caner to the Secretary.*]

Fairfield, in New-England,

May 19*th*, 1743.

Reverend Sir,

It is the chief design of this to lay before the venerable Society my *Not. Paroch.* For the last half year we have had no considerable alterations in the affairs of the Church of Fairfield, every thing remaining quiet and composed; though the constitution of this colony, both civil and ecclesiastical, has received sundry violent shocks from the effects of enthusiasm; but as I don't enter into affairs not immediately under my inspection, I have endeavoured to apply myself with diligence to cultivate a spirit of piety and sound religion among the members of my own charge. As the business of catechising is, confessedly, an important part of the pastoral care, so the experience I have had of its success in bringing both children and adults to a just and worthy apprehension of religion, has encouraged me to proceed in it with greater diligence. It would be of much use, for the furthering and promoting these, my labours, if the venerable Society would be pleased to bestow upon these children a few Catechisms, a dozen or two of Lewis' Exposition of the Catechism, half a dozen of Dr. Bray's Catechetical Instructions, and a dozen of Common Prayer-Books, with Tate and Brady's Version of the Psalms. I mentioned this request to the venerable Society about a year ago, but not succeeding, the necessity of the children obliges me to repeat it.

I am, with the utmost respect and veneration,

The venerable Society's most dutiful and obedient,

And, Sir, your most humble servant,

HENRY CANER.

[*Rev. Mr. Johnson to the Archbishop of Canterbury.*]

Stratford, in New-England,
May 22*d*, 1743.

May it please your Grace,

This will wait on your Grace by Mr. Ebenezer Thomson, whom I have several times mentioned to the Society, and who may truly be recommended as a person who (having been bred and graduated in our neighbouring College) has for these several years undergone much hardship and done much service, as far as his lay capacity would admit, in promoting the interest of religion in general, and the Church of England in particular, in these parts, having thought nothing too much to do or suffer that has fallen in his way for the sake of so good a cause, and who now goes home, with a good character from all the Clergy in these parts, in hope of a mission to Derby. But if New-London should be yet a vacancy, I should rather wish him to be sent thither. And on this occasion I humbly entreat your Grace's interest with the Society, that whenever any vacancies happen to be made in this country, either by death or removal, the people may have leave, before they are filled, to procure the Clergy to recommend some young gentleman, if any offers from hence, as there scarcely ever fails to be several (as there are now) who would gladly serve the interests of the Society, to the utmost of their power, at any possible rate, and are generallv much more acceptable to the people, and, consequently, more successful in promoting the great ends of the Society, than those who come hither, strangers to the condition of things in these countries. I beg your Grace will excuse me that I mention this, and that I again suggest the necessity of Bishops, which I have fresh reason to do, from the great prevalence of enthusiasm, and especially that mad sort of it which obtains among the Moravians to the westward, who are likely to make the greater progress, to the unspeakable damage of true religion, by means of having the Episcopal government among them. It is, indeed, very hard, that when enthusiasm and heresy have the advantage of Episcopacy to propagate them, the truth of the orthodox Church of England should not have the like advantage, for the defence and propagation of that. I beg your Grace's prayers and blessing, and remain, may it please your Grace, your Grace's most dutiful son and most obedient, humble servant,

SAMUEL JOHNSON.

[*Rev. Mr. Seabury to the Secretary.—Extract.*]

New-London, June 5th, 1743.

Reverend Sir,

But truth obligeth me to say that the prospect of a large Church at Hebron is not so good as formerly, because the followers of Mr. Whitefield, Mr. Tennant, &c., do extremely abound there; the dissenting teacher at Hebron having gone the greatest lengths in pretensions to inspiration and the sensible feeling of the Spirit, as well as into the greatest excesses of meetings almost every day and night. And I should the more rejoice in a resident minister there, because the same spirit of Methodism prevails mightily at New-London, increaseth my care and labours, and renders my absence on Sundays of dangerous consequence. The conformists, both at New-London and Hebron, indeed, are steadfast to the Church.

though they are very much alarmed by the new doctrines and new propagation of religion, the effects of which are really surprising. Those people have meetings in New-London almost every night or day, and 'tis not uncommon (as I am apprised by persons of good sense and integrity) to see ten or more seized at once with violent agitations, many incapable of any decency, crying out for their damned estate, so past speaking at all, or so much, indeed, as being unable to stand, fall down, as they pretend, with the weight of their guilt; and the most of those continuing thus violently exercised (as they say with conviction) but a few hours, do then receive comfort. The Spirit of God, they say, witnesses with their spirits, that they are converted and born again; then follow immediately such raptures and transports of joy as are more surprising than their distresses. New-London has been for a week together in such a tumult that I was afraid the people would have been beside themselves. I have had my house full of people, some under those distresses, and others surprised at the conduct of their neighbours, though I thank God I have never seen any person in this way, but, by cool reasoning and by plain expositions of the terms of reconciliation with God, they have been brought off from their amazing apprehensions to a just notion of the doctrines of repentance and remission of sins; and, beside my attendance at home for many days together on people thus frighted, I have been invited to preach to a numerous congregation at Lyme, about seven or eight miles from New-London, who never heard the Liturgy many of them, and who expressed great satisfaction in my explanation of those doctrines, about which New-England seems at present so much perplexed.

I remain your poor, though faithful servant,

SAMUEL SEABURY.

[*Rev. Mr. Johnson to the Secretary.*]

Stratford, in New-England,
September 30th, 1743.

Reverend Sir,

I am most humbly thankful to his Grace and the rest of the honourable Board, for their kind reception of my letters and for the favourable notice they have taken of what I suggested, and the excellent scheme they have concerted for providing for such young men as offer themselves candidates from hence, (of whom the number is still increasing,) as well as that of places where they might be advantageously situated; and people seem, in several places, well disposed to give all the security they can for £20 sterling per annum, and are contriving to lay out uncultivated lands for glebes, which, in the course of time, may be very valuable, though it must be some years before they can be cultivated so as to do much toward the support of an incumbent. An hundred acres have been lately laid out for the perpetual use of the Church, within the bounds of this town, which is now worth about £20 sterling.

I lately opened a new Church at Ripton, where the people hope, in due time, to have some young man to be placed as my assistant. On the Sunday following, the dissenting teacher, one Mills, whose praise is in the journal, being a great admirer of Mr. Whitfield, reviled and declaimed against my sermon, which was on the subject of relative holiness and the reverence due to the house of God. He insisted that there is no more holiness in a Church than under an oak tree, &c.; and soon after some of his followers put his doctrine in practice, by defiling the Church with ordure in several places.

This zealous man gave out, when Mr. Whitfield first appeared, that their employing and encouraging that great reformer would utterly destroy the Church, root and branch; but now finding the event to be the entire reverse of his predictions, he is grown out of all patience with us. In the mean time, while they are daily spitting out their impotent venom against us, I thank God we have a blessed spirit of peace and charity, and of zeal and unanimity, while every other Christian virtue is happily prevailing among my people, who are carrying on our new Church in the neatest manner, and with great dispatch, it being within a few months raised and now almost covered, and we have had several new families added, and more seem likely to follow them; but I cannot expect any enlargement of my salary from the people here till they have got through the great expense of building.

I am in much concern for the great damage I fear the Church in these parts will sustain by Mr. Seabury's removal, and Mr. Morris' succeeding him at New-London. This gentleman had the misfortune to have but little esteem among the people where he had officiated, and to be much despised by many others. I have faithfully laboured, both with him and them, to prevent this misfortune, but so the event has proved, which put the people of New-London into a terrible consternation, when they heard he was appointed for them, so that they were unwilling to admit him into their Church till his character should be cleared up; and applied to the Commissary to inquire into the grounds of that general disesteem he laboured under, but nothing has yet been done about it. They were advised by the Clergy here, in the mean time, out of duty and gratitude to the Society, to admit him into their Church, which, upon our advice, they immediately did, but yet depend upon the Commissary to take cognizance of the affair. What he proposes to do I have not heard, but whatsoever the result be, (though I earnestly wish otherwise,) I doubt there is little reason to expect the people there will be happy in him, or he in them, and I believe it would be well for both if they were otherwise provided for. New-London is a place of considerable importance to this government, and the Church there was likely to flourish in a good degree; and it grieves me very much, that this unhappy affair should be an hindrance to it. I should not have said this much, but that I have been earnestly solicited by that people to mention something of it, and that it looks unavoidable that the Society will be troubled with it first or last; but I shall add no more, unless the Society shall have occasion to inquire of me and my brethren about it, and shall only subjoin my *Not. Paroch.*, which is as follows:

I.	No. of families within the bounds of this town, I am told, is about........................	400
II.	No. of baptised here and in places adjacent by the minister of this town,..................	644
III.	No. since my last, of which three were adults,..	12
IV.	No. of actual communicants here and at Ripton, about................................	170
	Of which, admitted this last half year,.........	10
V.	No. of those that profess the Church, families,..	92
VI.	No., all the rest Presbyterians and Independents, Papists, none.	
VII.	No. of heathens, beside many unbaptised negroes,................................	10
VIII.	No. of converts, &c., no remarkable instance, they being generally a sober, virtuous people.	

I have drawn on the treasurer for my salary to Michaelmas, and remain the Society's most faithful and obliged,

And, Reverend Sir,

Your most obedient, humble servant,

SAM'L JOHNSON.

[*Rev. Mr. Beach to the Secretary.*]

Reading, in New-England,
October 20th, 1743.

Reverend Sir,

I beg the venerable Society's direction in an affair I am just now perplexed with. There are about twenty families professing the Church at New-Milford and New-Fairfield, which are about fifteen miles hence. I preach to them several times in a year, but seldom on the Lord's day. They frequently come to Church at Newtown, but, by reason of the distance, they can't attend constantly, and their families very seldom, and, when they can't come to Church, they meet together in their own town, and one of their number reads some part of the common prayer and a sermon. They are now building a Church, and hope in time to have a minister settled among them. But the Independents, to suppress this design in its infancy, having the authority in their hands, have lately prosecuted and fined them for their meeting to worship God according to the common prayer, and the same punishment they are like to suffer for every offence in this kind, although it is the common approved practice of the same Independents to meet for worship in their own way when they have no minister; but what is a virtue in them is a crime in our people. The same is like to be the case in many other towns, in which people professing the Church are so far distant from a settled minister, that they cannot constantly attend the worship of God with him.

The case of these people is very hard; if, on the Lord's day, they continue at home, they must be punished; if they meet to worship God according to the Church of England in the best manner they can, their mulct is still greater; and if they go to the Independent meeting in the town where they live, they must endure the mortification of hearing the doctrine and worship of the Church vilified, and the important truths of Christianity obscured and enervated by enthusiastic and antinomian dreams. Now I should be thankful if the venerable Society would direct me what course to advise these people to, and if I might receive a particular instruction to take care of those professing the Church in New-Milford and New-Fairfield as part of my parish. I believe it would put me into a better capacity to protect them from the insults of their Independent neighbours. I have, this half year, baptised eighteen children, and admitted several more persons to the Lord's Supper. The inclosed is the state of my parish. I have this day drawn for my half year's salary.

I am, Reverend Sir,

Yours and the Society's

Most obedient servant,

JOHN BEACH.

[*Rev. Mr. Caner to the Secretary.—Extract.*]

Fairfield, in New-England,
November 30th, 1743.

My parish has received no diminution and but little increase since my last; I beg leave, therefore, to refer to my *notitia parochialis* inclosed for what may be expected as to the present state of the Church in Fairfield. At Norwalk, Stamford and Ridgefield, where my brother chiefly officiates, there have been large accessions made to the Church of late, chiefly of persons who appear to have a serious sense of religion, and whose good example will, I trust, have a happy influence upon others. Where the late spirit of enthusiasm has most abounded, the Church has received the largest accession. Many of those deluded people, having lost themselves in the midst of error, wearied in the pursuit, as their passions subsided, sought for rest in the bosom and communion of the Church; and others, reflecting upon the weakness of their former dependence, which left them exposed to such violent disorders, have likewise thought proper to take shelter under the wings of the Church. Norwalk, Stamford, and the neighbouring towns, have been much visited with this spiritual malady, but at Fairfield it has never obtained, though it has been often attempted to be introduced by Mr. Whitfield, and many of his followers. An epidemical sickness has prevailed in the towns last mentioned this fall, and, among others, my brother has been confined by it above two months, which has greatly increased my burthen, the care of all these western Churches thus falling upon me, so that my time has been wholly taken up in visiting the sick and preaching from town to town.

[*The Churchwardens of Wallingford to the Secretary.*]

Wallingford, in New-England,
December 1st, 1743.

Reverend Sir,

We, the inhabitants of Wallingford, members of the Church of England, make bold on behalf of ourselves and at the request of our brethren inhabiting in the neighbouring towns of Guilford and Branford, to inform you that we are twenty-five masters of families that are members of said Church, and meet together every Lord's day and edify ourselves, as well as we can, by reading; and while the Reverend Mr. Morris was in these parts, we were edified to our great comfort; our number then increased, and many more were coming in to join us, but he being removed from us, and Mr. J. Lyon cannot attend us, we are now destitute, and our dissenting brethren from year to year are distressing us with executions for meeting-houses, rates, steeples, and bells for them; so that our present melancholy circumstances crave your good offices with the honourable Society. We are willing to do the best we can toward the support of a minister, and make no doubt but in two or three years' time we shall be able to raise £20 sterling per annum toward the support of a minister. We humbly pray we may be assisted with a minister, and, might we choose for ourselves, we having experienced the Rev. Mr. Morris, would heartily wish he might be the person; and could a method be found for quelling the perpetual demands of our dissenting brethren for meeting-houses, rates, &c., it would greatly add to the growth and consolation of our distressed Churches, and we, as in duty bound, shall ever pray.

HENRY BATES, } *Churchwardens,*
JOHN WARD, } *and several others.*

[*Rev. Dr. Johnson to the Secretary.*]

Stratford, in New-England,
January 10th, 1743-4.

Reverend Sir,

I most humbly thank you for your good offices to Mr. Thomson, and for your kind and affectionate letter by him, and your readiness therein expressed, to do any thing in your power toward promoting the interest of our holy religion and the best of Churches in these parts of the world; and, among other things, I was much obliged to you for what you kindly suggested to Mr. Thomson about the report you had heard of my going to meetings, and suffering my son to do so; and I beg leave to make my apology, and explain to you the truth of this matter, and entreat you would make that use of it, in my behalf, which you shall think proper, and may seem to you needful; and even to read this letter to the Society, if there appears to you occasion for it, in order that I may be freed from any mischief that may arise to me from any misrepresentations that may have been laid before them; for, I find I have enemies disposed to do me a damage, and those, I believe, some whom I have endeavoured to serve to my utmost, and for whom my tenderness and compassion has sometimes put me upon doing kind offices, even when I had too much reason to fear the public might suffer by it, an instance of which may possibly come into your hands. It is true Mr. Morris, in his great zeal, did complain of me to the Convention on those accounts, but I wrote to the Commissary, and gave him such an account of my conduct as I presume satisfied him, he having never remarked any thing to me, to the contrary, since.

As to my own going to meeting, the fact is, I did go to hear Mr. Whitfield once, which I presumed it would not be offensive for me to do, he being in orders in our Church, and not then under any censure: and, indeed, I thought it my duty so to do, that I might be under the better advantage to prevent the mischief I apprehended from him and his followers among the people; and the event has proved that I have, by this means, been under the greater advantage to withstand and quiet the late madness and enthusiasm that has prevailed among us, and make it turn to the great increase of the Church.

It was for the same reason that I, with two or three of my brethren of the Clergy, went one night in the dark, and perfectly *incognito*, among a vast crowd, to see and hear Davenport's managements, whom we heard rave about a quarter of an hour, and then went away, without having been known there; and twice in my travels, by mere accident, I happened, in the night, (for these mad meetings were chiefly in the night,) to come unexpectedly upon private houses where these wild meetings were carrying on, but soon left them, unknown; by which means I happened to be an eye-witness of those strange doings, which I gave the Society an account of, and have since made an advantage of my observations on those occasions to their confusion. Such have been the instances of my going to meeting, for which I have been faulted by some over-zealous people, whose venomous spirit toward the Dissenters has very much hurt the Church, while I have made the best advantage of what I observed, and with very good success, to do her service; and this much for myself.

As to my son, it is indeed a great mortification to him and me, that I am obliged to send him to a dissenting College, or deny him any public education at all; and rather than deny him a collegiate education, I confess I do not forbid him going to meeting when he can't help it, to which he is himself so averse, that nothing but mere necessity would put him upon it. He comes home to Church once in three weeks or a month, at least, at the communion, if possible, being fourteen miles distant, and as often as there is Church there, he goes to West Haven, which is four miles distant; at other times he stays at home in his chamber as much as he can, and the rector and tutors indulge him as much as they dare, being friendly disposed to serve me as much as they are able without hazarding the resentment of the government that supports them. This is the fact with respect to my son. And after all, if my method of proceeding is not what the Society approves of, I am heartily willing to stand corrected, and entirely to conform to their instructions, and in hopes of a line from you, on this subject, for my direction.

I remain, Reverend Sir,

Your most obliged and obedient,

Humble servant,

SAM'L JOHNSON.

P. S.—Since my last, here is an ingenious gentleman, one Mr. Prince, of very considerable learning, having been fifteen years a fellow of Harvard College, in Cambridge, who has conformed to the Church, and lives at present in this town, and desires to serve the Church in holy orders, and would willingly go home in the spring; and here is an honest neighbouring dissenting teacher, who will very soon appear for the Church, and probably bring the greatest part of his congregation with him, and I wish it may be in the Society's power to settle a small pension upon him, and send him back in holy orders to his people, if he should wait on them for that purpose.

Yours, as above,

S. J.

[*Clergy of Connecticut to the Secretary.—Extract.*]

Norwalk, March 28th, 1744.

Reverend Sir,

And we can with the same integrity recommend the people of Stamford, Greenwich and Horse Neck, whose petition for a minister to reside among them was laid before the Society by the Rev'd Isaac Brown, when he went home for orders. These people have been much persecuted by the dissenting government, for when they would have rewarded the Rev. Mr. Wetmore for his monthly attendance in officiating among them, by paying their proportion of the rates, according to an express law of the colony, they were prevented by a very oppressive judgment of the court; and though they have been put to great difficulties, yet the Church has much increased, especially since Mr. Richard Caner was sent to Norwalk, and there is a good prospect of their increasing much more, if they can obtain Mr. Miner to settle among them, now the confusions of Methodism are prevailing, as they have done very much of late, in that part of the government.

Mr. Miner is a gentleman well qualified to serve that people, and they have an earnest desire to obtain him. He is a late convert from the Dissenters, convinced of the necessity of conformity, chiefly by occasion of the late mischiefs of enthusiasm. He was for above twelve years a teacher among the Dissenters, much esteemed by them both for his preaching and good behaviour.

We subscribe, with our humblest duty to the Society,

Reverend Sir,

Your most obedient, humble servants,

S. Johnson, Richard Caner,
Jas. Wetmore, James Lyons,
Henry Caner.

[*Churchwardens, at Simsbury, to the Society.—Extract.*]

Simsbury, April 10th, 1744.

Reverend Sir,

We have built a convenient Church, and purchased a glebe of fifty acres adjacent to our Church, and in good order; we have been a Society for four years, and have almost constantly for that time carried on sermons and a form of prayer, and yet, notwithstanding all this, the Independents, by force and under a pretence of authority, have carried away our estates, to support their teachers, to build their meeting-houses, and procure their parsonages. Enthusiasm and error have much prevailed among us; but of late they have run into parties, so that, in a meeting-house adjacent to us, they cannot agree about calling a teacher, and many of them and of our neighbours, by the occasional visits of the Reverend Mr. Lyons, incline to the Church, having nothing so much to object against as the want of a settled minister. Our Clergy have advised us to Mr. Gibbs, as a modest, virtuous gentleman and well qualified to serve us, but as we are not able to support him suitably to the dignity of that station and character, we trust that the venerable Society, in their great wisdoms, will allow us their charitable assistance.

We are, Reverend Sir,

Your most obedient, humble servants,

WILLIAM CASE,
JNO. CHRISTIAN MILLER, } *Churchwardens.*

[*Rev. Mr. Punderson to the Secretary.—Extract.*]

N. Groton, April 9th, 1744.

Reverend Sir,

As I am at present the only missionary in this half of the government and part of Rhode Island, I would earnestly recommend it to the venerable Board, as soon as possible, to supply the vacancy at New-London, and, if possible, to erect a mission at Stonington and Charlestown, where the harvest would, undoubtedly, be very plenteous, were there a resident labourer of a virtuous character. I preached at Charlestown last Sunday to a considerable congregation.

I am, Reverend Sir, yours,

And the Society's real friend and servant,

EBEN'R PUNDERSON.

[*Rev. Mr. Lyons to the Secretary.—Extract.*]

Derby, *May* 8*th*, 1744.

Reverend Sir,

At a place called Guilford, where there are two Independent congregations in the compact part of the town, and where, also, the worship of our Church has not till lately made its entrance, I have preached several times, baptised three children, and eight families (consisting of thirty-six children beside adults) have declared their conformity, and in testimony thereof, have subscribed a paper which I formed for that purpose, and many of them have occasionally communicated since that time. At Milford and New-Haven there are a few members of our Church, but care is taken, at the last of those places especially, that they should not increase, the rector and tutors of the College there having, of late, suffered none of the students (except the children of professed Churchmen) to attend my lectures. At West Haven I have baptised two children and officiated frequently. At Derby and Oxford I have had sixteen new communicants, at the last of which places I have baptised seven children, and catechised at Derby; but having committed the care of registering the baptisms there to one of the Churchwardens, he obstinately refused to show me the lists, which naturally induces me to present my venerable patrons with a short sketch of my grievances at this same Derby. As soon as they had advice of my appointment, and from what country I came, and, indeed, before I arrived among them, they abused me, calling me an "Irish Teague and Foreigner," with many other reflections of an uncivilized and unchristian kind; they boasted they should soon discover me, meaning, I suppose, they would either find or fasten some thing upon me relating to my character or conduct whereby they might get rid of me. Under these disadvantages I entered on that part of my mission, but, by care and diligence, conciliated myself to them, 'till the Reverend Mr. Thompson, of Scituate, came up amongst them, whose conduct kindled a fire that is not extinguished. In my absence, and while he was among them, they appointed a vestry without my privity, and let me know nothing of their intents till four days before that meeting, of their own appointment; meanwhile, they secreted from me the Society's letter, and when I insisted on seeing it, asserted they had no occasion to consult me, nor make me privy to their purposes, so I did not see it till two days before that meeting. From Mr. Thompson's conduct and theirs, I became clearly convinced that they were mutually of the mind to bring him into my mission. At their instance, I indicated a regular vestry, and at that, the appointment of a committee to find a suitable tract of land for a glebe. I encouraged them all in my power, and exhorted them to order, peace and unanimity, but to little effect, for at a vestry held in Easter Week, some of their leading men asserted they would not assist in getting a glebe unless on condition to have their own countryman to fill the Church. They alleged they were acquainted with the venerable Society's mind in that matter, which, they said, had left them to their choice, and had agreed to make it a rule that every country should be furnished with missionaries of their own raising (as they phrase it.) It would be too tedious to record all the abuse and insults I have received at Derby; so many and so severe, that some of themselves, more moderate than the rest, remonstrated to them the danger they were in of losing the mission by their abuses to me. They answered, they did not care if it was sunk, they could soon renew it, and had rather have it sunk in the deepest part of the sea than have it in an itinerancy; though I have officiated in that place above one-third of my time, and am, through God's goodness, hitherto irreprovable in doctrine and practice. My New-England brethren of the Clergy here are so fond of their own countrymen that, were there never so much occasion for it, either here or at the Board, they would be at little pains to do my character justice; and in a little time they hope to get rid of missionaries that are not country born, or, at least, that no more of European education be sent; and then what face the Church here will put on, is as easy as it is unpleasant to foresee. If the insults of Derby are not redressed, it will be in vain to send any European, especially into this colony, whether as resident or itinerant.

I am, Reverend Sir,
Your most obedient, humble servant,
JAMES LYONS.

[*Rev. Mr. Caner to the Secretary.—Extract.*]

Fairfield, in New-England,
May 10*th*, 1744.

Reverend Sir,

The present state of my own parish does not yield me all the satisfaction I could wish. The late enthusiasm never made much progress here, and, indeed, the temper of the people is generally rather faulty in the other extreme, a cold Laodicean disposition, an inconsiderate neglect of the great duties of religion, a visible deadness and formality, is what, at present, gives me most concern, and prevents the success of my administrations.

I am, Reverend Sir, your most obedient,
And most humble servant,
HENRY CANER.

[NOTE.—It may be a question worth examination, whether the enthusiasm complained of was not, in its reactionary effect, the occasion, if not the cause, of the Laodicean coldness complained of.]

The Members of the Church in Northbury to the Secretary.]

Northbury, May 28*th*, 1744.

The representation and humble petition of the members of the Church of England, in Northbury, in the township of Waterbury, in the colony of Connecticut, in New-England, and the members of said Church, dwelling in other places nearly adjoining, humbly sheweth :

We were all educated in this land, under the instruction of Independent teachers, or (as they would be called) Presbyterians; and consequently, we were prejudiced strongly against the Church of England from our cradles, until we had the advantage of books from your Reverend missionaries and others, whereby we began to see with our own eyes that things were not as they had been represented to our view; and Mr. Whitfield, passing through this land, condemning all but his adherents, and his followers and imitators, by their insufferable enthusiastick whims and extemporaneous jargon, brought in such a flood of confusion amongst us, that we became sensible of the unscriptural method we had always been accustomed to take in our worship of God, and of the weakness of the pretended constitution of the Churches (so called) in this land; whereupon, we fled to the Church of England for safety, and are daily more and more satisfied we are safe, provided the purity of our hearts and lives be conformable to her excellent doctrine; and that it is the best constituted Church this day in the world.

Henry Cook, Isaac Castel,
Barnaby Ford, John How,
Thomas Claselee.

[*Rev. Mr. Caner to the Secretary.—Extract.*]

Fairfield, in New-England,
November 13*th*, 1744.

Reverend Sir,

We daily expect a new storm from the daily irregular excursions of Mr. Whitfield; he has not yet begun his progress, having been under afflictions for the loss of his only child, and, since that, visited with dangerous sickness himself; his sickness still continues, and whether it shall please God to continue him a scourge to these Churches is yet uncertain.

[*Rev. Mr. Johnson to the Secretary.—Extract.*]

Stratford, in New-England,
February 12th, 1744–5.

Reverend Sir,

I observe the Society has come to a resolution not to receive any for the future, without liberty first obtained for them to go home, &c. This order, as far as I was concerned, I shall dutifully observe; but, as it is expressed in the most general terms, I beg leave to ask whether it is to be understood of any at all, even though their view were only to supply any vacancy that may happen, or whether it be not rather the Society's meaning, that none shall go with a view to any new mission to be erected, without leave first obtained. It is of this last case, I humbly presume, the Society would be understood, because it would seem hard, and might be very detrimental to the Church, for the people to be so long destitute, as the time would require to send and receive the Society's answer.

I humbly hope this resolution of the Society will not be understood to look back so as to defeat the hopes of Messrs. Miner and Lamson, when it shall please God to deliver them from their captivity.*

As to Mr. Prince, who is now teaching a school, all I can say of him from my own knowledge is, that ever since he has been in those parts, which is now almost two years, his behaviour has been not only entirely unexceptionable, but very amiable. He was, it is true, rejected from Harvard College, but I understood it not to be from immorality, but for his resolutely, and, perhaps, too warmly adhering to what he thought right, and publishing his reasons (not since answered) in a controversy among them relating to the government of the College; which occasioned, indeed, great obloquy

* They had probably been captured on their passage, and carried prisoners to France, as several of those who went for orders were.

against him, and made the Convention doubtful about employing him, but they at length came to this conclusion, (if I remember right,) that if he brought sufficient certificates of his good behaviour for two years from that time, which was last May, they should be willing to recommend him. As to his writing against the three creeds, it is utterly groundless; all the pretence for it was, that about twelve years ago he published a piece upon the resurrection of Christ, wherein he has a slant of two or three words about composing creeds, or something to that effect, and he told me at that time he had imbibed some loose latitudinarian notions from reading Chubb, and the Independent Whig, &c., which he had long since been convinced were very erroneous, of which he gave satisfaction to Dr. Cutler by a letter to him. However, as to all these things, I beg leave to refer you to the Rev. Mr. Davenport, a very worthy member of the Society, now going home, who is much better acquainted with what concerns Mr. Prince, in that government, than I am.

I remain, Reverend Sir,

Your most faithful and most obedient servant,

SAMUEL JOHNSON.

[*Rev. Mr. Johnson to the Secretary.—Extract.*]

Stratford, in New-England,

March 30*th*, 1745.

Reverend Sir,

And as there is such a growing disposition among the people in many places to forsake the tenets of enthusiasm and confusion, so there is a like disposition increasing in the College, where there are already ten children of the Church, and several sons of dissenting parents, that are much inclined to conform. I was there last week, and was much pleased with their exercises; among the rest, there was one layman, a person of good character, (beside Messrs. Marsh and Mansfield, mentioned in my last,) who desired me to mention him to the

Society as a candidate for the ministry. Thus, *the harvest is large and the labourers* not a *few*, who would gladly be employed, and be content with as moderate wages as can be thought tolerable, whenever the Society shall be in a disposition to employ them, or any of them.

Though the madness of the late enthusiasm has much abated, the venom of it still continues, and, I fear, rather increases, and operates in a violent manner in many places against the Church; so that no sooner does any person in authority appear for the Church, but he is soon displaced, and some bitter creature set up by the government in his room; and in some places, notwithstanding the law they had made in our favour, they have of late taxed the lands of the Church people in common with the Dissenters, toward the support of their ministers. I have myself lately had no less than ten pounds of our money forced from me, toward maintaining three of the worst creatures in the government, being taxes raised upon some lands I had in the places where they were teachers. But what I would mention as the greatest grievance of this kind, is the case of the Church people at Derby, who are forced to pay such a land tax in their own town to a dissenting teacher and meeting-house in one of their villages, (when they have a Church of their own to finish and a minister to provide for,) the amount of which, in the whole, will be very considerable.

I am, Reverend Sir,

Your most obliged, obedient, humble servant,

SAMUEL JOHNSON.

[*Rev. Mr. Lyons to the Secretary.—Extract.*]

New-Haven, May 30th, 1745.

Reverend Sir,

The conformists at West Haven increase, and they have almost finished the Church. In many other places (too tedious to mention) our Church begins to gain ground in spite of many disadvantages. At Wallingford and Cheshire, the Dissenters take, by distress, the Churchmen's estates, to build, repair, and keep clean their meeting-houses; and, though they have had several trials in our courts, they always lose their cases. The people of Derby still continue divided by a national spirit that prevails, and is industriously propagated by some of them and the neighbouring Clergy; however, after all attempts made, and unchristian means used, by some to render me unacceptable, (by hauling me once and again before an Independent justice of the peace, as I mentioned in some former account,) yet, through the goodness of God, my innocence and integrity protected me, and I continue irreprovable, having a good understanding with the most of my extensive mission, and even with many of Derby, who are grieved with the irregular proceedings of that National party.

I am, Reverend Sir, yours, &c., &c.,

James Lyons.

[*Rev. Mr. Gibbs to the Secretary.—Extract.*]

Simsbury, June 26th, 1745.

Reverend Sir,

The Church seems to be in a promising condition, and I am not without hope that there will be a great increase in time. I have now twenty communicants, and have baptised eight. The Churchmen here have been much oppressed by the Dissenters, who have taken from them seventy pounds toward building their meeting-house and settling their minister.

I remain, Sir,

Your most humble and obedient servant,

William Gibbs.

[*Rev. Mr. Johnson to the Secretary.—Extract.*]

Stratford, in New-England,
September 2d, 1745.

Reverend Sir,

I am very glad the Society has made the providing a parsonage-house the conditions of the continuance to old missions. This is a very reasonable and happy exchange for a former proposal of making an house and glebe the condition of opening new missions, which was very difficult and discouraging to many new places.

I have, by favour of Mr. Vesey, seen the sermon and abstract you mention relating to the Moskito Indians, but do not know of any missionary willing to move to that distance, it being very remote from these parts, and thought to be an unhealthy climate. Mr. Prince, however, is willing to undertake, if the Society shall think proper to employ him, and I am informed that the Commissary is well satisfied with respect to the objections that were alleged against him, and is willing to recommend him; and in order thereunto, I have sent him a good testimonial from these parts where he has resided chiefly above two years. I hope he may be the bearer of this letter, or, at least, go home in the spring, and am persuaded if he can have his health, he may do very good service in such a mission as you propose.

As I may not have opportunity again after Michaelmas, I beg leave to add that I have continued, once in awhile, to visit Middletown and Guilford, where there continues to be a good prospect, and the College remains in the same disposition as when I wrote last. Another promising youth offers his service, one of Bishop Berkeley's scholars, whose name is *Colton*, and he, with the other two I mentioned before, *Mansfield* and *Lyman*, beg leave to hope they may be employed by the Society about two years hence, when they will be of full age, and in the mean time are devoting themselves to pursue such studies, under my direction, as may qualify them for it.

It is a mighty grief to us to hear of the death of our friend, Mr. Miner, the case of whose disconsolate widow and fatherless children is very pitiable; he would have been a very useful man if he had lived; nor do we yet hear since of Mr. Lamson. Would to God we had a Bishop to ordain here, which would prevent such unhappy disasters.

I remain, Reverend Sir,

Your most obedient and humble servant,

SAMUEL JOHNSON.

[*Rev. Mr. Punderson to the Secretary.—Extract.*]

N. Groton, October 8th, 1745.

Reverend Sir,

Since my last I have been to Stafford, preached and baptised some children. Mr. Payne, of whom I acquainted the Society in my last, proposes, by divine permission, (having obtained leave from the Society,) to come home next summer. He has only a wife and two children, and there is no missionary within near fifty miles, and the country pretty well inhabited.

The third Sunday in September I preached in New-London, desired the congregation to meet upon the next day, which they did, and voted to procure a house as soon as possible for their next missionary. One of the members of that Church has given a convenient and valuable spot of land for that purpose; they have generously subscribed to the building of said house, which I hope will be fit to live in by the beginning of next summer. I verily think it a piece of justice due to that congregation in general, to assure the Society that, according to their abilities, they are a generous good sort of people, and they continue firm and unshaken.

Reverend Sir, yours, and the Society's

Most obedient and obliged servant,

EBEN'R PUNDERSON.

[*The Churchwardens of West Haven to the Society.—Extract.*]

West Haven, October 26th, 1745.

Reverend Sir,

We beg leave to represent the state of our part of the mission to the venerable Board, as the parish of West Haven is small, and the inhabitants poor. The Dissenters were not able, after our conformity, to support their teacher by a ministerial rate, so that they have sold the glebe land, and had money out of the treasury, which, with some additions made by the parish, founded a bank, the interest of which supports their teacher, which weakens our hands and hinders the conformity of Dissenters, as they expect to contribute to the support of ours if they conform.

We are, Reverend Sir,

Your most obliged, humble servants,

JOHN HUMPHREVILE, } *Churchwardens.*
JOSEPH PRINDLE, }

[*Rev. Mr. Johnson to the Secretary.—Extract.*]

Stratford, in New-England,
26th March, 1746.

Reverend Sir,

I have once or twice mentioned the case of the people of our Church at Ripton, a parish of this town, under my care, where there are fifty-one families that have built a Church about eight miles from hence. They have been so undeniably importunate to have the service and sermons read among them to prevent their children from straggling and going to meeting, that I have this winter indulged their importunity in permitting my son to read to them, whose services therein have been very acceptable to them, and they beg me to mention him to the Society, with their earnest desires that he may be allowed as a catechist and reader for them, and would allow him seventy or eighty pounds our currency, which is equal to about ten pounds sterling. As to my son, I shall only beg leave to say, that I thank God he has good abilities, and that I have spared no pains to cultivate them in the best manner circumstances will admit of. He will shortly enter his 20th year, and has took his Bachelor's degree almost two years ago; the chief Greek and Latin classics were then so familiar to him, that he merited Bishop Berkeley's premium in this College, and he has taken much pains to qualify himself in all other parts of learning; particularly, he has read much of our best English philosophers and divines for his years, and is now studying the Hebrew, and Antiquities, both sacred and profane. But whether he will make divinity or law the business of his life, he has not yet resolved.

I am, Reverend Sir, your most obliged,

And most obedient, humble servant,

SAMUEL JOHNSON.

[*Rev. Mr. Caner to the Secretary.—Extract.*]

Fairfield, in New-England,

November 10*th*, 1746.

Sir,

As to Norwalk and Stamford, I am afraid the interest of the Church loses ground in those places, for want of a more constant service than I can supply them with. And I cannot help repeating my earnest desire that the Society will either supply these places, or, by some further provision, enable me to supply them by an assistant. Here are sundry young gentlemen, ready to enter into the Society's service, who would be very acceptable to these people. The Society will excuse me that I am solicitous for the welfare of a people, chiefly, under God, the fruit of my own diligence, that I may not see the labour of almost twenty years bestowed in vain.

I am the venerable Society's
Most dutiful and obedient, and, Sir,
Your most humble servant,
HENRY CANER.

[*Rev. Mr. Gibbs to the Secretary.*]

Simsbury, New-England,
October 22*d*, 1746.

Reverend Sir,

I presume to write, at the same time hoping and wishing for the prosperity of the Church here, which is environed among a number of its enemies, who are continually wishing for its overthrow. The Independents, who have been heretofore very rude, bold and insolent toward those of the Church, by forcing and obliging them to pay to the Dissenters, do yet, some of them, persist in the same manner, and have obliged a communicant of my Church, though, indeed, belonging to another town, viz., Farmington, about fifteen miles distant, to pay toward the repairing of their meeting-house, and threatened hard for his refusing to pay.

And another communicant of mine, of the same town, do they very much threaten. Thus bold and daring are they to all that profess themselves of the Church.

I would further acquaint the honourable Society that the prejudices of the people toward the Church wear off by degrees, and they begin to be more enlightened about it, and I am not wanting in my endeavours to instruct them as to the same.

I have baptised, since the eighth of May last, ten children, one of which I baptised at Litchfield, near thirty miles west of Simsbury, where I was desired to preach; and another at

Middletown, twenty-seven miles southward, and I have five new communicants added.

I pray God for the enlargement of the Church in these parts, and hope it may increase more and more, which is the earnest wish of him who subscribes himself,

The Society's most obedient

And humble servant,

WILLIAM GIBBS.

[*Rev. Mr. Punderson to the Secretary.*]

N. Groton, 6*th October*, 1746.

Reverend Sir,

As I am the only missionary the Society have at present in the eastern half of the government, I think it my duty, in the most pressing manner, to solicit the Society's further assistance to New-London, Charlestown and Hebron; especially New-London. In behalf of that people I can plead with great assurance of success, as they have complied with the terms on which the venerable Society suspended their assistance; having set up and covered a very good house which, in a few weeks, may be made a comfortable habitation.

With regard to Hebron, which I visit twice a year, and therein administer the Sacraments, I have this to observe, that when I was there last, which was the last day of August, there were about forty communicants, and six children baptised. The day following I preached them a sermon, after which they unanimously subscribed £303 10s. for the purchase of thirty acres of exceedingly good land, (the donor gave £30,) a deed of which I shall transmit with this letter, and beg leave earnestly to recommend to the venerable Board the supply of a people so steadfast and zealous, and who have not a missionary within near forty miles of them. I presume there would be as large an addition to them as to any congregation in the government, if they were supplied with a pious and faithful minister. The Thursday following, I preached a sermon in Litchfield, about eighty miles from my house, where there is a considerable number of conformists, who performed their part of the divine service with propriety and reverence. I furnished them with some books, and trust there will be additions to them.

I must also beg leave to refresh the memories of the venerable Board with respect to the melancholy state of Charlestown, where there is great need of a resident missionary. The deed of forty acres of good land given to that Church, I hope has reached the Society 'ere this, having been sent with my letters of April 4th. The state of the Church in Groton and the adjacent towns remains much the same, but I hope will soon increase, the Independent teacher in this place having left his people, and 'tis the general opinion that they will not be able to settle another.

I am, Reverend Sir, yours, and the Society's

Most faithful friend and servant,

EBEN'R PUNDERSON.

[*Rev. Mr. Johnson to the Secretary.—Extract.*]

Stratford, in New-England,

October 1st, 1746.

Reverend Sir,

Since my last, I have received the Bible and Common Prayer-Books safe, for which we are all very thankful. My son continues to read and instruct the youth at Ripton with good success, and the Church there flourishes. I continue to visit them, and administer the Sacraments to them once in two or three months, and they are going on to finish their Church. My Church also flourishes in this parish, where two new families are added, and I have baptised twenty-four, and admitted eight communicants since last March, whereof one is a negro man. I have also visited Middletown and Guilford, where the Church keeps its ground, though I cannot say it much increases for want of ministers. A love to the Church is still gaining in the College, and four more, whose names are Allen, Lloyd, Sturgeon and Chandler, have declared themselves candidates for holy orders; and there seems a very growing disposition toward the Church, in the town of New-Haven, as well as in the College, so that I hope there will, 'ere long, be a flourishing Church there. I have heretofore desired leave for Messrs. Dibble and Leaming to go for orders, and am now desired to ask the same for Messrs. Mansfield and Allen, as soon as the Society can be in a disposition to receive them. Mr. Cole, for whom I wrote long since, is, I doubt, discouraged, having heard nothing from him in a great while. I presume it probable, that leave was given him to go home, by Mr. Dean; but as we have not heard a word of him since he left London, we have too much reason to fear he is lost. If this should prove to be the case, (as Mr. Lyons is said to be removed, and Mr. Dean to have been appointed to succeed him at Derby,) the people there are very desirous that Mr. Mansfield may have leave to go for them, where they are providing a glebe; and Waterbury having also provided one, begs to have a minister for themselves, with Northbury and Litchfield, and that Mr. Cole may have leave to go for them, or one other of the candidates, if Mr. Cole be otherwise provided for. New-London is also providing a house, and Mr. Cole or Mr. Lloyd would do well for them.

I am, Reverend Sir, your most obliged
And most obedient, humble servant,
SAMUEL JOHNSON.

[*Rev. Mr. Caner to the Secretary.—Extract.*]

Fairfield, in New-England,
May 12th, 1746.

Sir,

I have not been favoured with an answer to either of my two letters of November and December past, requesting some further provisions for the Church at Norwalk. The suffering condition of that Church, notwithstanding my utmost care, obliges me to renew my request, and humbly beg that the venerable Society will give that people leave to recommend some young gentleman home, in their own favour, or make such other provision for them as the Society shall think proper. I mentioned in my last their having purchased a new house and garden spot for the use of a minister, to which they propose to add some convenient pasturage as soon as they have finished their new Church, which at present lies pretty heavy upon them. Beside the provision already made, they offer to raise twenty pounds sterling per annum, which I think they will be able to advance, because the taxes levied by the government here in favour of a minister amount to about fifteen pounds sterling, and they will doubtless exert themselves to raise five pounds more than what is exacted of them by law.

The Church of Norwalk is, I think, the largest and most promising Church in this colony, which makes me the more solicitous to have some better provision made for it than I am capable of bestowing that way consistently with a proper care of other Churches; and this, also, will, I hope, plead my excuse with the venerable Society for the repeated trouble I give them upon this subject.

As to Fairfield, nothing new or uncommon has occurred since my last. The condition of the Church is, I think, nothing worse, I am afraid I must add, nor much better, since my last account. Indeed, in these times of war and confusion, (in which we also have had our share,) which are often attended with greater degrees of licentiousness and corruption of manners, I am apt to flatter myself that our labour is not wholly lost, if we may be instrumental in preserving religion from decay, even though no great progress should be made in its advancement.

The particular state of these Churches will appear from the *notitia parochialis* enclosed, and to which I beg leave to refer.

I am the Society's most dutiful and obedient,

And, Sir, your most humble servant,

Henry Caner.

[*Rev. Mr. Gibbs to the Secretary.*]

Simsbury, May 8th, 1746.

Reverend Sir,

I take the freedom to write, and, at the same time, represent the condition of the Church here. It is situated back of the great river Connecticut eight miles; close by are a number of large commodious towns, Hartford being the chief and a county town, and about ten miles from Simsbury. The Church here seems to be well situated, and I am not without hopes of its growth, notwithstanding it is environed and surrounded by so great a number of staunch enemies to it, and those who call themselves "new lights," who are of a bitter and inveterate spirit toward the Church. I have not been wanting since my being here in my endeavours to enlighten these people, in the Church, as to the feasts and fasts of the Church, and in teaching and catechising their children. I have spread about several books of the Society's, which have been very beneficial, Dr. King being very much in request.

I have belonging to the Church here forty families, twenty-six persons, communicants, and have baptised since July last thirteen children. I hope to see the Church prosperous and flourishing here; people's prejudices begin to wear more off, and I pray God to open their eyes that they may see and know better, and that they may be brought into the Church, that so we may glorify God with one heart and mind.

I beg leave to subscribe myself the Society's

Most obedient, humble servant,

WILLIAM GIBBS.

[*Rev. Mr. Punderson to the Secretary.*]

Groton, *April 4th*, 1746.

Reverend Sir,

It is with a very sensible pleasure that I can acquaint the venerable Society with the almost daily increase of our Church, and that the opinions of most sober, considerate persons grow more favourable toward it; particularly, I am rejoiced upon Mr. John Whitney's embracing the Church, and resolving, by divine Providence, with the Society's aid, to come over in the fall for holy orders. He is a person of an excellent moral character, good sense, and of a mild disposition. The people in New-London are very desirous (if they should not be supplied before) that he may be appointed for them. The conformists, also, of Stonington, where he lives, together with those of Charlestown and Westerly, are fond of having him, if the Society are able and willing to erect them into a mission. The harvest is truly great, and at present no labourer in this half of the government but myself, of the Episcopal order, and, with the most sincere gratitude, I bless God that my labours are not in vain. I esteem it a singular Providence, that in New-London the Church have lost none in their long vacancy, but wait with patience. A deed of the land given by a worthy member of the Church, which is, I suppose, worth £300 our money, will be transmitted with my letter; a frame of a house worth £100 is already got, and they are daily forwarding it.

Capt. Mumford, with whom Mr. Dean embarked, is not yet arrived; we fear he is taken or foundered. By him I had expectations of a letter from the venerable Society, whom I fervently pray God daily to enlarge, and make a more extensive blessing to mankind in general, and this land in particular.

I am, with the greatest respect, Reverend Sir,

Yours, and the Society's faithful friend and servant,

EBEN'R PUNDERSON.

[*Rev. Mr. Beach to the Secretary.*]

Reading, in Connecticut, in N. E.,
April 2d, 1746.

Reverend Sir,

All that I have at present to acquaint the venerable Society with, beside what is contained in the enclosed, is, that we have erected another Church at Newtown, which is forty-six feet long, thirty-five broad, and twenty-five up to the roof. It is a strong, neat building, and though it be small, yet, considering the poverty of people in these new settlements, and that the parish being sixteen miles in length, we must have two Churches in it, it is a considerable charge to that part of the parish, who have contributed cheerfully, some thirty, some fifty, and one man two hundred pounds this currency; while our neighbours of the Independent persuasion have their meeting-houses built by a tax laid by the government upon all the land in the parish. And in this parish all who go to *meeting* are exempt from paying any thing toward the support of the government, but as soon as any join in the worship of the Church of England they immediately lose that privilege. But the more we are oppressed, though there may be several professors of the Church of England, yet, I hope, we shall be the more sincere in our profession; and it is very certain that our people generally expend more by far for the support of religion than their neighbours of the dissenting persuasion.

If the venerable Society would think it reasonable to send me four dozen Common Prayer-Books, with Tate and Brady's version of the Psalms, and two dozen of the Whole Duty of Man, they should be carefully distributed among the poorer people, by,

Reverend Sir, yours,
And the venerable Society's
Most obedient and humble servant,
JOHN BEACH.

[*Rev. Mr. Lamson to the Secretary.*]

North Castle, in the Parish of Rye,
February 10th, 1746-7.

Reverend Sir,

The mission at Fairfield having become vacant by the Reverend Mr. Caner's acceptance of an invitation to Boston, the Episcopal congregation at Fairfield, by advice of the Reverend Mr. Caner, have invited me to accept that mission, if the venerable Society will be pleased to bestow it upon me at their request and mine, in which, there being such a universal concurrence, without an exception, I could not but think it an encouragement to hope that my labours among them may be attended with good success, (by the blessing of God,) and, therefore, I do cheerfully concur with them in their application to the venerable Board, that I may be removed into the Reverend Mr. Caner's place, according to the request of that Church, provided I may be allowed the same salary that Mr. Caner received. For, although Mr. Caner's benevolence and the people's purchase have provided a very decent glebe house, yet, fifty pounds sterling, added to what may be expected from the people, will not be a decent subsistence in a place where living must be more expensive than in most other country places. My present situation can't be thought a settlement, inasmuch as no house or glebe is provided, nor my support sufficient to enable me to purchase one. I have endeavoured, since my arrival, to do what service I can among a great number of poor people scattered about in the woods, who have little ability, and, most of them, as little inclination to reward me. I compassionate their circumstances, and the more, because so many of them have very little sense of the importance of religion and virtue. The Reverend Mr. Wetmore has been treating with a worthy young gentleman, Mr. Thomas Bradbury Chandler, who is willing to perform the service of a lay Catechist among these people, if the honourable Society, upon my removal, will be pleased to bestow upon him the ten pounds sterling salary that was formerly allowed to Mr. Flint Dwight, deceased. I am of opinion that such a provision is as much as these people can expect at present, and I believe it may, in a great measure, supply the place of a minister in orders, considering that Mr. Wetmore, with Mr. Chandler's assistance to read in the Church at Rye in his absence, may more frequently visit the Churches at North Castle and Bedford, and administer the Sacraments among them. And some of the people have expressed a satisfaction in the hopes of having so ingenious a man as Mr. Chandler to labour among them in such a method after my leaving them. They find as little fault as I could expect at the talk of my removal, knowing that my present income is too small for a support. I shall be glad to know the honourable Society's resolutions, in answer to this humble request of mine and the Church at Fairfield, as soon as may be; and as that place will be the more acceptable to me for its nearness to my friends, being but eight miles from my father's house, I hope my request will be granted; which, if the venerable Society shall think fit to gratify me in, no diligence shall be wanting on my part, according to my best abilities, to serve the great designs of their charity, God's glory, and the good of immortal souls.

The sectaries will be very busy in endeavouring to seduce the people when they have no minister among them; for which reason I beg leave to repeat my urgency to have this affair considered and expedited as fast as proper, and only add my humble duty to the venerable Board, and, with hearty prayers for the success of their extensive charity,

I humbly subscribe myself,

Reverend Sir, your most obedient,

And most humble servant,

JOSEPH LAMSON.

[*Rev. Mr. Caner to the Secretary.*]

Fairfield, in New-England,
February 12th, 1746–7.

Reverend Sir,

I having lately received an invitation from the congregation of King's Chapel, in Boston, to succeed the Reverend Mr. Commissary Price, who has resigned, I take the first opportunity to ask the venerable Society's concurrence and dismission from the present service in which I am now engaged. I have long laboured under infirmities of body, which made it very difficult for me to perform the services required in such an extensive cure. The frequent colds I have taken, and disorders consequent thereon, have made traveling to me pretty much impracticable.

I humbly thank the venerable Society for their favours to me and to the people whom I have served, and because I am much concerned that the interests of religion should be carried on as well as begun here, I humbly hope the Society will agree to the request of the people of this Church (herewith transmitted) and appoint the Reverend Mr. Lamson to succeed in this place. I should conceive a good prospect of this gentleman promoting the interests of religion and piety here, from the great harmony that appears between him and this people. A custom of being indulged this way has made it matter of consequence in this part of the world, that the people should, as much as possible, be gratified in the choice of their ministers; and frequent observation has confirmed me in it, that little can be done toward the advancement of piety where a good understanding does not subsist between minister and people. I omit at this time to mention the present state of these Churches, a full account of which I propose shortly to transmit. In the mean time, I beg leave to observe that, as this Church is situated at the head of the county, a very small vacancy may prove of much disservice, especially at this time, when very few Churches this way are supplied. One thing further I humbly move to the Society, which is, that they will be pleased to continue the full salary to this place, for, though the people are generous according to their circumstances, yet the expensiveness of the place makes the whole but a necessary support; this town, and that of New-London, being more expensive than any others in the colony.

I expect to be called upon from Boston Lady-day next; but propose to continue my labours here, with neighbouring assistance, till May or June, by which time I conceive hopes the Society will grant me a dismission, and remove Mr. Lamson to this place. In regard to salary, I shall not presume to draw further than Lady-day next, till I have the Society's express leave how far, or to what term, I shall be indulged to draw.

The people of Fairfield, to recommend themselves as much as possible to the Society's favour, have, upon this occasion, purchased a large and convenient house, with suitable accommodations, for a parsonage house, worth about one hundred and fifty pounds sterling, and have, by the will of a charitable person, Mrs. Jerusha Sturges, lately deceased, received an addition of fifty pounds of this currency, to their bank, which I formerly made mention of. I hope, upon the whole, their honest industry and zeal will engage the Society's compassion, and the continuance of their favour, in supporting a very promising mission.

For myself, I beg leave to assure the Society that I am

Their most dutiful, most obedient

And most humble servant.

HENRY CANER.

[*Rev. Mr. Punderson to the Secretary.—Extract.*]

N. Groton, September 29th, 1747.

Reverend and dear Sir,

I have the satisfaction to inform the venerable Board, that the ministry house in New-London is nearly finished. I have contributed something, and endeavoured to my utmost to forward it.

They are building a Church in Norwich, the largest and most flourishing of any town in this colony. There are about thirty families of conformists. The town has always had the character of the most rigid Congregationalists in the government. 'Tis really surprising how much their dispositions are softened toward the Church; and, indeed, 'tis so almost every where.

Reverend Sir, yours, and the Society's

Most obedient, humble servant,

EBEN'R PUNDERSON.

[*Churchwardens of St. John's Church, in Stamford, Connecticut, to the Secretary.*]

Colony of Connecticut, Stamford,
March 25th, 1747.

Reverend Sir,

We, the subscribers, churchwardens and vestrymen of St. John's Church, in Stamford, with the unanimous concurrence, and in behalf of all the professors of the Church of England, in the towns of Stamford and Greenwich, in Connecticut, beg leave to represent to the venerable Society the state of our Church, and with humble submission request their patronage, and that the effects of their extensive charity, which hath brought the means of salvation to many thousand souls, may preserve us and our posterity from wandering in error and darkness, and guide our feet in the way of peace, by assisting us to procure a settlement of the worship of God among us, according to the pure doctrines and wholesome rites and usages of the Church of England, which we highly reverence and esteem. We have struggled with many and great difficulties in advancing to the state in which we now are, to have a Church erected and so far finished as to be fit for our assembling in it, and with accessions to our number of professors sufficient to be enabled to purchase a glebe, and to pay twenty pounds sterling per annum to a minister, which we have obliged ourselves to do by subscription under our hands, and hope to make some additions, so that the whole may be worth thirty pounds sterling per annum, which is the most that we are able to perform at present, and too little for a decent support for a minister. We have been much oppressed by the Dissenters among whom we live, who, under the protection of the laws of the colony, have obliged us to pay taxes to their minister, and to build them meeting-houses, even when we had obliged ourselves to contribute, according to our abilities, to reward ministers of the Church of England for coming to preach among us, and administer to us the Holy Sacraments; and several have been imprisoned, and others threatened with imprisonment, to compel them to pay such taxes; and we could get no relief from the courts of justice here. This has made us very desirous to obtain a minister in orders among us, which is the only means to obtain exemption from such taxes, according to the express words of the colony act. We, therefore, exerted ourselves to the utmost of our abilities to assist Mr. Miner to go for orders, who was taken by the French upon his passage with the Reverend Mr. Lamson, and afterward died in England, which proved a very melancholy disappointment to us; and before, we had contributed considerably to assist Mr. Isaac Brown, when he went home for orders, with hopes that he might have been sent to us, but were disappointed by his coming back for Brook Haven. Since Mr. Miner's death, we have applied ourselves to Mr. Ebenezer Dibble, by the advice of the Reverend Mr. Caner and others. This gentleman has read prayer and sermons among us, to our very great satisfaction, for near a year and a half, and being willing to go home for holy orders, and return to us to be our minister, we have again exerted our utmost power to procure a glebe, subscribed for his support annually twenty pounds sterling, and do assist him further to defray the expense of his voyage. We have applied to the Reverend Clergy to represent our state, who all of them approve well of Mr. Dibble, and having giving him testimonials to the Lord Bishop of London, we earnestly hope he may obtain holy orders, and humbly entreat the venerable Society to compassionate our circumstances, and admit Mr. Dibble to be their missionary to us, with such salary as they may think fit to allow, which we hope will contribute to the glory of God and to the salvation of many poor souls; and we, your poor petitioners, as in duty bound, shall ever pray for the enlargement of Christ's kingdom by the extensive charity of your venerable Society.

We are, Reverend Sir, your most obedient, &c.,

John Lloyd,
Thomas Youngs, } *Churchwardens.*

And others.

[*The Churchwardens of Litchfield, Connecticut, to the Secretary.*]

Litchfield, April the 4th, A. D. 1747.

Reverend Sir,

We, the subscribers, inhabitants in Litchfield, in the County of Hartford, in Connecticut, in New-England, humbly beg the favour that our following requests may be laid before the venerable Society for the Propagation of the Gospel in foreign parts, and that those declarations that hereby we make, (which you in your wisdom shall think worthy their notice, may be made known to them. We shall, therefore, take leave to begin with our declarations. Above two years past a great number of us declared our conformity to the Church of England by subscribing a letter to the Reverend Mr. Beach, inviting him amongst us, attending divine service with him, owing to the excellency of the doctrine and the manner of worship in the said Church, and openly defending them to the utmost of our power; but even now the Dissenters have executions out against us for rates, due long sinec, and daily threaten to take us to the gaol if we refuse to pay them; and this, notwithstanding we bring and offer them a discharge in full under the hands of the Reverend Mr. Beach; and one of us, who had been a communicant in the Church above a year, hath lately been actually seized by their collector, and on the way to the gaol was freed by his own brother, who paid the rate to the collector. We meet with many subtle contrivances amongst almost all of every degree among them, to suppress and confound us, but we shall not be particular for fear of being tedious. We persist with resolution, being convinced of the goodness of our cause, and gain ground daily, being now about double the number of conformists since a year from this day. We are remote from all our Reverend missionaries except the Reverend Mr. Beach and Mr. Gibbs, Mr. Gibbs being the nighest, who lives twenty-seven miles, and Mr. Beach between thirty and forty miles from us. We have already purchased a glebe of fifty acres of good land, which lyeth about three miles distant from the town, and have begun to improve upon it, and design yearly to proceed therein, and hope yearly to make it profitable in time. We are willing to contribute toward the support of a missionary amongst us, according to the dignity of the office and our abilities, which we confess are small; we have hopes of additions to our number, for many people in the country, and especially in this town, are weary of the Independent scheme, but, whether we have additions or not, we design to build a Church; consequently much can't be expected from us at present.

There are a great number of new towns northward and westward from us, and hardly a town without some conformists to our excellent Church; and we humbly conceive it would promote the joyous design of the honourable Society if a missionary were placed in these parts. Northbury and we are willing to be included in the same mission; and since Mr. Samuel Cole is going for orders, (with whom we are personally acquainted,) who has been helpful to us in many respects, our humble request is, that he may be the person that may be sent to us, and that he may be the person, rather than any other. We shall only add our hearty thanks to the honourable Society for their care of this land, and after, that we may be still greater partakers of it, who are, Reverend Sir, your most obedient and humble servants,

JACOB GRISWOLD, } *Churchwardens.*
JOSEPH WILLBORN, }
And others.

[*Rev. Mr. Johnson to the Bishop of London.*

Stratford, April 28th, 1747.

My Lord,

About a month ago I gave your Lordship some account of a College undertaking in New-Jersey with a Royal Charter, which I apprehend would be of very ill-consequence to the Church, it being entirely in the hands of the most virulent

Methodists.* Since that, I have procured a copy of their charter, and I apprehend it would not be unacceptable to your Lordship to have a sight of it. This is the occasion of my so soon troubling you again, and accordingly I here enclose a copy of it, such as I could get; there may, perhaps, be some small defects in it, but, on the whole, it is doubtless genuine, and your Lordship can judge whether it be fit that absurd and mischievous sect should have such an ample and unlimited power given them. I am told, the best sort of people in that province do as much dislike it as we do.

My Lord, I had about two years ago a letter from the Society forbidding any one to go home for orders without leave first obtained. This I was willing to understand only in case of any new mission, or any new charge to the Society. I desired it might not be understood to preclude us the liberty of sending home proper persons to supply vacancies by death or removal; but I had last week a letter, by which it appears we are in *no* case to send any home without having first obtained leave. This, my Lord, is a very great discouragement to the Church in these parts, especially under our present circumstances. The death of the Reverend Mr. Commissary Vesey, Mr. Davenport, Mr. Richard Caner, and his removal from Norwalk before his death, and that of Mr. Lyons and Mr. Morris, and the resignation of Mr. Commissary Price, have occasioned a number of vacancies, four of which are in this colony, so that I am now alone here on the seacoast, without one person, in orders, beside myself, for more than one hundred miles; in which compass there is business enough for six or seven ministers; and those northward have their hands full, so that my burthen is at present insupportable, nor have we yet leave for any to go home, though there are five or six valuable candidates. Unless, therefore, the Society can provide, or your Lordship can think proper to ordain on such titles as can be made here, (which, in some places, though not without much hardship, may, I believe, be made equal to thirty pounds sterling per annum,) the Church must soon decay apace; mean time it is

* That is, the followers of Mr. Whitfield, though, by profession, Presbyterians.

really affecting to hear the cries and importunities of people from several quarters, and not have it in one's power to help them. I humbly beg your Lordship's compassion, prayers and benediction,

And remain, may it please your Lordship,
Your Lordship's most dutiful son,
And most obedient, humble servant,
SAMUEL JOHNSON.

TO MY LORD OF LONDON.

[*A Petition from the Churchwardens of Norwalk to the Secretary.*]

Norwalk, Connecticut, March 5th, 1748.

We, the Churchwardens and Vestry of the Church of England, in Norwalk, most humbly beg leave to lay our case and request before this venerable Board, which is as follows, viz.:

That in the year 1742, in the month of June, the Reverend Mr. Richard Caner, by the honourable Society's great favour, for which we are humbly thankful, came to us in holy orders, at which time the Church in Norwalk consisted of about thirty families; and the Church under his ministry greatly increasing, about Christmas following we concluded to build a new Church of the following dimensions, viz., fifty-five feet in length, beside steeple and chancel, and thirty-five feet in width, which was raised in March following, and we provided with great cheerfulness in carrying on the work in order to finish, till the time of Mr. Caner's removal from us, which was in the month of October, 1745, at which time our Church had increased to the number of ninety families. Immediately after Mr. Caner's removal from us, we applied to Mr. Henry Caner, and upon his advice, procured Mr. Jeremiah Leaming, who came in December, 1745, and continued with us two years, and for his service in the Church we paid him more than twenty pounds sterling per annum, and the Church has increased even to the number of one hundred and five families, which exceeds the number of any other Church in the government except the Church in Stratford. Furthermore, upon advice of the Reverend Henry Caner, we purchased a good house and small glebe, with another lot of land at a small distance from the house, of five acres of land, the deeds whereof were sent to the Society last summer by the Rev. Mr. Commissary Price, and we have since that time purchased two acres and a half of land in addition, and adjoining to said five acres; and since Mr. Leaming, who is truly a worthy gentleman, for whom we have a sincere regard, has, however, thought best to leave us, having some other views, we are very thankful to the Society for committing us to the care of the Reverend Mr. Lamson, whose labours are always very acceptable to us when he can attend here; but as this cannot be very frequently, by reason of the distance and his extensive charge, we have, with the approbation of the Rev. Clergy, unanimously agreed with Mr. John Ogilvie to read the service of the Church, with a view of his settling in the ministry among us, and obliged ourselves to pay him fifty pounds, New-York money, per annum, equal to three hundred pounds in our unsettled currency, and he is now, with the approbation of our Reverend Clergy, reading the liturgy and sermons among us to our entire satisfaction. What, therefore, we beg leave to ask of this venerable Society is, that, as we have thus endeavoured to our utmost to qualify ourselves for a mission, they would be graciously pleased to erect us into a mission, and give leave to the Reverend the Clergy to recommend the said Mr. John Ogilvie, as soon as may be, for holy orders; and that he may be appointed missionary for this town, together with Ridgefield, which desired to be joined with us, and we shall be most humbly thankful for any salary which this venerable Society, according to their wonted goodness, shall please to grant to them. Praying with great earnestness for God's blessings upon the pious undertaking of this most charitable Society, and that we may no longer remain without a missionary,

We are, venerable gentlemen,

Your most obliged, most dutiful,

Most obedient, humble servants,

JOHN BELDEN,
WILLIAM JOHNSON, } *Churchwardens.*

And others.

[*Churchwardens of Stamford to the Secretary.*]

Stamford, April 26th, 1748.

Reverend Sir,

We, the Churchwardens and Vestry of St. John's Church, in the united parish of Stamford and Greenwich, beg leave, in behalf of ourselves and the professors of the Church of England, in Stamford and Greenwich, to return our hearty thanks unto the venerable Society for the Propagation of the Gospel, for their charitable notice and care of us, expressed in your letter to the Churchwardens and Vestry of Norwalk, dated December 27th, 1747, giving liberty for Mr. Dibble to go home for holy orders, and to take the charge of our Church, with that of Norwalk, on consideration of our paying ten pounds sterling per annum toward his support, as Norwalk was to give security for twenty, with the actual possession of their glebe. As this resolution of the venerable Society is said to be consenting to their request in favour of Mr. Dibble, we are willing humbly to hope our request in favour of Mr. Dibble, referred to in our petition, dated March 25th, 1747, (which we transmitted by Mr. Commissary Price,) is granted; for we don't know that the people of Norwalk ever requested in favour of Mr. Dibble, nor has he read service among them; but, among us, steadily for two years and a half, for whom we have great esteem and regard, and shall be very much gratified, if we can obtain, from the venerable Society's great charity, his being appointed their missionary for *our* Church. Our congregation voted cheerfully to comply with the Society's directions, in your letter to the Church of Norwalk, which Mr. Dibble will communicate to you, in expectation that, in Norwalk, they would have readily done their part; but when we found that the people of Norwalk declined coming to a positive determination to do, in favour of Mr. Dibble, what the honourable Society required as the condition on their part, our people, from a hearty affection to Mr. Dibble, resolved cheerfully to undertake the expense of his voyage, and we have effectually secured the payment of twenty pounds sterling per annum to the Society's missionary, according to our bond in Mr. Dibble's hand, and promise hereby to put him into possession of our glebe, which is better than that of Norwalk; or, however the honourable Society shall determine as to uniting us with Norwalk, we humbly submit, and shall be heartily thankful for any share of Mr. Dibble's ministry, that the honourable Society shall be pleased to allot for us; so that, by being put under his care, we may be sheltered from the persecutions we have suffered from the Dissenters, because not included in any of the missions, as we set forth more largely in our petition above mentioned, and to which we beg leave to refer; and with earnest prayers that God would bless all the charities of that venerable Board, we subscribe,

Reverend Sir,

Your most obedient, humble servants,

JOHN LLOYD,
THOMAS YOUNG, } *Churchwardens.*

And others.

[*Rev. Mr. Graves to the Secretary.*]

New-London, September 7th, 1748.

Good Sir,

I have wrote so lately, that were it not in obedience to my instructions, I would not so suddenly have occasioned this second trouble. Since my last, I have visited and spent a fortnight at Hebron, in which time I read prayers and preached nine sermons in the Church, and at their houses; in the latter, I had every day several Dissenters, some of whom told me they had never before attended, and expressed a satisfactory approbation at our service. However, the people continue to deny my authority over them, because I can't produce it under your hand but as I mentioned this before, I doubt not but I shall soon be favoured with your determination in that affair. The Presbyterian divisions are very rife and warm, and will certainly add to our hearers in these parts. At my return, I did duty in the new Church at Norwich, baptised a child and churched its mother. The parent used many arguments to stand surety, but I told him the canons and rubricks, and the practice of others, was my rule. The week before I went to Hebron, I received an earnest invitation from the inhabitants of Branford, which is above forty miles hence. I happily, on my way thither, met Dr Johnson ten miles this side, at a place called Guilford, where he read prayers, and baptised three children, and I preached to a large congregation. Two days after, I performed service at Branford to a most agreeable sight of auditors, who behaved very well, and some of the chief of the Presbyterians came to my lodgings and returned me thanks. As for the people of New-London, I am afraid they will never be unanimously reconciled to a regular minister; I despair, though I shall continue to act in the best manner I can for the glory of God and their edification. I am sorry to say, but from duty am obliged to inform you, that they think the Society has not used them very well, in obliging them to build a house and sending them a missionary, before they desired one, as they say you wrote you would not, which desire they did not intend to execute in less than two years hence. I cannot, from their behaviour in Church, conclude that ever they had an orthodox minister among them, as my manner of performing seems strange to them; so does their religious deportment to me, but I'll endeavour to perform it, [*i. e.*, the service.] I have given Mr. Livingston, merchant, at New-York, one bill of fifteen pounds sterling, due the 25th of June last, on the treasurer, and promised another for the 25th of this month. The heads of families here are about seven hundred and thirty; for want of a registry I don't know yet how many are baptised. Since the 7th of March, I baptised eleven, and a girl of eleven years old; communicants are about thirty. The number of heathens and infidels are as much too numerous as the converts are too few. I really have not found out yet the number of hearers or Dissenters at Hebron. I had each time about forty communicants. I have baptised only two children there. I hope, Sir, if this account is defective, you will condescend to pardon and remove my ignorance, since I shall be all attention and obedience to your commands and instructions. I pray God to direct and prosper the consultations and proceedings of the religious, august and venerable Society, and reward their earthly services with eternal joys. As they may depend upon my best performances, I desire you will be so kind as to present to them the duty of their unworthy missionary, and, good Sir,

Your most obedient servant,

And affectionate brother,

MATT. GRAVES.

[*Rev. Mr. Johnson to the Secretary.*]

Stratford, in New-England,

September 29th, 1748.

Reverend Sir,

I most humbly thank you for yours of June 23d, by Mr. Leaming, who, I thank God, is already safe returned. I hope he will do good service at Newport, where he is much wanted by reason of Mr. Honeyman's great age and infirmities, and I hope it will not be long before Mr. Dibble and Mr. Mansfield also arrive. I know not how these gentlemen can well subsist upon so small salaries; however, I hope the honourable Society, who doubtless would do better for us if they could, will be well satisfied of their sincerity and zeal for promoting the interests of the Church and true religion from their gladly going so far for holy orders, upon so slender worldly encouragement. I thank you for your good wishes for my health, which, I bless God, is very good, but I am yet lame, having been ill-served in the setting of my leg, so that it is yet very infirm.

I now proceed to give my Michaelmas account of the state

of my parish and the country adjacent, where I have preached. As to the Church in this town, it is in a flourishing condition, one family having been added and more looking forward, and thirty-one have been baptised and eight added to the communion since my last; our new Church is almost finished, in a very neat and elegant manner, the architecture being allowed in some things to exceed any thing done before in New-England. We have had some valuable contributions, and my people have done as well as could be expected from their circumstances, which are generally but slender; but there is one of them who deserves to be mentioned in particular for his generosity; Mr. Beach, brother of the Reverend Mr. Beach, who, though he has a considerable family, has contributed above three thousand pounds, our currency, to it already, and is daily doing more, and designs to leave an annuity, *in perpetuum*, toward keeping it in repair, beside what he intends toward a glebe, to which purpose one Mr. Birdsey, a worthy person, lately deceased, left twenty acres of pasture about two miles off, worth a hundred pounds in our currency.

As to Ripton, they continue to [strive] under the small encouragement I am able to give them of having a minister to themselves; they purpose, however, to lay their case before the Society, in hopes of being in due time provided for, and, I believe there will be sixty families join, within five or six miles of their Church, and they have purchased a house and two acres of land toward a glebe. I wish they could be provided for.

Scarce ever was there a people in a more bewildered, confounded condition than those in this colony generally are, as to their religious affairs, occasioned by the sad effects of Methodism, still in many places strangely rampant, and crumbling them into endless separations, which occasions the most sensible of them to be still every where looking toward the Church as their only refuge. I have this summer been much solicited to visit several places. I have rode as much as I could, particularly to Guilford and Branford, where I have preached to great numbers, which Mr. Graves also has done, and I believe those two towns will, in a little time, be prepared to make a mission; at the former, they are building a Church, and designing it at the latter.

Middletown and Wallingford are also joining, in order to be another mission in due time, and they are going forward with their Church at Middletown, where a sensible, studious and discreet young man, one Mr. Camp, bred at our College, is reading service and sermons, and begs me to mention him to the Society as a candidate, and that he may hope in due time to be employed in their service. Mr. Colton still reads at Hebron, and those people with him have lately been with me, begging my interest with the Society, that Mr. Colton may have leave, as soon as may be, at least by next fall, to go for orders for them, which I very much desire in their behalf, there being a good prospect there.

Mr. Punderson and I, who were together at New-Haven, have both directed them to wait on Mr. Graves, to draw an address for them, and recommend their case; and I have written to him in their behalf to desire his assistance in forwarding their affairs, and they truly need and deserve the Society's notice, being thirty miles from any missionary.

There were nine of our Clergy together at the Commencement, at New-Haven, about a fortnight ago, among which the worthy Mr. Commissary Barclay favoured us with his company. We all consulted the best things we could for the Church's interest. Among the candidates for their degrees, there were no less than ten belonging to our Church, five Masters and five Bachelors; among the former, two in orders, Messrs. Sturges and Leaming, and two candidates, Chandler and ———, of the Bachelors, beside my youngest son and Mr. Ogilvie. Seabury had a promising son, and as he designs him for the Society's service, he desires me to mention what I know of him; and as he has lived four years much under my eye, I can truly testify of him that he is a solid, sensible, virtuous youth, and, I doubt not, may in due time do good service.

Mrs. Dean desires me to give her duty and thanks to the Society for the liberty granted her to draw on the treasurer for fifteen pounds sterling, which she has drawn accordingly. My eldest son, also, gives his duty and thanks for your good wishes; he and I have also drawn on the treasurer to this Michaelmas, and my *Notitia Parochialis* is as follows.

I am, Reverend Sir,

Your most obliged, obedient, humble servant,

SAMUEL JOHNSON.

Notitia Parochialis, for Michaelmas, 1748.

I.	No. of families inhabitants within the bounds of this town, near	500
II.	No. of baptised here, and in places adjacent, in the Church,	349
III.	No. of baptised since Lady-day,	31
IV.	No. of actual Communicants here and in Ripton, about	200
	Of which admitted, since my last, (of which one negro woman,)	8
V.	No. of those who profess the Church, families, about	145
VI.	The rest called Congregationalists; Papists, none.	
VII.	Heathens, beside many unbaptised negroes, about ten.	
VIII.	Of converts to a sober life, no remarkable instance, they being generally a sober, regular people.	

[*Rev. Mr. Lamson to the Secretary.—Extract.*]

Fairfield, November 10th, 1748.

Reverend Sir,

I have formerly mentioned a Church built at Stratfield, a village within the bounds of Fairfield, in which they are very urgent to have me officiate every third Sunday, because we have large congregations when I preach there. The people living in the town and westward, are very much against it, because Mr. Caner used to keep steadily to the Church in town, but then there was neither Church nor congregation at Stratfield.

Norwalk people have been imprudent in their conduct relating to the honourable Society's appointment for them. I am sorry for their imprudence, and I believe they are so too, but at present are so much in a ruffle, that 'tis hard to guess what the conclusion will be, and I hardly know what method I shall be able to take to quiet the commotions among them. I shall be glad of your directions, and will endeavour, to the utmost of my abilities, to answer the design of my mission from the venerable Society, whose charitable purposes that God would every where bless and prosper, is the humble prayer of,

Reverend Sir, yours,

And the honourable Society's

Most obedient and dutiful servant,

JOSEPH LAMSON.

[*Address of the Inhabitants of Huntington, &c., to the Society.—Extract.*]

WE are inhabitants of a town which, till of late, has been under great prejudices against the Church of England, a few excepted; but by late enthusiastic confusions, which mightily prevailed here, some of us have been awakened to consider the consequence of those principles in which we had been educated, and by the assistance of the Reverend Mr. Seabury, the Society's missionary at Hempstead, who has been very ready to visit us on week days, and to perform divine service among us, we have most heartily embraced the established Church, and think it our duty, for our own improvement in true religion, for the good of our country, and for the honour of God, to join with our neighbours, conformists, and do all in our power for the promotion of the interests of the established Church; in our zeal for which, we have built a Church that, in a little time, will be commodious for public use; but as we are eighteen miles distant from Mr. Seabury, who is the nearest missionary, and he being obliged to attend two Churches in his own parish, viz., those of Hempstead and Oyster Bay, we, therefore, most humbly beg the Society to attend to our prayers, which is, that Mr. Samuel Seabury, the son of your worthy missionary, a young gentleman (lately educated and graduated at Yale College) of a good character and excellent hopes, may be appointed the Society's Catechist at this place, and perform divine service among us in a lay capacity, with some allowance from the honourable Society for that service.

In testimony of our sincerity, we have to this affixed our subscription of such sums of money as each of us respectively promise and oblige ourselves to pay to Mr. Samuel Seabury aforesaid, yearly, in half yearly payments, for the space of three years, for officiating amongst us; which subscription, we beg the honourable Society to believe, will be punctually paid by the honourable Society's most humble petitioners, the subscribers,

H. Lloyd,
And others.

[*Churchwardens, &c., to the Society.—Extract.*]

Ripton, in Connecticut, New-England,
September 14*th*, 1748.

Gentlemen,

As the distance from the Church, at Stratford, is eight or ten, or for some, twelve miles, it is exceedingly difficult, especially in the winter season, to go to Church there with our families; and being fearful that the Church will diminish among us, as the case now is, having no other means when we cannot attend at Stratford, only the Rev. Dr. Johnson to be with us about four times in a year, excepting some time past, when the Reverend Dr. Johnson's son did read to us, for which we are heartily thankful to the honourable Society; but he is now become a student at law, and follows the courts, and has declared that he will not be a Clergyman; and has not officiated here for several months; indeed, while he did, we were laughed at by the Dissenters for having a lawyer for our priest, which discouraged many of our people, so that they would not go to hear him. Now, if there be a probability of our having a minister, which we heartily desire and earnestly petition for, we hope the Society will send us a true son of the established Church, who may have the prosperity of the Church at heart, which, if we should obtain, we doubt not but that the Church would be likely to flourish among us, but if not, we fear that many of our young people will turn to the Dissenters as many have done already.

[*Rev. Mr. Dibblee to the Society.*]

Stamford, November 14th, 1748.

Reverend Sir,

I take this opportunity, the first that conveniently offers, to acquaint you that, by the blessing of God, Mr. Mansfield and I arrived safe and in good health, at New-York, the 23d of October, and to my mission, at Stamford, on the 25th. My mind is impressed with a sense of the divine goodness to me in my voyage, through so many dangers as I have been happily preserved, and returned successfully to my family; and, I think it my duty to return my thanks to the venerable Society, for the expression of their favour and goodness in the reception I had from the honourable Board, and the charitable assistance afforded to the good and well-disposed people who had so earnestly desired that I might be their minister, in the holy order, of the Church of England; and the Churchwardens and Vestry of St. John's Church, in Stamford, desire me to return their very sincere and hearty thanks to the Society for their favour to me, and the grant of their humble request, by admitting them into the number of the Churches under the honourable Society's charitable protection and assistance, and particularly for the library allowed their Church, and the pious tracts sent by me, to be dispersed for promoting religion and virtue among them; and 'tis a pleasure to me to acquaint the Society, that my people have every way manifested their great satisfaction and joy at my return to them, and I have reason to hope that, by God's blessing attending my honest endeavours, I may do much good among them, which I shall not fail to use my utmost application to effect, and pray God to give success. I have already preached at three distinct parts of my mission to pretty large congregations, have baptised two adult persons, one aged sixty-seven years, and the other above forty, and also five infants; have once administered the Lord's Supper at Stamford, had but 16 communicants, but expect more at Christmas. I hope I may be excused for not sending a *Notitia Parochialis* at this time, not being able as yet to give it in form. I find the people of Norwalk are much ruffled, as Mr. Ogilvie now talks of leaving them, (they say,) after he had promised to be their minister, with such a support as they could give him. This promise, I suppose, induced them to neglect the provision the honourable Society made for them, against the advice of sundry of the Clergy, and particularly of Mr. Wetmore, to whom both I and the people of Norwalk are indebted, for his friendly and good advice at that time, according to which I entirely conducted myself, and gave not the least occasion of umbrage to that people, who, I perceive, manifest some offence at me, as well as at others that don't deserve it, because they are unwilling to lay the blame of their misfortune where it is only due. I only add my humble duty to your venerable Board, with the earnest prayers to almighty God, to give his blessing to all their charitable designs, and, with much respect, beg leave to subscribe, as I am sincerely and heartily,

Reverend Sir, your most obedient,

And most humble servant,

EBENEZER DIBBLEE.

[*Rev. Mr. Punderson to the Secretary.—Extract.*]

N. Groton, 25th March, 1749.

Reverend and dear Sir,

Since my preaching last September, at Cohasset, about eight miles north of Guilford, and which was the first sermon preached in that place by a Clergyman of the Church of England, they have almost ever since read prayers and sermons to upward of forty persons. I have promised them a visit the beginning of April.

[*Rev. Mr. Johnson to the Secretary.—Extract.*]

Stratford, in New-England,
March 28th, 1749.

Reverend Sir,

I have little that is new to say of the state of my parish, but a disposition among the sectaries toward the Church, seems here, and in many other places, still increasing, particularly at Guilford and Branford, where I baptised a man and his wife and five children, and seven children in the family of another person, who is a man of considerable weight in thta last mentioned town, where twenty-nine families have, within two or three years, conformed to the Church, who, with eighteen families at Guilford, (which is within ten miles,) are in hopes they may, within a little while, become a mission; and a young man who took his Bachelor's degree last commencement, whose name is Stocking, is desirous to be admitted as a candidate for the Society's service, and they are about procuring him to read to them 'till he is of age, which will be about two or three years hence, by which time there will probably be a considerable addition to them. I have already mentioned the desires of Middletown and Wallingford, where the Church has further increased since my last, and Mr. Camp has continued to read there with good success, and, I think, will be a worthy and useful person, and he and they are about addressing the Society for leave for him to go home for them next spring, and would be humbly thankful if leave would be given him to go, by next fall, that he may embark early in the spring. They are near raising their Church, and two more new Churches are building, viz., at Norwich and Litchfield. The Church is very considerably increasing at New-Haven, where the College is, and a considerable sum is already subscribed toward building a Church, and it is not doubted but between that town and West-Haven (a village within four miles, where there is already a neat little Church) there will soon be forty or fifty families. My younger son has read lla the last fall and winter, chiefly at West-Haven, and sometimes at Branford and Guilford, as well as Ripton, but as he lives at the College, the chief place of his usefulness is there and at West-Haven. And I doubt not, by the time of his being of age, and perhaps before, there will be a flourishing Church there, which will be a place of much importance.

The dissenting gentleman's pernicious answer to Mr. White has, by the zeal of our sectaries, been reprinted, both at Boston and York, and scattered all over the country, which does much damage in prejudicing people against the Church; and they are now reprinting (I suppose) the same gentleman's piece against subscription to explanatory articles; it would therefore be of great use if we had, each of us, a few copies of Mr. White's answers, to lend about as an antidote, and Mr. Harvest's, or some other author's, defence of subscription, against Chandler.

[*Rev. Mr. Beach to the Secretary.—Extract.*]

Reading, in Connecticut, New-England,
April 1st, 1749.

Reverend Sir,

I have about four hundred constant hearers, all of whom, excepting a very few, adorn their profession by a sober, righteous and godly life. Almost two-thirds of the inhabitants of this parish are Independents, who have two ministers of their own persuasion. I baptise about sixty or seventy children commonly in one year, and some few adults, and am now preparing two whole families for baptism who were bred Independents. My parishioners are poor, and have but few negro slaves, but all they have, I have, after proper instructions, baptised, and some of them are communicants, and appear to be serious Christians. Our Church here, like the house of David, waxes stronger and stronger.

[*Rev. Mr. Gibbs to the Secretary.—Extract.*]

Simsbury, New-England, July 4th, 1749.

Reverend Sir,

New-Cambridge and Cornwall. As to the first of these places I have attended nigh two years, and yet do, as often as I well can, and for which they willingly reward me and to my satisfaction; yet, nevertheless, the Dissenters do oblige them to pay to the dissenting minister, and which they have refused, and for their refusal, were, four of them, committed to Hartford gaol, and in a place where they keep malefactors; upon which they then paid their money to the collector,

Thomas Hart, of New-Cambridge. I accordingly demanded the money of said collector, but he refused, by reason, as he said, of my mission not extending thither. Six more are now threatened, and whom I fear they will imprison. As to the other place, Cornwall, I have taken care of it near one year and a half, and they have taken the money from them also. I demanded the same of the collector there, but he refused to pay me; one of these men, viz., Stephen Lee, being firmly attached to the Church, refused paying the collector for the support of the dissenting minister of the place, and for this, was committed to the gaol of Hartford, at the news of which, I being but twelve miles distant, went and visited him; the man being poor, I took pity on him and released him, by paying his rate, which was seven pounds, and the charges likewise, which, with the rate, amounted to twenty-one pounds; and this is the usage of Dissenters toward Churchmen here, which very much grieves me. I therefore humbly beg the honourable Society would, as soon as they think it best and convenient, relieve the Church under its present circumstances, and so free it from all its grievances and trouble. If the Society were pleased to appoint me over these places I have now the care of, it might put a stop to the Dissenters interfering with us more, for they at present seem to be resolutely bent to hurt, (and if it were possible,) to ruin the Church in these parts; and as to my mission, they look upon it to extend no further than Simsbury.

[*Rev. Mr. Punderson to the Secretary.—Extract.*]

Groton, 25*th September*, 1749.

Reverend Sir,

In May I made another tour to the Union, about forty-five miles from my house; preached at Mr. Lawson's, where between sixty and seventy persons were convened; seven then declared conformity, and they have ever since upheld the worship of God according to our most excellent liturgy; in the evening returned sixteen miles to Mansfield, preached, and administered the Sacrament of the Lord's Supper, the next day, to sixteen communicants; on Friday, performed service in the Church at Norwich. During the heat of summer have visited Charlestown, Preston, Stonington, Norwich, and South Groton.

[*Rev. Mr. Dibblee to the Secretary.—Extract.*]

Stamford, in Connecticut,
September 29th, 1749.

Reverend Sir,

I bless God that I have not laboured among them without some visible success in each of the places where I have performed divine service. I preach at Horse Neck the second Sunday in each month, about six miles from Stamford; have had some converts to the Church there, and the people have zealously exerted themselves to build a small chapel, of about thirty-six feet in length and twenty-five feet in breadth, to accommodate our assembly at these times, which they have enclosed and glazed, and if they could be favoured with a Bible and Common Prayer-Book for that Church, it would be a very welcome present, their Churchwardens having humbly desired me to request the same. Greenwich being not above five miles from Stamford, I have only occasionally officiated there upon week days, except two Sundays the year past; and as they have no settled dissenting minister among them, they have invited me into their meeting-house, and the inhabitants of all sorts generally attend Church when I preach there; and at Stamford there is a very visible alteration in the temper and disposition of the dissenting party; in so much, that at sundry times when their meeting-house chanced to be destitute of a dissenting minister, our Church has been crowded by the attendance of Dissenters, and many of them cheerfully united in the services of our holy Church, which, together with the sundry converts already obtained, gives me great encouragement to hope, by the blessing of God, for abundant success in my ministry.

[*Rev. Mr. Watkins to the Secretary.—Extract.*]

New-Windsor, in the Province of New-York, in America, October 16*th*, 1749.

Reverend Sir,

Having for three years past been in a very low state of health, in April last I took a journey into New-England to see if by that I could in any measure recover my health; and in my journey I was very earnestly requested by the people of Norwalk to preach on Sunday, and administer the Holy Sacrament of the Lord's Supper to them, which accordingly I did, and was much pleased to see such a large congregation and so many communicants; the number of which was about seventy, who behaved very decently. From thence, as I have passed through Stratford, I was very much urged by the Reverend Dr. Johnson and some of the good people of Ripton to preach in a new Church in Ripton, and administer the Holy Sacrament there, which I likewise did; there I found a congregation of about three hundred people of the Church of England, where I also administered the Holy Sacrament to about sixty communicants, who behaved very devoutly and with much decency.

I find the people of New-England, and especially in Connecticut, generally are of a more zealous turn of mind than in those provinces which are to the west and south of it.

HEZEKIAH WATKINS.

[*Rev. Mr. Gibbs to the Secretary.—Extract.*]

Hartford Gaol, December 28th, 1749.

Reverend Sir,

In my last, which was but lately, I acquainted the Society of the Dissenters' ill usage toward the Churchmen of New-Cambridge, in obliging them to pay to them, and when, having demanded the money of the collector, was refused the same, and which put me upon sueing him before John Humphreys, Esquire, one of his Majesty's justices of the peace, in Simsbury town, for my Churchwarden's rate of Caleb Matthews, but was cast, and for my refusing to pay the cost, an execution has been out against me for some time, and is now brought and served by Jonathan Humphreys' constable, of that place, (Simsbury,) and I am by him taken and brought to Hartford, and so put into the gaol where I now am; thus presumptuous and bold are these men in these parts.

[*Rev. Mr. Punderson to the Secretary.*]

March 27th, 1750.

Reverend and dear Sir,

There was some time since a statute, made in this government, to exempt the professors of the Church of England from paying taxes to dissenting ministers and meeting-houses, but expressed in such limited and ambiguous terms as to be the occasion of many disputes and difficulties to the messengers of peace, to whose care they belong. I have been obliged to take out six or seven writs upon that statute, which, with my other papers, I shall soon transmit to the venerable Society, and in two of which I have been with-

17

stood and cast, and could have no appeal, and have been at more than £70 expense, and lie under an execution for £11, which was served on me not many days since. I cannot but believe that the venerable Board will speedily employ their interest, not only to put an end to such presumptuous and outrageous conduct from those who breathe by toleration, but also that the expense I have been at in those suits, and in defence of my children, for as such I look upon those who have committed the care of their souls to me, might be ordered to be returned. At present, being very much unwell, having last Saturday rode to Charlestown, part of the way in the rain, preached two sermons on Sunday and yesterday in Stonington, upon my return, got to my own house about nine. At present, I add only my fervent prayers to Almighty God for prosperity and success to that venerable Board, and an increase of liberty and peace to the professors of our most excellent Church,

And am, Reverend Sir, yours,

And the Society's laborious servant,

EBEN'R PUNDERSON.

[*Rev. Dr. Johnson to the Secretary.—Extract.*]

Stratford, in New-England,

March 30th, 1750.

Reverend Sir,

The little hopes we can have, Sir, of having any of our candidates or destitute places provided for even ever so slenderly, and *for a long time*, is a very great damp to the Church in these parts, which, however, would not be wholly discouraged, provided it were practicable for them to obtain orders, if it were only upon such title as the people could make, which, though it would be very hard for them to do, they would, in some places, engage £30 per annum, and the candidates would accept of it, at least for the present, till more could be done for them, either by the Society or the people themselves, as they should increase. This is the case at Norwalk, Hebron, Middletown, with Wallingford and Guilford, with Branford, and I am desired by sundry of both people and candidates, to beg the direction of the Society how to proceed; whether £30 from the people can be accepted for a title, and, if so, to whom they can apply for orders, since they can have no title from the Society *for a long time.* They would, however, in the mean time, do as they best can; and I beg to be under the Society's direction, and entreat, that if no Bishop should come over into these parts, we may be advised time enough for them to go home in the fall, whether orders can be had upon such a title, and from whom.

They are the more solicitous for this, for the reasons I gave in my last, viz., that the people must be forced to pay to the Dissenters till they have ministers of their own in orders. We intend, indeed, to apply to our next assembly for relief, but I doubt the success; mean time many of our people are frequently persecuted and imprisoned for their rates to dissenting teachers, which they never had been in any stipulation with. The case of great numbers is extremely hard, if they can have no ministers in orders, neither from any title of the Society, nor from any that themselves can make, and, at the same time, cannot have the excellent liturgy and sermons of the Church read to them by candidates of their own, whom they would gladly support to the utmost of their power, if they could have their own money for their own purposes. In these straits, Sir, I beg you would tell us what we should do.

And to add to all our other griefs, it seems we have some enemy or other that has represented us to the venerable Board, *as presuming to vary from the established form of Prayer, omitting, adding or altering, &c.* This is very hard indeed, when we have given so much proof of our inviolable attachment to it, and that the established Episcopacy and liturgy is dearer to us than any thing in the world besides; so dear as to make us leave *fathers, mothers, brothers, sisters, houses and lands,* and venture our lives to the greatest hazards for it; twenty-five of us having gone a thousand leagues for Episcopal orders, of whom no less than five have lost their lives, and several others suffered the most dangerous sickness, and all at the expense of more than we could well afford; and all this, when we might have had the greatest applause of all our friends and acquaintances, if we could have made our consciences easy as we were, and the best preferments they could give.

I have diligently inquired what foundation there could be for this report, and can find none. Most of the Clergy and readers have read in my Church in my absence, and my people tell me they never heard the least variation, nor can I find any thing of this kind in the Clergy or lay readers. One, indeed, tells me he has sometimes added two or three words in the prayer after sermon, *Grant us, we beseech thee*, &c., in which he had followed a great example he heard in London. Perhaps the first lesson, or some of the latter part of the liturgy may have been omitted on some extreme cold day, or in the collect of the day, for the gunpowder treason; it may have been read, *giving his late Majesty, King William, a safe arrival in England*, instead of *here*, which could not be true; and I should be glad if the informer were put upon proof, that if there ever was any thing worse than these it might be made to appear, that the offender might receive condign punishment. Sure I am there is nothing we have more at heart than to receive the free enjoyment of the English establishment without variation, and the immediate inspection of a worthy Bishop, to whom we would gladly account for all our behaviour and conduct; and, till any thing material is made out against us, I simply beg the Society's charity for us, and I believe I may safely challenge the informer to make any thing of this kind to appear, and I am freely willing and shall be glad to leave this or any other controversy he may think fit to have with us, to the wisdom, candour and justice of the venerable Society to judge between us.

Reverend Sir, your most obedient servant,

SAMUEL JOHNSON.

[*Rev. Mr. Beach to the Secretary.*]

Reading, in Connecticut, New-England,
April 9th, 1750.

Reverend Sir,

As I take three small congregations professing the Church of England, at New-Milford and New-Fairfield, being betwixt eighteen and twenty-five miles distant from my dwelling, so I last week visited them, and found that many of their neighbours from Independents are become a sort of extravagant enthusiasts, which, as yet, want a name. For their minister they have an ignorant mechanick, not able to give a tolerable açcount of the first principles of natural or revealed religion, as I have found by conversing with him; his praying and preaching, as they call it, is performed by screaming and hallooing to such a degree, that he may be heard at above a mile distant. He administers the Lord's Supper (as he says) to persons who profess to be unbaptised, and to small children; and at the time when he presumes to administer that holy Sacrament, as credible spectators inform me, there is such a hideous and horrible screaming and howling among his communicants, that one would be tempted to suspect that the devil was come visibly among them. I have taken some pains with this presumptuous man and his hearers, but to little purpose, for they have renounced reason as carnal, and pretend to inspiration. I have baptised this half year fifty-eight, of whom five are adults; some few of them were Indian children. My congregations are in a peaceable and growing condition, and, I think, do increase in knowledge and virtue. I this day draw upon the treasurer for twenty-five pounds, and am, Reverend Sir,

Yours, and the venerable Society's

Most obedient servant,

John Beach.

[*Rev. Mr. Gibbs to the Secretary.—Extract.*]

Simsbury, May 24th, 1750.

Reverend Sir,

The Dissenters remain yet insolent, as is manifest by their attempting to take away rates from some of my parishioners, who are scarce two miles distant from the Church; their plea is that they are out of the bounds of Simsbury. I did at first promise myself the satisfaction and pleasure of seeing a large growth of the Church here, but am now something scrupulous of the same, as things at present are, and which I impute mainly to the want of a house, and which my people have not so much as attempted after, and which I am now altogether out of hopes of.

WILLIAM GIBBS.

[*Rev. Mr. Punderson to the Society.*]

N. Groton, 25th June, 1750.

Reverend Sir,

As the venerable Society have appointed me an itinerant missionary in New-England, the members of the Church of England, at Middletown, Cohasset, Guilford, Wallingford, Mansfield, Stafford, &c., have submitted themselves to my pastoral care, and whatever ministerial taxes they have been assessed to pay, I have ordered to be entirely applied toward building their Churches and maintaining readers among them, without taking any part of them myself. My discharges they have accepted in Middletown, Guilford, Wallingford, Mansfield, Stafford, Canterbury, &c.; but in Branford and Cohasset they have, in the most violent manner, been distressing, and imprisoning the members of the Church of England. The last winter, taking encouragement from my ill success in endeavouring to recover the taxes taken about three years ago from one Jonathan Wood, and last year from Matthew Paul, of the Union, (who lost upward of twelve pounds of our money, taken from him, as will appear by the enclosed receipts,) great has been the expense and many the hardships I have been at in endeavouring to protect the Church in that liberty only which the Baptists and Quakers universally enjoy in the government; and I now despair, without the venerable Board will interpose and procure an express order that the professors of the Church of England shall enjoy, at least, the same ease and liberty that Dissenters are indulged in. There are so many coming over to the Church on the one hand, or going over to the Independents on the other, that the Presbyterians (as they call themselves) imagine oppression and violence the only method to support their declining interest, as appears by their taking by distress more than five hundred pounds from the Independents in a less space than fifteen miles square, annually, for some years past, which sufferings greatly excite my pity; since both, though equally involved in schism and error, have, or ought to have, the same indulgence from the act of toleration.

Since mine of the 26th of March last, upon the 14th of May I set out upon a long journey; went to Hartford to forward a memorial to the Assembly in favour of the Church; the next day rode to Middletown, sixteen miles, and preached them a sermon; the day after went down to Cohasset, fourteen miles; preached the day following to a pretty congregation of sincere Church people, all brought over to the Church by God's blessing on my labours there; the next day and following, preached in Guilford, christened four children, and went to Branford; preached to at least three hundred persons, administered the Sacrament of the Lord's Supper to about thirty communicants, baptised four children; the next day rode to Wallingford, preached to a pretty congregation, baptised three children; the next day went to Middletown, and the day following, preached there; the next day went to

East Haddam, where probably there never was a minister of the Church of England before, had a congregation of near one hundred persons, one child christened, and one couple married, added two to our Church, who received the communion the first Sunday of this instant, and are persons of an excellent character ; the next day arrived at my house, so that in the space of twelve days I travelled near two hundred miles, preached nine sermons, and had near one thousand persons attend divine service in the several places. Upon the 12th of this instant, I preached at Windham, two persons declared for the Church ; the next day in Mansfield, christened a child ; the next day at Hebron, preached to a large congregation ; after service twenty of them signed a bond for thirty pounds sterling to Mr. Colton, annually, earnestly entreating the Society that he may have leave to come home in the fall. Above all things, I earnestly entreat the venerable Society to have such compassion upon the members of the Church of England, as to procure immediately a toleration for them from all such unrighteous oppression, that the messengers of peace they send into this government may not be perplexed and harassed by endless law proceedings. I have drawn for £8 of my last quarter's salary, in favour of the Reverend Mr. Broughton, and the rest in favour of Mr. Woodbridge,

And am, Reverend Sir, yours,

And the Society's obedient, humble servant,

EBEN'R PUNDERSON.

[*Rev. Mr. Graves to the Bishop of London.—Extract.*]

New-London, July 20th, 1750.

My Lord,

To vindicate the cause of oppressed innocence, and relieve those who suffer for righteousness sake, is the command of our Saviour and a grand characteristic of His holy religion ; how far I have succeeded in this noble design, which now, in all humility, sues for your Lordship's consummating approbation, Mr. Copp, the bearer hereof, is both a witness and example. This gentleman, who has had a liberal education, according to the methods practised in this place, was descended from Presbyterian parents, and was brought up in the utmost prejudice to our religion. At my coming to this mission, I found him the publick master of a grammar and mathematical school, supported solely by Presbyterian donations. By report he was a bigoted Independent, but a strict moralist. Curiosity at first led me into his acquaintance, and conversation informed me of his parts. His aversion to our Church, I easily apprehended, arose from zeal without knowledge—zeal for his own sect and ignorance of our reasonable service; thence I applied myself to treat with him in an easy manner, and by degrees more closely upon topics of religion, and afterward induced him to read some books wrote in vindication of our discipline, the happy consequence of which was, he admired and ingenuously owned his ignorance, confessed the purity of our Church, and has reasoned and read himself into a conscientious conformist, as I verily believe; so that he is deprived of his office, and the very house he rented for some years is hired to another. However, he resolved to persevere in his well-grounded resolution, and to rely entirely upon the providence of that God, who has changed his darkness into light, and hence he presumes to cast himself at your Lordship's feet, and, if found worthy, to implore the sacred imposition of your hands. God forbid that I should, from any motive whatsoever, recommend an improper labourer into Christ's vineyard; and, therefore, am I humbly of opinion that this gentleman will make a very useful missionary. If it be for His glory, may God incline your heart to add him to our number, otherwise not.

'Tis reported, my Lord, that you intend to appoint a new Commissary in these parts, and that a native of the place is to discharge that office; but I hope your Lordship (for God's sake pardon my well-intended freedom) will be pleased to consider that, as an American is Commissary in the western, so to condescend that a European may be impowered in the eastern part of this continent; for my part, I am not at all fit for that honourable post, but will be bold to say, that Dr. McSparran is every way qualified for it. All Europeans, especially ministers, meet with a very ungracious reception here; and certain I am, that there is a plan already formed to extirpate us entirely; a plan which, in its embryo, I zealously opposed, and, by the help of God, hitherto have been enabled to defeat it; a plan which, I doubt not to affirm, would shake the foundation of these infant Churches, by casting us absolutely upon the mercy of the populace, and reduce us into a Presbyterian, servile dependence. It would be too tedious to trouble you with a recital of the whole affair, which the bearer, being perfectly acquainted with, will, at your Lordship's command, impartially relate.

'Twould be too long as well as tragical to repeat the several difficulties, severities and affronts which our hearers are harassed with, in many parts of this colony, by rigorous persecutions and arbitrary pecuniary demands, inflicted on the conscientious members of our Church by domineering Presbyterians, the old implacable enemies of Zion's prosperity and peace. These, your Lordship's sons, are imprisoned, arrested and nonsuited with prodigious cost, contrary to the laws of God and man. All professors of the Church of England, over whom there is not a particular missionary appointed, are obliged to support Presbyterian teachers and their meeting-houses—a cruel injustice and usurpation imposed on no other Society. This is solemn truth. As your Lordship is not only Bishop of these parts, but also one of his Majesty's most honourable privy council, I am confident a letter from you to some of your Clergy, with your Lordship's order or request to our General Assembly, that all the professors or members of the Church of England be exempted from all rates and demands whatever, collected for the support of other Churches and ministers than their own, would obtain the desired effect, and every day gain proselytes to our holy communion, who are now restrained through fear of additional taxes.

am, my Lord,

Your Lordship's humble servant,

MATT. GRAVES.

[*From Minutes of the Society.*]

20*th July*, 1750.

At a general meeting of the Society for the Propagation of the Gospel in Foreign Parts, held on the 20th of July, 1750—

It was reported from the Committee, that they had read a letter from the Reverend Mr. Mansfield, missionary at Derby, in Connecticut, dated "Derby, December 26th, 1749," acquainting that the people of Derby and Oxford, as well as those of Waterbury and Westbury, have been sharers in the great oppressions which are laid upon the members of the Episcopal Church in that colony, by means of the dissenting collectors distraining their goods toward the support of the dissenting teachers, and their meeting-houses; but notwithstanding this, his congregation adheres steadily to the Church, and the number of communicants in Derby is sixty-nine, in Waterbury seventy-seven, and he had baptised, in the preceding half year, twenty-four children.

Whereupon, the Committee inspected the minutes of the Society of the 17th of November, 1749, wherein the Society resolved to protect the members of the Church of England in all their just legal rights.

N. B.—These sort of complaints come by every ship almost; there are now some ministers of the Church of England in prison on account of their persecutions from the Dissenters.

[The original of this N. B. is in the handwriting of Archbishop Secker.—Ed.]

[*Memorandum of Dr. Bearcroft, (the Secretary,) about the Charter of Connecticut. From the Society's papers.*]

The Charter of the Colony of Connecticut, in New-England, was granted on the 23d day of April, in the fourteenth year of the reign of King Charles the Second, and power was given by it to John Winthrop, John Mason and others, to become a body corporate and political, by name of the Governors and Company of the English Colony of Connecticut, in New-England, in America, and, as such, to have a perpetual succession and common seal, and to choose annually, on every second Thursday in May, a governor, a deputy governor, and twelve assistants, to make reasonable laws, not contrary to the laws of England, and to revoke the same as by the General Assembly, or the major part of them, shall be thought fit; and to do all other matters and things whereby the people, inhabitants there, may be so religiously, peaceably and civilly governed, as that their good life and orderly conversation may win and invite the natives of the country to the knowledge and obedience of the only true God and Saviour of mankind and of the Christian faith.

Complaint is made that several members of the Church of England, in this province, have been cast into prison by the magistrates for the non-payment of taxes, expressly assessed and raised for the building and support of Presbyterian meeting-houses and their teachers.

N. B.—It is asserted that the Independents also are thus harassed on the same account, but Quakers and Anabaptists are excused.

[*Rev. Mr. Mansfield to the Secretary.*]

Derby, *July*, *A. D.*, 1750.

Reverend Sir,

I have continued this last half year constantly to officiate in the several parts of my mission, and occasionally, especially on holy days, at six or seven other towns, which are destitute of a missionary. The Church seems to be in a flourishing condition in the places which I visit, notwithstanding the hardships which some of them labour under in being distrained by the dissenting collectors of money to support their teachers; which, at the desire of the Church people of Brantford particularly, I mentioned in my letter of December 12th. This severity of the Dissenters will, I fear, ruin the interests of the Church in some places; the people, by reason of heavy taxes laid upon them for the support of dissenting ministers, being unable to make any provision for the building of Churches and buying glebes, and, consequently, almost despairing of enjoying the privileges of the Church. Some of these towns are about thirty and forty miles distant from Derby, the place of my residence; yet as the people express a very great desire of having the missionaries of the honourable Society come among them, I visit them as often as the care of my large mission will permit me. I have annexed my *Notitia Parochialis* for Derby and Waterbury, and have drawn upon the Society's treasurer £10 toward my support,

And am, Reverend Sir, the Society's
Most obliged and obedient servant,
RICHARD MANSFIELD.

[*Rev. Dr. Johnson to the Secretary.—Extract.*]

Stratford, in New-England,
October 15*th,* 1750.

Reverend Sir,

As to our petition to our Assembly for power by law to tax ourselves, and collect our tax independent of the Dissenters, I am sorry to tell you that it is defeated. All the Clergy and people were unanimous in it, except the Reverend Mr. Graves, but he could not see reason to approve of it, thinking it best the law should stand as it is, and we be subject to the Dissenters to tax us and collect our taxes, though the law forbids us a vote in raising them, with which many of our people were very uneasy. However, as the rest were agreed in it, they thought proper to go on; but as he was pleased to oppose it by writing to some of the members of the Assembly, it was postponed till we had a meeting last fall, when he objected to the draught that had been made. At length we agreed, and he with the rest, as we thought, that a new draught should be made, and to leave it to our attorney to make the draught as he thought best, by leaving out any mention of catechists or candidates, which also Mr. Graves had objected to; but as the attorney (who was now the sole draughtsman) petitioned for taxing and collection powers, within ourselves, which Mr. Graves disliked, he appeared at our last Assembly and entered his protest against it, as what he called a "spurious address."

Upon this, again it was laid aside till this fall, and at our meeting last month he did not come, but sent a draught of his own, wherein he only petitions that the law, as it is, might be extended, and not that we might have power to tax ourselves and collect our taxes for the support of ministers; and let us know if any other form of a draught was offered, he should appear at the Assembly and oppose it. We were all of opinion that his draught was not sufficient, because it left us still under the power of the Dissenters to tax us and collect our taxes, without our having a vote in raising them, or choosing the collectors; so, rather than have an open opposition before the Assembly, we thought it best to drop the whole affair, and still be at the mercy of the Dissenters, as we were, though our case is very difficult.

I remain, Reverend Sir,

Your most humbl

And most oвedient servant,

Samuel Johnson.

[*Rev. Mr. Punderson to the Secretary.*]

Groton, October 18*th*, 1750.

Reverend Sir,

I have the pleasure to assure the venerable Society that a greater success has attended my ministration for some months past, than has in any half year since employed by the Society, and a more general concern to acquaint themselves with our best of Churches prevails among the people than at any time heretofore. As an evidence of which, I shall only mention two journeys I have taken in said time. Upon the 14th of May I rode to Hartford, near fifty miles; the next day to Middletown, sixteen miles, gave them a sermon; the next day went to Cohasset, where I performed divine service the day following to a considerable congregation; the next day at Guilford; the day following at an out-house in said Guilford, and christened three children; in the evening rode to Branford, where, the day following, (*i. e.*, Sunday,) preached to near three hundred persons, and administered the Holy Sacrament to upward of thirty persons; the next day preached to a considerable number in Wallingford; upon Wednesday at Middletown; and upon Thursday at East Haddam, where probably there never was a minister of the Church of England before, to near 100 persons, married one couple, and christened one child; the next day visited a person of excellent sense and unspotted life at Middletown, who was at the Church the day before, who, together with his wife, declared for the Church, and have both been at our communion, in Norwich, twice since. So that in twelve days I rode 200 miles; preached nine sermons; added eight to our communion; christened ten children. The 5th of September rode to Middletown, and preached there the next day; the day following at East Haddam; on Sunday at Middletown, in their town house, it being quite full; administered the two Sacraments; their Church is a beautiful timber building, and will soon be fit to meet in; a folio Bible and Common Prayer-Book would be very acceptable to them; the next day in a small Church in Wallingford; the day following gave private baptism to a poor, weak child, as I went to my native place, New-Haven; the Sunday after the commencement, preached in the State house, in that town, to a numerous assembly, notwithstanding Brother Thompson preached the same day in the Church at West Haven; the day following at Branford; upon Tuesday in the Church, at Guilford, to abundance; the next day at Cohasset; upon Friday, at Millington, added there two more to our communion; the next day christened three children. I travelled in this journey about one hundred and sixty miles; preached eleven sermons; christened seventeen children; the Sunday before last was at Charlestown, and the last at Norwich; the Church greatly increases at both those places.

I shall trespass no longer on your and the Society's patience, save only to entreat their attention to what I transmitted last June, that the professors of the established Church may have ease and rest from such as delight in oppression; and that I have drawn for my last quarter's salary in favour of Mr. Dudley Woodbridge,

And am, Reverend Sir,

Yours, and the Society's faithful servant,

EBEN'R PUNDERSON.

[*Rev. Mr. Graves to the Secretary.—Extract.*]

N. London, January 20*th*, 1751.

Reverend and good Sir,

'Tis a truth, I presume, self-evident, that invention is as necessary in letter writing as in composing sermons, and that a connection of thoughts, as far as the subject will admit of, is equally necessary in both, with this distinction, that we may compose, having topics in abundance, when we will, but not write, for the contrary reason, when we please. The latter is my misfortune frequently, as at present. In my two last letters I exhausted my poor treasury of invention, so that there's scarcely one reflection behind worthy your reflection and review. What to do in this emergency I know not. Prudence advises me to be mute, "*nescit vox missa reverti;*" obedience to the instruction of my venerable superiors, to write. "*Principibus placuisse viris non ultima laus est;*" and sure I am 'tis better, in all lights and at all hazards, to demonstrate my best, though imperfect duty, by a cheerful compliance, than to incur the censure of ingratitude by a guilty silence.

The Church of New-London certainly increases, and though those Dissenters who attend most constantly are not open, declared professors, yet their frequent appearance is, to me, a proof of their intention; and the repeated desertion of their own, shows their tacit approbation of our religion. I have baptised about five since my last, but before my next shall have baptised a Quaker of about fifty years old and upward, and his two adult children. The communicants increase but slowly. A letter just come from Hebron has revived my decaying spirits, and enlarged my thoughts. Sure no man had ever such a knotty people to engage with, for nothing but persecutions, afflictions and bonds, in the most literal sense, for the Gospel's sake, are my certain lot among that people; but I hope there are five righteous to be found there, for whose spiritual interest I beg leave to intercede for the rest. One Mr. Thompson, who is a gentleman of very great estate, desires his duty and services to be presented to the honourable and religious Society, and that I may acquaint them that if they will either send them a missionary, or permit them to send a candidate home, he will, out of his own estate, give a glebe of twelve acres of good land, and cause a house to be built for a minister, and enter into bonds for the performance thereof. I desire you will be pleased to intimate this to the honourable Society, for I am persuaded 'twill be the certain means of propagating the Gospel in these parts. 'Tis his opinion and mine, that the most certain way to accomplish that glorious end, would be to authorize the missionary of Hebron to take care of Bolton, which lies at one end of it, and the adjacent parts, and to preach one Sunday in the old Church at Hebron and the other in the new; for this gentleman, who is very able, is very desirous, also, to have two Churches, [one] at each end of the parish, about eight miles distant from each other. I must add that 'tis my conscientious opinion Mr. Colton is quite unfit for holy orders, unless a covetous man, a farmer, an apothecary, a merchant, and a usurer, is qualified for the ministry, for such and all these he surely is; but I solemnly declare there are more and more notorious reasons why such a man should never be ordained. All that I shall add about Hebron is, that inasmuch as they are very wicked, they have the greater necessity for a good resident minister, and, therefore, I humbly desire you will be pleased to consider this good design of Mr. Thompson, and give it all the weight you can before the venerable Society,

And I am, good Sir,

Your most obedient and very humble servant,

And affectionate brother,

MATT. GRAVES.

[*Rev. Mr. Dibblee to the Secretary.—Extract.*]

Stamford, Connecticut, in N. England,
April 2d, 1751.

Reverend Sir,

The Church at Norwalk appears very thankful that the Society is pleased to determine in their favour, and to grant them, in conjunction with Ridgefield, to be a mission. At their instance and request, I preached in the Church of Norwalk the fourth Sunday in March last, to a large congregation, and gave the communion to upward of sixty persons. I have appointed Sunday after Easter to be at Ridgefield, where the poor people have been entirely destitute of the publick administration of religion the year past, except once a quarter on Sundays, and oftener on week days. I have officiated among them on the Sunday after Christmas. I gave the communion at Ridgefield to upward of forty persons. Truly, Sir, the harvest is plenteous, but the labourers are few, and our earnest prayers to the Lord of the harvest is, that a door may be opened for a further supply of faithful labourers. I have been obliged, in a great measure, to act the part of an itinerant missionary ever since my return in holy orders, by reason of the destitute circumstances of the poor people scattered abroad, as sheep without a shepherd, as there are many twenty or thirty miles back into the country who frequently sent for me. Brother Lamson has taken the principal care of the Church of Norwalk for the year, excepting visiting them on special occasions in case of sickness, &c., on which occasions I have been frequently sent for. I have complied with the request of sundry poor people living back on the "oblong," so called, a tract of land, as it were, lying between the governments of New-York and Connecticut, twenty or thirty miles. I have engaged to travel up amongst them the first week in May next, where there is no settled minister of any denomination among them, and, I am informed, many of them are professors of our holy Church, but destitute of the means of salvation, and seldom have an opportunity to devote their children to God in covenant. I have appointed to preach at three different places that week on the "oblong." My parish remains, by the blessing of God on my labours, in peace and unity. We have sundry accessions to the Church since my last of the 29th of September. I preached last Christmas to a numerous assembly; multitudes of the Dissenters came to Church and behaved with great decency. Seven heads of families have declared conformity since my last account, in Stamford, and some at Horse Neck and Stanwick. I baptised but one adult; twenty-six infants, white; one, black; three added to the communion.

The duties of my parish are considerable; and these, together with the additional duties which, in compassion, I have performed among the poor people at Ridgefield, and at other places, as I have been occasionally sent for, have rendered my family circumstances difficult, so that the principal discouragement I labour under is with respect to my support. My people truly contribute according to their ability to my support, but there are many whose circumstances are so indigent, that I am obliged to remit their taxes, or suffer them to be distressed by the dissenting collectors; for, by the laws of this government, the professors of the Church are taxed as their dissenting brethren are; the tax is gathered by a collector of their appointing, and he generally, by a too great remissness in doing his duty, or by unreasonable severity upon the professors of the Church of England, endeavours to distress the Church and hurt the minister of it, and in some parts of my parish, I have been no small sufferer in this respect.

I am most sincerely, Reverend Sir,

Your most obedient, most humble servant,

EBENEZER DIBBLEE.

[*Rev. Mr. Johnson to the Secretary.*]

Stratford, in New-England,
April 14th, 1751

Reverend Sir,

As this will probably go by Messrs. Camp and Colton, whom we have recommended to my Lord of London for holy orders, I would take this occasion to suggest that, as it is now much less a charity to provide for a school in this town than heretofore, since the schools are of late better provided for by law than formerly, by money arising from the sale of some uncultivated publick lands, Mr. Browne tells me he is willing to resign his salary from the next Michaelmas. I know Ripton people will hope to have it converted to them for a minister. I wish it could be so; but whether the venerable Board will be pleased to admit of this, or add £5 to it and divide, for a little stipend to each between these candidates, or whatever other disposition they shall please to make, I entirely submit to their wise goodness.

I now proceed to answer the other parts of your kind letter of October 19th. What gave me uneasy apprehensions relating to the order you mention was, that it seemed to relate to such as were *in the Society's service*, as the words were. I had been informed that I was censured myself by some invidious person on account of my making some little additions and variations in adapting some of the prayers of the liturgy to the use of families for country people, in an appendix to a sermon I published at the opening of our Church, in which I followed such examples as Mr. Nelson, and other devotional writers of good credit; and as I have good reason to believe that this, with an invidious spirit toward me and some others, was the occasion of that information, I presume to enclose here a copy of that poor sermon, (which I had not otherwise ventured to do,) for I would do nothing but what I would willingly submit to the correction of the venerable Board, my benefactors.

As to such young readers as are not in the Society's service, I cannot yet find any fact; however, they are sufficiently cautioned.

As to New-Cambridge, the fact was as Mr. Gibbs represented it; but as they are much nearer to one of Mr. Mansfield's parishes, viz., Waterbury, than to Mr. Gibbs, and so he can better recover their rates by our law, they have since put themselves under his protection, and so that matter is accommodated; but there are many in several places that are at such a distance from *any* incumbent in orders, that they cannot have the benefit of the law, and so they are still imprisoned for non-payment to Dissenters.

I am very glad, Sir, to understand by your letter, that the *Society are determined to support the members of the Church here so far as they can, &c.;* but, indeed, I do not know what they can do, so long as the charter of this government stands as it does; by virtue of which they esteem themselves an independent Legislature, and so not only do not send home their laws to be confirmed by the King and Council, but insist that they are by no means obliged to do so; whence it comes to pass, that they pass many acts highly detrimental even to themselves, to trade in general, and so to the nation as well as to the Church, especially relating to their paper money, which is a source of very great injustice in many respects, as they manage it. On which account, I humbly conceive it would be happy, for themselves as well as the Church, if the legislature at home should reduce them to a state of mere dependence on the Crown, by obliging them to accept of a new or explanatory charter, by which nothing should be allowed to pass for law without his Majesty's assent, as in Massachusetts; for want of which, the wiser and better part are so dependent on the people, that they dare not exert themselves as they would for the best, and so are run away with by a prevailing mob, and the law is a universally vague and uncertain thing, both in legislation and execution, and the government is so popular, that they scarce know what it is to be governed, and so are extremely apt to run into endless factions, and that in the affairs of religion as well as in State.

But as you desire a *particular account*, &c., that the Society may have a clear notion of the condition of things in this colony, I here enclose No. I., a copy of our charter, by which it may be judged whether they have any right to make any establishment of religion; and the rather, as we humbly apprehend that the *Church of England is already established* in these plantations, by the act of union with *Scotland;* and the Lord's justices, in a letter to Lieutenant-Governor Dummer, in the year 1725, declared it to be an invasion of his Majesty's prerogative for any of his subjects to presume to make any establishment of religion without his royal assent. No. II. You have a copy of their law by which they have made a kind of establishment of religion without his royal assent. No. III. will show what their law is about supporting their minister and collecting the rates. No. IV. contains a law that fear extorted from them by a jail full of our people, who at the same time addressed the late Bishop of London, from thence giving an account of their sufferings. This law provides only for such as *can and will attend*, which is such a vague expression that, to what distance or frequency it shall extend, depends on the judges who favour us more or less, according as they are affected. Sometimes a case has been lost in suing for the rates of such as lived within four, five or six miles of a Church, with an incumbent in orders; and what made this law the more grievous, or rather less easy, was that, by the law No. V., our people were excluded from their Society, or parish meetings, and so, from any vote in raising the rates or choosing the collectors, and this, we think, inconsistent with the English constitution, that they should be obliged to pay money they had no vote in raising: upon which we offered the memorial No. VI., in which we petition to have leave to be embodied into Societies within ourselves, and so to have the same powers by law with our neighbours, and to extend to all the people of our Church, though they have not an incumbent near them in orders, &c.; and we had some reason to hope it would have been granted if it had gone on; and, if it had been negatived, I intended (which I thought the only course we could take) to have sent it, with a copy of their negative; but as I intimated in my last, we could not bring it to the trial by reason of the violent opposition of the Rev. Mr. Graves. And, lastly, that the Society may see their treatment of us, I enclose No. VII. An account sent me of the present case of one little collection of people, by which that of many others may be easily conceived, and I thought it best to send it in its native simplicity, as they sent it. And these people never were in any stipulation with the dissenting minister, and at the same time, at a great expense (with others in the neighbouring towns of Guilford and Branford, whose case is the same) in building a Church, and providing for the support of a minister.

Thus, Sir, I have given as exact and clear a state of our case as I am able. I would only humbly beg leave to suggest whether it would be advisable to mention any thing of my writing in this manner in the "abstract," as it may be a prejudice to the Church, should it be known among us, of my writing so particularly about the government; and, indeed, I doubt whether it be best that any greater number of the "abstract" be sent hither than to each minister a copy or two, since our adversaries have of late been making such wicked work from them, in misrepresenting and abusing both the Society and us.

I am, Reverend Sir, your most humble,

And most obedient servant,

SAMUEL JOHNSON.

ENCLOSURES.

No. II.

(Referred to in the foregoing.)

ANNO REGNI ANNE REGINÆ, SEPTIMO.

An act in approbation of the Agreement of the late Rev. Elders and Messengers of all the Churches in this government, made and concluded at Say-Brook, Anno, &c., 1708.

The Reverend ministers, delegates from ye Elders and messengers of the Churches, in this government, met at Say-

Brook, September ye ninth, one thousand seven hundred and eight; having represented to this Assembly a confession of faith, heads of agreement and regulation, in ye administration of Church discipline, as unanimously agreed, and consented to by ye Elders and messengers of all ye Churches in this government.

This Assembly do declare their great approbation of such a happy agreement; and do ordain yt. all the Churches within this government, that are, and shall be thus united in doctrine, worship and discipline, be, and for the future shall be, owned and acknowledged, established by law:

Provided always, that nothing herein shall be intended or construed to hinder or prevent any Society or Church that is or shall be allowed by the laws of this government, who soberly differ or dissent from the united Churches hereby established, from exercising worship and discipline in their own way, according to their consciences.

No. III.

An Extract from the Act for the Settlement and Support of Ministers, &c.

And when any such rate or tax is granted and made, as aforesaid, viz., by the major vote of each parish or Society, the said selectmen or committee shall apply to some assistant or justice of ye peace, in ye same county, for a writ or warrant, directed to the collector or collectors, chosen and appointed to collect such rate or tax, enabling him or them to levy and collect ye same, which assistant or justice shall forthwith proceed to grant our said writ.

And every such collector or collectors shall, with convenient speed, levy and collect every such rate committed to him or them; the whole of which they shall do, and pay unto ye said minister or ministers, within two months after ye yearly salary becomes due, for ye payment of which such rate or tax is or shall be granted.

No. IV.

Anno Regni Regis Georgii Decimo Tertio. Anno, 1727.

An act providing how ye taxes levied on ye professors of ye Church of England for ye support of ye gospel shall be disposed of, and for exempting said professors from paying any taxes for ye building meeting-houses for ye present established Churches of this government.

Upon the prayer of Moses Ward, of Fairfield, Churchwarden, and ye rest of ye Churchwardens, Vestrymen, &c., praying this Assembly, by some act or otherwise, to free them from paying to dissenting ministers, and from building dissenting meeting-houses, complaining that money has been lately taken from them by distress, &c.; further urging that there might be some provision made by ye law, for obliging the parishioners to pay to the support of their ministers.

Be it enacted, by the governor, council and representatives, in General Court assembled, and by the authority of the same, that all persons who are of the Church of England, and those who are of ye Churches established by ye laws of this government, yt. live in ye bounds of any parish allowed by this Assembly, shall be taxed by ye parishioners of ye said parish, by ye same rule, and in ye same proportion, for ye support of ye ministry in such parish; but if it so happens, that there be a Society of ye Church of England, where there is a person in orders, according to ye Canons of ye Church of England, settled and abiding among them, and performing divine service so near to any person yt. had declared himself of the Church of England that he can conveniently, and doth attend ye publick worship there, then the collectors, having first indifferently levied ye tax, as aforesaid, shall deliver ye taxes collected of such persons declaring themselves, and attending, as aforesaid, unto ye ministers of ye Church of England, living near unto such persons; which minister shall have full power to receive and recover ye same, in order to his support in the place assigned to him.

But if such proportion of any taxes be not sufficient in any Society of ye Church of England to support ye incumbent there, then such Society may levy and collect of them who profess and attend, as aforesaid, greater taxes, at their own discretion, for the support of their minister.

And the parishioners of ye Church of England, attending, as aforesaid, are hereby excused from paying any taxes for ye building meeting-houses for ye present established Churches of this government.

No. V.

An Extract from the Act for Forming and Regulating Societies or Parishes, May, 1746.

Be it further enacted, by the authority aforesaid, that no person shall presume to vote in any Society meeting aforesaid, unless such person hath a freehold in the same town or Society, rated as fifty shillings or forty pounds on ye common list; or is a person of full age and in full communion with the Church; nor shall any person who is or shall be, by the law of this government, freed or exempted from ye payment of those taxes granted by any town or Society for ye support and ye worship and ministry of ye Presbyterian, Congregational or Consociated Churches of this government, and for the building and maintaining meeting-houses for such worship, on account or by reason of his dissenting from the way of worship and ministry aforesaid, be allowed or admitted to act or vote in any town or Society meeting, in those votes which respect or relate to ye support of ye worship and ministry aforesaid, and ye building and maintaining of ye meeting-houses aforesaid.

No. VI.

A Memorial offered to the Assembly in 1749.

To the honourable the General Assembly of his Majesty's Colony of Connecticut, to be held in Hartford, in said colony, on ye second Thursday of May, 1749, the Memorial of ye Churchwardens of several Societies of ye Church of England, in behalf of said Society, in said colony, humbly showeth:

That your memorialists, entirely sensible of, and highly thankful for ye many favours and advantages which they enjoy, under the influence and government of this legislature, and cheerfully use every opportunity to express their gratitude therefor, and in particular for ye happiness they have long enjoyed under ye act of 1727, exempting them from paying taxes to other than the ministers of their own profession, which act was well calculated, as we conceive, so long as it answered the good purposes intended by the enactors of it; but the late act of May, 1746, having excluded ye members of ye Church of England from voting in Society meetings, and from having any hand in raising those taxes which they are obliged to pay, and ye circumstances of ye Church of England, in this colony, being in some measure altered since ye making that act, particularly in that whereas, at ye time of making that act, there were few members of ye Church of England but what were regularly embodied, and had a Clergyman in orders, abiding among them, for which case only said act provides. There are now in many places numbers of that profession, who, through unavoidable difficulties, cannot procure or maintain Clergymen among them, who would and do maintain Catechists or candidates for holy orders, according to the practice allowed and approved of by ye Society, in England, for propagating, &c.; which, creating a very considerable expense to them, they cannot but esteem it a heavy burthen on them to be obliged, at ye same time, to pay rates to the ministers according to the establishment in this colony; and whereas, ye collectors of rates in ye parishes where there are Societies of ye Church of England, complain that it is a burthen on them to collect indiscriminately ye rates of both professions, without any advantage or reward arising from ye collection of ye rates of ye professors of ye Church of England; and whereas, the disproportionate numbers of professors of ye Church of England and ye Presbyterians require taxations in different proportions for ye support of their respective ministers, according to their different numbers, and ye members of one and ye same Church of England are differently taxed by reason of their living in different ecclesiastical Societies, and whereas, should the law of '27 be repealed, and no provision made in lieu thereof, it might be of ill consequence, as tending to weaken ye obligation men are under to pay to ye support in some way or other of worship and ministry, it might greatly unhinge ye minds of ye people by seeing so great a number of their neighbours entirely exempted from paying any rates. Your honour's memorialists are humbly of opinion that to prevent these inconveniences is a matter not unworthy the attention of this honourable Assembly; and do therefore humbly pray your honours to take these things into your wise consideration, and by an act of this Assembly for that purpose, provide that wherever there be any Societies of ye professors of ye Church of England within the limits of ye parishes by law established, who have ministers ordained according to the Canons of ye Church of England, abiding among them, or candidates for holy orders with them residing and performing divine service, who are approved and allowed by ye Clergy of ye Church of England within this colony, or are at charge in building Churches or procuring glebes, that in all such cases, such professors of ye Church of England, having certified their professions to ye Clerk of ye Society in which they dwell, and voluntarily caused their names to be enrolled as such professors, shall be exempted from paying any taxes toward the building meeting-houses, or to the support of ye ministers of any other denomination, and shall have granted to them parish privileges, and have power, within themselves, to meet and tax themselves, in what manner and proportion they think proper for ye support of their ministers or candidates and for building their Churches, &c.; and to choose collectors, who shall have power to collect such taxes, and to be governed and directed by the same laws that collectors of Society rates in this colony are, or in some other way, as your honours, in your wisdom, shall judge proper to grant relief to your memorialists, who, as in duty bound, &c.

N. B.—This was signed by a number of Churchwardens of the several Churches, or by their order, as many as could have opportunity, except New-London.*

[*Rev. Mr. Gibbs to the Secretary.—Extract.*]

Simsbury, March 25th, 1751.

Reverend Sir,

Whereas the Dissenters have been, as I have represented to the honourable Society, very insolent as to their oppressing the members of the Church, there now appears in them a relaxation and respite as to the same, and there seems a great fear of an after scourge. This may, I believe, prevent them from any further proceedings, not but that their wills are as good as ever, and which is apparent by their late threat, even this winter, toward some of the Church people living out of Simsbury four miles; but they at present do forbear, and, I am apt to think, will cease meddling with the Church any more.

One of my parishioners, a late conformist, whose residence is but a little way from Simsbury, and in the bounds of Farmington, has met with some kind of oppression. I have not as yet undertaken to defend him, by reason that I fear justice will not be allowed me, though, according to the law, it should and ought to be. I have, therefore, thought it best to forbear a while longer.

As to the Church here, it is as I represented; it lays very open and unfinished, and which grieves me much. Were my people but resolutely bent and engaged, they might then do according to what is expected of them, and there might probably then be large additions to the Church; but then, again, that which may deter some of them from embracing it is the oppression it is under, and meets with, and thus is the growth of it in some measure retarded.

I remain, Reverend Sir,

The Society's most obedient, humble servant,

William Gibbs

---

* Mr. Graves was the minister at New-London.—Ed.

[*Rev. Mr. Gibbs to the Secretary.*]

Simsbury, July 19th, 1751.

Reverend Sir,

I received your letter in June, and as to these laws you are desirous of knowing, I can give no fuller account of them than what the Reverend Dr. Johnson has, having lately consulted him on that affair; but it may not be amiss to send that which the Dissenters have so greatly insisted upon, viz.:

Be it enacted, by the Governor, Council and Representatives, in General Court assembled, and by the authority of the same, That all persons who are of the Church of England, and those who are of the Church established by the laws of this government, that live in the bounds of any parish allowed by this Assembly, shall be taxed by the parishioners of the same parish, by the same rule and in the same proportion, for the support of the ministry in such parish. But if it so happen that there be a Society of the Church of England where there is a person in orders, according to the Canons of the Church of England, settled and abiding among them, and performing divine service so near to any person that hath declared himself of the Church of England, that he can conveniently, and doth, attend the public worship there, then the collectors, having first indifferently levied the tax, as above said, shall deliver the taxes collected from such persons declaring themselves and attending as aforesaid, unto the minister of the Church of England living near unto such persons, which minister shall have full power to receive and recover the same in order to his support in the place assigned to him; but if such proportion of taxes be not sufficient in any Society of the Church of England to support the incumbent there, then such Society may levy and collect of them, who profess and attend as aforesaid, greater taxes, at their own discretion, for the support of their minister; and the parishioners of the Church of England are hereby excused from paying any taxes for building meeting-houses for the present established Churches of this government.

Now, from this, the Dissenters' plea is: That those of our communion who live remote, do not answer this law, by reason of their not *conveniently* attending, as they say. I hope there will be no more difficulties, but yet I am not without fear. Two persons of this town have lately conformed to the Church, and I am satisfied several more would come, if the people would but build a house, and which there are no signs of.

The house which I at present inhabit has been sold some time ago, and I do expect the person will move into it by the fall; and whether my people do intend to provide for me, I can't really say. They will not, or they care not, to give me a satisfactory answer when asked, so that this must make a removal very necessary, and which, I hope, the Society will consider.

I remain, Rev. Sir, your affectionate servant and brother,

And the Society's most obedient, humble servant,

WILLIAM GIBBS.

[*Rev. Mr. Graves to the Secretary.*]

N. London, October 10th, 1751.

Reverend and Good Sir,

It is impossible to describe the satisfaction I received upon reading the animating letter to poor Mr. Gibbs. Surely, he as well as others of us have suffered religious persecution in the most literal sense. As the letter is wrote with a truly Christian sympathy and necessary indignation, as well as an unchangeable resolution to support the missionaries, and protect our oppressed and worthy converts, so I presume it will, in the mean time, be of great service to enable us to carry on the blessed work of propagation and conversion, if the wisdom of the venerable Society will judge it proper to send each of us in Connecticut such another letter, empowering us to preach in all the neighbouring parts, that the envious, bigoted Dissenters of this colony, so oppressive and notorious for stifling and perplexing our growing religion, may know you have a power of explaining your own words and to assert your liberty of your own charter; a charter whose nature is purely spiritual, whereas, that of this jealous colony is wholly civic. I have lately carefully canvassed it, and there is no clause in it respecting religion except this following sentence. They have a power to "direct, rule and dispose of all other (viz., civic) matters and things whereby our said people, inhabitants there, may be so religiously, civilly and peaceably governed, that their good life and orderly conversation may win and invite the natives of the country to the knowledge and obedience of the only true God and Saviour of mankind and the Christian faith, which is our royal intention and the adventurer's free profession, is the only and principal end of this plantation."

Mr. Punderson has lately been cast in our Superior Court, suing for his rates; and I assure you, one of the principal leaders of this government told me expressly, that the courts are determined to overrule all our proceedings in such cases. I lately waited upon our deputy-governor, and told him plainly, that though the law about rates was very equal and just in its beginning, yet the conclusion was full of ambiguity, snares and deceit; that we missionaries were greatly abused and despised by this government, as persons exposed to publick contempt, and our hearers to exactions and oppression. He told me we were treated according to law, and deserved no other usage; that imprisoning Mr. Gibbs and casting Mr. Punderson were just acts, and that their laws should be executed. I answered, their proceeding against us and our hearers, who lived remote, were arbitrary, and contrary to the practice of Europe, and that no English history could produce an instance of any dissenting teacher being so scandalously and barbarously dealt with. Upon the whole, I find that he (who is in principle an Independent) is resolved to baffle the authority and crush our endeavours. May God restrain the remainder of his wrath.

I am, good Sir, your most obedient and grateful servant,
And affectionate brother,
MATT. GRAVES.

[*Rev. Mr. Punderson to the Secretary.—Extract.*]

Groton, in New-England,
December 6th, 1751.

Reverend Sir,

Our blessed Lord having assured us that a good shepherd will lay down his life for his flock, I thought best to spend some of my temporal interest in defending my flock from the cruel oppression of their adversaries; and as £77.10 has been distrained from nine persons, who were brought over to the Church by me since my complaint of June, 1750, £40 of which was taken from four persons in N. Guilford, who, with many others, declared for the Church in September, 1747, and have ever since attended the service of the Church, to whom Mr. George Bartlett (before this a Deacon among the Presbyterians and brother-in-law to Dr. Johnson) has constantly read prayers and sermons, I have sued for their taxes, and obtained judgment against most of the collectors before the Justices' Court, but, by writ of error and an appeal, I have finally recovered but twelve pounds. In the case of Deacon Bartlett, although these concessions were made by the opposite party at the County Court, to which they appealed, viz.: 1. That I was an itinerant missionary in New-England; 2. That in the year 1747 a number of people made declaration of conformity to the Church of England in said N. Guilford, forty-four miles from Groton, and submitted themselves to my charge; 3. That I ordered them to attend divine service, which they have constantly done ever since, said Bartlett being their reader; 4. That their collector for the year 1748 took of said Bartlett upward of eleven pounds, he being a professed Churchman; 5. That I have constantly attended them every half year, except last spring; after an attendance of ten days, judgment was given against me in direct opposition to the enclosed maxims upon law and for the construction of statutes and reasons annexed; and as I observed to the judges, 'tis very surprising that a statute, professedly made at the desire and in favour of the Church, should be used to the oppression and vexation of it, as the venerable Society gave me assurance of their interposition to put a final period to this violent oppressive spirit, which is not only peculiar in this government, but also peculiarly displayed against the Church of England. Quakers and Baptists are in this government universally exempted from paying taxes to them,

And am, Reverend Sir, yours and the Society's
Most faithful, humble servant,
EBEN'R PUNDERSON.

[*Rev. Dr. Johnson to the Secretary.—Extract.*]

Stratford, New-England,
April 8th, 1752.

Reverend Sir,

Nor hath the condition of the Church within the whole of this colony much altered, save that it hath so far increased at New-Haven (with West-Haven at about four miles distance) that they have this winter got timber to build a Church of the dimensions of sixty feet by forty, beside the steeple and chancel; and as this is a place of very great importance on account of the College being there, it would be very happy for them if the Society were able to assist them in providing for a minister, as I doubt they will not be able to do more than £25 sterling per annum themselves, especially while building. The Church is also gaining at Guilford and Branford, which being but twelve miles asunder, propose to join for the present in procuring a minister, to whom they would also engage about £25 per annum, and therefore stand in like need of assistance; and there are two worthy candidates likely to offer for these places, but if the Society be not able to assist them, they must perhaps be content for the present to have but one over them all.

[*Rev. Mr. Gibbs to the Secretary.—Extract.*]

Simsbury, June 23d, 1752.

Reverend Sir,

I have lately met with some opposition from the Dissenters. One of my parishioners, at Farmington, and about seven or eight miles distant, has been made to pay to the support of the dissenting minister. I demanded the rate of the collector, but was refused it, upon which I sued him before his Majesty's justice of the peace, in this town, John Humphreys, Esq., and it going then in my favour, they appealed to the County Court, and recovered of me, by reason that two evidences took their oath that said parishioner acted with them in the settling of their minister, which he denied, (as I am informed by one whom I appointed to act in my stead.) The man is an elderly man, and attends the Church as often as he can, and especially on Sacrament days, and this for three years past, and which was vouched for in court by two or three evidences. The distance of the place and the badness of the weather is a great hindrance to his attending oftener than he does. I am sorry my people act in the manner they do, and that they are so careless of complying with the Society's demand. I have no place to abide in but one room in the Churchwarden's house, and which is a great incumbrance.

[*Rev. Mr. Wetmore to the Bishop of London.—Extract.*]

Province of New-York, in America,
Rye, August 11th, 1752.

My Lord,

That in the colonies called New-England the people are mostly Dissenters of one sort or other, must be well known to your Lordship, and that they use their power in compelling the professors of the Church of England among them, as if themselves were an *established* Church; and, indeed, so their controversial writers assume, very positively, and treat the constitution of our national Church, and the professors of it in this country especially, with such rudeness and indecency as tries the patience of the most mortified Christian. Mr. Hobart, of Fairfield, a few years ago, preached and printed a sermon, which began a controversy that is yet subsisting. After an attack upon the Episcopacy of the Church, as inconsistent with that equality, which, by Christ's institution, ought to subsist among his ministers, he charges schism with great boldness upon the professors of the Church of England, and urges the awful guilt of it to deter his hearers from such a dangerous communion; this has produced vindications, addresses, &c. It has been urged on our side that the colonies are part of and belong to the English nation, which is of the Church of England, and are, therefore, in duty bound to submit to the government thereof, in things religious as well as civic, and not to separate from its communion; that the establishment of the Church of England, extending to all its parts, reaches hither, which is especially evident in the act of Union, and his Majesty's patent granted to the late Bishop of London, to exercise spiritual jurisdiction in the plantations. Against this has been urged the authority of a passage in a letter of the Lords Justices, in the year 1725, to Lieut. Governor Dummer, that there is no regular establishment of any national or provincial Church in these plantations, and of a passage in a letter from the late Bishop of London to Dr. Coleman, a Presbyterian minister in Boston, May 24th, 1735: "My opinion has always been, that the religious state of New-England is founded on an equal liberty to all Protestants, none of which can claim the name of a national establishment, or any kind of superiority over the rest." These passages were both written without having in view the present subject of controversy, but to answer a quite different purpose; being written to and for the information of one domineering sect, which claims the privilege of an establishment, and would treat all others, even the professors of the Church of England, as Dissenters and Separatists. That all the various Sectaries should enjoy entirely the benefit of toleration, is what nobody gainsays, what nobody, I hope, envies them. But when the legislature of Boston was applied to for *convening a provincial Synod*, the Lords Justices wrote to the then Lieutenant-Governor, directing him to put a stop to such proceedings, as being an invasion of the King's prerogative, in which letter was the above paragraph, or at least the sense of it, which, in my view, was only to deny any establishment that could be made of Dissenters, and with respect to the Church of England to insinuate no more than what we are but too sensible of, viz., that what the act of Union provided with respect to an establishment of religion in the plantations, has had no other effect than to declare us members of our mother Church, the Church of England, and permit us to adhere to her communion, and receive the sacred influences of her Episcopacy, without being liable to insults and criminations on that account; and to await what our gracious Sovereign may do toward a more particular establishment and regulation, when we shall be so happy as to see a Bishop appointed for us. *This establishment* of Episcopacy is indeed wanting. What may be done for us in consequence of the act of Union, is as yet undone; this seems to be what is signified in the preamble of the late Bishop's patent. *Cum Coloniæ Plantationes, Cæteraque Dominia Nostra in America* NONDUM *divisa, vel formata*, &c. The dispute is, whether the act of Union, *Anno quinto Annæ reginæ*, Section 8, providing for the preservation of the English establishment "within the Kingdom of England and Ireland, the dominion of Wales, and the town of Berwick upon Tweed, and the territories thereunto belonging," under the word *Territories*, does not comprehend the English colonies. Your Lordship's opinion, if in our favour, and we have leave to divulge it, would be at this time a consolation to many who not only esteem the constitution of the Church of England preferable in itself to any other, but think they discharge a good conscience by professing themselves of that communion, in the face of insults and many inconveniences, because they think they must thus follow peace; but their adversaries tell them that they contract the awful guilt of *schism*, and that neither God nor their King will approve their zeal for conformity. A short paragraph from your Lordship would be of equal authority with those alleged against us, and carry the same reverence and respect; and, for my own part, I shall most humbly submit to correction from your Lordship's hands if I have gone into mistakes.

Begging your Lordship's prayers and benediction, and craving pardon for this presumption, I most dutifully subscribe,

My Lord, your Lordship's most dutiful and obedient Son,

And very humble servant,

JAMES WETMORE

[*Rev. Mr. Graves to the Secretary.—Extract.*]

New-London, September 2d, 1752.

Reverend Sir,

That you, Sir, was pleased to write to me I am sensible of, and thankfully acknowledge the signal favour; but it was intercepted and opened by one Captain Durfey, which I proved and demanded, but in vain, before Mr. Stewart and two justices of the peace. I have heard some of the contents, and shall follow your kind advice. I have not received one letter from England since last fall. 'Tis a solemn truth, however, his Lordship resents it to Dr. Johnson; every charge against poor Mr. ——— was literally true, and will, unless he has repented of them, be found so at the last day. Let those who certified the reverse answer for themselves; but I determine never to write against another, though most undeserving.

With pleasure I can say my hearers rather increase, notwithstanding the open wickedness of some among them. The enclosed are specimens of their late revived behaviour, and the continued disturbance and perplexities and abuses I receive in my person and office, without the least prospect or glimmer of their amendment. Here it is publickly and frequently asserted that neither the Bishop of London nor the Society have any power over the people; that this Church is not upon the same footing with other Churches of England; (this Mr. Stewart openly declared in court, pleading in vindication of Captain Durfey's behaviour of the fifth of July last;) that the minister has nothing to do in parish affairs, only to read and preach; that his Church is vested in lay patrons; that it is now in Mr. Mumford, of Groton; (which was attempted to be proved in court by a written instrument from the donor of the Church land;) that it is not subject to the canons; that the Vestry and Churchwardens are the minister's directors, and could place and displace him at their pleasure; that no minister can or shall do any duty in this Church, though at the request of the incumbent, without the knowledge and consent of the Vestry, which in open court they (foolishly) endeavour to prove from the 50th and 52d canons. These, with several other wild Independent principles, are their invincible rules, and to such I am sure my regular patrons will not expect my compliance; and therefore I hope they will, in mercy, remove me to South Carolina, where I hope to give them more satisfaction than it's possible any European can in New-England. Your last letter I received in March, 1750-1, and the proceedings in October encourage me to make this request, and to hope for success.*

* How I have done my duty and resolutely discharged my conscience, though among briars and thorns, I can confidently declare that no minister was ever better beloved by all his hearers. Two leading men and four or five of their creatures and dependents, who are obstinately resolved to harass and perplex me, excepted, I am sure, I have acquired the love and favour of all the Dissenters, who are pleased to express great concern at my difficulties and thoughts of removing.

[*Rev. Mr. Dibblee to the Secretary.—Extract.*]

Stamford, Connecticut, in New-England,
October 2d, 1752.

Reverend Sir,

An earnest invitation from the good people of Newtown and Reading to succeed the worthy Mr. Beach; and from him I am informed, no one would give them better satisfaction. But, although the prospect of mending my living, thirty pounds sterling per annum, is an argument of great weight to me in my low circumstances, yet being assured that the ruin of this infant Church would be the consequence of my removal at this juncture, so soon after the good people, though poor, have exerted themselves in building their Church, and are just now engaging themselves in a great expense to finish it, having been obliged (by reason of the great expense in sending Mr. Minor home; the purchase of the glebe lot, and assisting me to go for holy orders) to meet in it under very indecent circumstances, I am resolved (in submission to the venerable Board) to refuse this advantageous offer, and rely upon God's good providence to be provided for; whose honour and the interest of our holy Church, I think, will be advanced by this self-denial, as our enemies are ready, upon all occasions, to reproach us for showing even a necessary concern for our temporal interest, when, with any face, they can suggest that religion is disserved thereby.

[*Rev. Mr. Graves to the Secretary.—Extract.*]

N. London, October 26*th*, 1752.

Reverend Sir,

What difficulties I meet with from the turbulent spirits of some here, Mr. Bourse can easily inform you; though 'tis a hard task to desire him to describe the open wickedness and persevering impiety of Captain Durfey. I know he can, and I hope that blessed Spirit, whose influence he is now more immediately seeking, will animate him to declare the truth, without favour or affection, on all questions you shall be pleased to ask him, either concerning his reputation or mine. For my own part, the more freely and ingeniously he informs you or others of my real conduct or common administration, the more he will merit my thanks and esteem.

[*Rev. Mr. Camp to the Secretary.—Extract.*]

Middletown, in Connecticut, New-England
November 8*th*, 1752.

Reverend Sir,

At the importunity of the members of the Church, in North Guilford, (a place about fourteen miles from Middletown,) who have constantly upheld the worship of God by reading prayers and sermons for these three years past, and have suffered much distress by the dissenting collectors; with a view to my better support and to ease them of their burden, I have taken them under my care, and steadily officiate there most of my time; but since, I find it will turn to small account, for notwithstanding this, the collectors are obstinately set to collect their rates to support their own ministers and to repair their meeting-house, pleading that I have no business there, as not being employed by the Society, and as not having any place in particular assigned to me in my license. In this case, I have advised with one of the ablest of our counsellors, (on whose judgment I much confide, he being a member of the Church,) who assures me that by the laws of the government, they can certainly get the money from us, which, if they can, I am confident they will, and if they do so, I very much fear that the Dissenters at Middletown and Wallingford will follow their example, for they have an equal power and right to do the same, the result of which is, that I shall be left without support.

The humble petition of the Mohegan Indians, in New-England, in Connecticut, to the most honourable Religious Society in London for Propagating the Gospel in Foreign Parts and Countries, 1756:

We, your humble petitioners, do beg leave to say, Captain John Mason, our guardian and great friend, that died in London on our business some years ago, when he was here amongst us did then teach many of our children to read and write, by which means we learned that the world would, some time or other, come to an end, and all dead folks would all come to life again, and that there is a place called heaven where all good folks will go when they die; and we understand that Mr. Cleveland is an English minister, who we hope the honourable Society will order to stay at Norwich Landing, about three miles distant from us; and the people at Norwich, being always our good friends, they always standing for our interests; and we humbly beg the favour of you, gentlemen, that we, the poor tribe of Mohegan Indians, not having money to hire a minister to teach us the way or path to heaven, may have a share in the Reverend Mr. Cleveland, that we may be taught to go to that good place when we die as well as white men. We are so poor we cannot give him much, without it is a few oysters, fresh fish, and now and then a bit of venison when we have good luck in hunting, except [unless] our well-beloved trustee and guardian, Mr. Samuel Mason, doth gain our case that he is now about in London; which gentleman can give your honors a more full account of our case and circumstances, who we hope will be ready and willing to inform you, he being our agent; there being about four hundred of our tribe that live about four miles from the Church at Norwich, and about the same distance from the Groton Church.

Dated at Mohegan, in Connecticut, this 19*th Jan'y*, 1756.

Wee nate at um nogum nocke Wiegon watch, tahlah boah wee be Sumbyah watuan nogum acode munch togio watabon Sumbya. Moy-wee no munch is Sawonake Matchoog che che gun.

In English:

We think he is a good true-hearted minister, that will teach us the right path to heaven, and not cheat us by showing us the wrong path, but will teach us the right way.

John Uncas, *Chief Sachem*,
John Manepoone,
Joshua Ocoon,
Jabez Jones,
Eben'r Tunner,
Daniel Cooper,
Peter Choozheegan.*

This is a true copy of what the Indians have sent to the Society, enclosed in a letter from the Churches in Norwich and Groton to Dr. Bearcroft. Please show this to Dr. Nicholls.

Joseph Tracey.

* This last was written with the subscriber's own hand.

[*Several Questions relating to the State of Religion in Connecticut.*]

Query 1.—If a hundred families living contiguous, but yet in two colonies, should desire to unite into a Church, in conformity with the Church of England, and those in each colony agree to pay their proportion to the support of a minister, licensed by the Bishop of London, naming the person, could such minister, residing in one colony, claim the benefit of such an act as No. 3 in the other colony, where he officiates attentively, though his habitation be only in one colony?

Query 2.—Is it not repugnant to the act of Uniformity, *Primo Eliz.*, (especially with reference to the last clause, that shows it was designed to extend to all the country belonging to the English dominions,) for any of the colonies to make laws, either to oblige the professors of the Church of England, or, indeed, any others, to support any dissenting way of worship, or to be present thereat?

Query 3.—Ought not the act No. 3 to be construed in a sense not repugnant to the laws of England, when capable of such a sense, rather than in a sense that implies a plain repugnancy, as compelling me to support Independency seems to be?

[*Rev. Mr. Beach to the Secretary.*]

Reading, Connecticut, in N. England,
November 2d, 1759.

Reverend Sir,

I beg leave to return my humble thanks to the venerabl Society for their instructions for our conduct in the late critical conjuncture, when we were in no small danger of becoming a prey to our barbarous enemies, which has had a good effect. Blessed be Almighty God, the snare which they had laid for us is broken, and we are delivered; the divine justice is very apparent in bringing off innocent blood, which, in a most shocking manner, they have been shedding for more ıan half a century. Upon this generation, as they have ione, so has God requited them. The people in New-England are very sensible that, under God, our preservation is owing to his Majesty's paternal care, and the great expense which our mother country has been at for us. My parish is in a flourishing state in all respects, excepting that we have lost some of our young men in the army; more, indeed, by sickness than by the sword, for this countrymen do not bear a campaign so well as Europeans.

As Common Prayer-Books, Duties of Man, and small devotional tracts are not to be purchased here, I therefore presume humbly to request (if it may consist with the wisdom of the venerable Society) that I might be entrusted with a few of such good books to be distributed among my parishioners.

I am, Reverend Sir, yours and the venerable Society's
Most obedient, humble servant,
JOHN BEACH.

[*Rev. Mr. Newton to the Secretary.—Extract.*]

Ripton, in Connecticut, N. England,
July 2d, 1759.

Reverend Sir,

I take this opportunity to inform the honourable Society of the success of the gospel, and of my labours in the propagation of it. Our liturgy is more favourably received and esteemed by the Dissenters than has been for some time past, and many of them frequently come to Church, and desire to be acquainted with it; and some of them who, a year ago, would not have been seen in a Church at publick worship no sooner than in a mass house, (they declared them to be one and the same.) Two families, of good character and conversation, have conformed since my letter of December last, and we have had some additions to our number of communicants.

The honourable Society's most obedient,

Humble servant,

CHRISTOPHER NEWTON.

[*Rev. Mr. Dibblee to the Secretary.—Extract.*]

Stamford, Connecticut, New-England,
September 29th, 1759.

Reverend Sir,

My people continue in a peaceful, united state, in all parts of my extensive mission, and I constantly attend the duties of my office in the various parts of my mission as formerly. There hath not been late accessions to the Church from the Dissenters; the sound of the trumpet and the alarms to war, together with a concern for the events thereof, principally engross the attention of the people. Indeed, the Church of Stamford is rather weakened than strengthened of late by enlistments into publick service, and by the surprising removal of a number of heads of families, through a very malignant disorder that has prevailed among my people. In less than a year past I have buried twelve heads of families, seven, males, some of them the best ornaments of religion and zeal for the Church, and the support of it among us, and of good esteem among our dissenting brethren. June 24th, second Sunday after Trinity, I preached in the lower district of Salem to a very considerable auditory, judged between three and four hundred people, old and young, who behaved very devoutly and attentively; I gave the communion to thirty-nine communicants. There is a hopeful prospect of the increase and flourishing state of religion among that scattered poor people, and no endeavours of mine are wanting to serve them in their best interest. I preached to them about two weeks before, upon a special fast appointed in that province, to implore the smiles and blessing of Divine Providence to attend his Majesty's arms the ensuing campaign, upon which occasion that people also gave a religious and devout attendance.

I am, Reverend Sir, your most obedient,

Most humble servant, and brother in Christ,

EBEN'R DIBBLEE.

[The war alluded to was what was familiarly known as "the old French war."]

[*Rev. Mr. Graves to the Secretary.—Extract.*]

New-London, in N. England,
November 23d, 1759.

Reverend and good Sir,

I understand Mr. Fairweather is appointed to Narragansett. God's will be done. Sure I am, had the naked truth been laid before you, my request had been preferred. I belive that none but Mr. Merritt would have presumed to impose upon such a glorious Society, in counterfeiting a whole parish's design; asserting a glaring falsehood, and condemning the innocent. May God grant him true repentance. Did they know the man, I really believe, though he's of a great family and very rich, they, as well as all considerate Independents here, would despise him. This is the second time he has falsely represented a parish, viz., that of Providence and that of Narragansett. Had I been a proselyte of Clark's Arianism, he had been my sure friend; but as it was in the beginning of Christianity, so it is now, that the great men of the world are always the greatest opposers of Christ and his disciples. The prospect of the recompense of reward is, and will, I trust, be my abiding comfort, in all the vicissitudes and disappointments of life.

Good Sir, your most obliged, grateful,

And obedient servant,

MATT. GRAVES.

[*Rev. Mr. Dibblee to the Secretary.—Extract.*]

Stamford, New-England,
April 1st, 1760.

Reverend Sir,

I thank you for your favour of the 3d of May last, which came to hand long since. If I should live to see an end of the present war, and this Church should be able to free itself from some particular embarrassments, I make no doubt of its future increasing and flourishing state. But one considerable discouragement they labour under is this: antecedent to the late trouble, and before our country was made the seat of war, they had run themselves in debt about one hundred pounds sterling toward furnishing their Church; and the burden of publick taxes, voluntary enlistments into publick service, and the death of many of its most considerable professors, have so weakened them that they still lie under the burden of that debt. This induced the Churchwardens and Vestry, with their minister, in October last, to prefer a petition to the General Assembly of the province, for liberty to draw a lottery in their favour, not to endow the Church, but to free the poor people from those troubles which were brought upon them by the pure providence of God; but, alas, no such favour could be obtained, not even to draw a lottery in the government, if we should not offer a ticket for sale in it; and why? not because it is repugnant to their principles, for they have given countenance to publick lotteries, even to repair the broken fortunes of private persons, and to help to build up and establish an Independent College in the Jerseys, when they could obtain no such favour in their own province. But, alas, this was too great an act of favour to the established Church.

I am, Reverend and worthy Sir,

Your very humble servant, and brother in Christ,

EBENEZER DIBBLEE.

[*Rev. Mr. Beach to the Secretary.—Extract.*]

Reading, in Connecticut, April 22d, 1760.

Reverend Sir,

Arian and Socinian errors, by means of some books written by Dissenters in England, seem of late to gain ground a great pace in this country among the Presbyterians, as they choose to be called, and some of our people are in no small danger from that infection. I have, therefore, at Dr. Johnson's desire and advice, prepared a small piece for the press, being *an attempt to vindicate Scripture Mysteries, particularly the Doctrines of the Holy Trinity, the Atonement of Christ, and the renovation by the Holy Spirit; also of the Eternity of the Future Punishment, with some Strictures upon what Mr. J. Taylor hath advanced on those points*, to which the Doctor hath written a short preface. If it should obtain the approbation of all my brethren at our Convention, (at which they desired me to preach upon these subjects,) and it should be published, I shall presume to send you over some copies, hoping it may make some amends for my former error.

[*Rev. Mr. Newton to the Secretary.*]

Ripton, N. England, June 25th, 1760.

Reverend Sir,

The state of the parish of Ripton is so much the same, as I have informed you in my letter of January last, that it would be but repeating what I have already wrote, to give any further account, except of baptisms. I have baptised this half year twenty white children, and one black, and, under the blessing of God, have been able to preach and catechise, not only on the Sabbath, but in the week, and have reason to think it has had a good effect upon many, and especially upon a number of families that live at the distance of about eight, and some ten miles from Ripton, to whom I have often preached; and of late they have been more ready to hear than formerly, and seem to be religiously disposed, and sensible of the importance of attending publick worship, and, accordingly, have built a Church thirty-six feet long and twenty-six feet wide; and in about six weeks from the beginning, so far finished it that we met in it for publick worship, and a large congregation attended, it was supposed upward of three hundred people. These people live at a great distance from any publick worship, and many of them are so poor that they have not horses to carry their families to worship if they would, and others, it seems by their conduct, choose to spend the Sabbath in hunting and unnecessary visits, and are not only dilatory in religious matters, but in secular affairs. Many live but little above the Indian, and are destitute of the comforts of life. This melancholy prospect influenced some persons that were able, to build a Church, as one of them declared to me, that has been a professor of the Church for some years, that he thought it his duty to expend part of his estate in building a Church, to prevent their becoming heathens. These people since have attended worship and seem very highly to prize the worship of the Church, and have desired me to take the care of them, and I have preached every fourth Sunday to them, and wait for the direction of the venerable Society. Those that have before been professors of the Church in these parts, have sent their requests to the Society; and as my duty will be attended with more trouble and expense, and very little can I expect from the people for my support, I humbly beg the Society would make to me some addition to my salary, and also give me some books for a library, which is allowed to every mission but Ripton; and permit me, Sir, to ask for some Bibles and Common Prayer-Books and Catechisms, to be distributed among the poor people that belong to the new Church. I believe people never stood in more need of charity than they, and a Bible and Common Prayer-Book for the Church.

Most obedient, &c.,

CHRISTOPHER NEWTON.

[*Rev. Mr. Scovil to the Secretary.—Extract.*]

Waterbury, June 26th, A. D. 1760.

May it please the Society,

I have contrived to officiate alternately in my several parishes; have had the satisfaction to find my labours so far successful as to promote a very good harmony among my parishioners, and engage them to give a regular and constant attendance upon our publick worship. There does also a pretty good understanding subsist between them and the Dissenters, who have, many of them, upon some occasions, given their attendance upon the worship of our most excellent Church, though the number of conformists from them to us has been but three families, who have publickly joined our Church, and put themselves under my care. Our number is not hereby enlarged, several families that were conformists having moved out of my parishes, within this half year past. I have visited Simsbury, and officiated there, as I informed the Society I had done in my last letters, and propose to give them all the assistance I can, consistent with the duty of my own particular parishes, till they shall be otherwise supplied. The good people of Simsbury have hired a young gentleman that was educated at Yale College, to read prayers and sermons for them, and have of late seemed to exert themselves as far as they could to support the interests of the Church. I have drawn my bills upon the Society's treasurer for my salary the last half year, and have herewith sent my *Notitia Parochialis*, and am,

May it please the Society,

The Society's most obliged,

And most obedient, humble servant,

James Scovil.

Notitia Parochialis.

No. of families belonging to the Church in Waterbury and Westbury,..........	57
In Northbury,..........	32
In New-Cambridge,..........	28
Communicants in Waterbury and Westbury,..........	88
In Northbury,..........	37
In New-Cambridge,..........	47
Baptised last half year,..........	15

[*Rev. Mr. Mansfield to the Secretary.*]

Derby, N. England, June 27th, 1760.

Reverend Sir,

I continue still employed in the care of my two parishes of Derby and Oxford, and I think I have good reason to hope that my labours are somewhat serviceable in promoting Christian piety and virtue among my parishioners; and I have had the satisfaction of the addition of two families of Dissenters and one single person, (all of them people of good reputation,) who, within the last half year, have professed for the Church of England, and constantly attend its worship.

I have lately been a journey to Simsbury, where, on a Sunday, I preached and performed divine service, and administered the communion to about forty communicants, and baptised three adults and nine children. The Church has of late much revived there under the care of Mr. Viets, a young gentleman, a candidate for holy orders in the Church, who was educated and has taken a degree of Bachelor of Arts at Yale College, in New-Haven, and who for some time past has read divine service and sermons in the Church at Simsbury. They have workmen now employed in finishing off their Church, and are making preparations to finish their glebe-house, each of them having been heretofore much neglected; and there seems at present to be a fair prospect of a flourishing Church in that town, where, for many years before, it had been gradually declining.

I propose to use my best endeavours to promote the interest of religion in my mission. I hereto annex my *Notitia Parochialis* for the last half year, and have drawn upon the Society's treasurer for fifteen pounds sterling toward my support, and am,

Reverend Sir, the Society's and your most obliged
And most obedient, humble servant,
RICHARD MANSFIELD.

In Derby and Oxford—

No. of families,...............................	74
Baptised last half year,........................	23
Actual Communicants of the Church of England,..	80

[*Extract from a Letter from Dr. Johnson to the Archbishop of Canterbury.*]*

May it please your Grace,

While I was in Connecticut, about six months ago, I had opportunity to know much of the condition of the Church in those parts, and therefore thought I would be a little more particular in giving your Grace an account of it. The Church is generally in an increasing and flourishing condition, and much the more so, on account of the violent contentions of the Dissenters among themselves, which in effect drive people into the Church. The Wallingford affair was again before the Assembly last May, and the lower house were still more zealous in the cause of the minor party, which seems the prevailing disposition of the country, so that there will probably be a great struggle to get out the governor and several of the upper house for not favouring them; and I here send your Grace two pamphlets relating to these controversies, that have been published since my last. The parties are

---

* This was written after Dr. Johnson had removed to New-York to take charge of King's, now Columbia College.

both upon bad extremes. Hart and Yale, &c., are followers of Taylor, Foster, &c.; and, I doubt Socinianism is at the bottom, and the President, Hobart, &c., are most rigid Calvinists, and intent at any rate to oppose the others to their utmost. Mean time the Church is every where in peace, and the Clergy orthodox; only I find there are some of the leading laity in good Mr. Palmer's district, that is infected with what is here called *Taylorism, i. e.*, Socinianism and Pelagianism, and they are somewhat disaffected, I believe, without reason, against their minister, for preaching against those errors; charging him with Calvinism, and, perhaps, he may be a little too warm on these accounts. I desired Mr. Beach to preach at their Convention, in Trinity week, in defence of the Trinity and against those loose notions, which he did to good acceptance, and the sermon is to be published; a copy of which I shall send your Grace when I next write.

It is a great detriment to the Churches at Middletown and Wallingford that Mr. Camp hath left them, induced partly by his necessities, and partly by the persuasion of Governor Dobbs, to move to North Carolina. How they are to be supplied I am at a loss to know; they ought each to have a minister, and I wish the Society were in a condition to settle at least forty pounds on the former and thirty pounds upon the latter, who hope for one Mr. Andrews, a candidate of good character, and one Treadwell, said to be a worthy youth, who has lately appeared for the Church, both bred at New-Haven College, where I found three or four hopeful young men preparing for orders. Mr. Punderson seems a very honest and laborious man; yet the Church at New-Haven appears uneasy, and rather declining under his ministry, occasioned, I believe, partly by his want of politeness, and partly by his being absent so much, having five or six places under his care. I wish he was again at Groton and some politer person in his place, and another at Guilford and Branford.

There are now thirty Churches in that colony, (though but fourteen ministers,) there being three or four new ones, one of which is a third within the bounds of Stratford, in a remote corner, ten miles from one and eight from another, under the care of Mr. Newton, who desires me to intercede for a few Prayer-Books and small practical tracts for them, being poor, and some of dissolute habits; and as he has this additional labour, I wish the Society could add ten pounds to his salary, he being both laborious and needy. The more I know of Mr. Winslow the more I am pleased in him as my successor. He excels all the Clergy in that colony as a preacher, and is behind none of them in discretion and good conduct; and being rector of the first Church, and otherwise duly, if not the best qualified, I wish, when Commissaries are appointed, he may be a Commissary, being also of the most creditable family and education; and as he has a large, young, growing family, and is obliged in that situation to live at the most expense of any of them, it would be highly expedient, if practicable, to add ten pounds more to his support.

And here, my Lord, I beg leave to add a few words of that colony in general, though perhaps it might hurt the Church were I known to write too freely. I am humbly of opinion, that every thing being taken into the account, that for its bigness is the best of all his Majesty's colonies in America. All the disadvantages it labours under are owing to its wretched constitution, being little more than a mere democracy, and most of them upon a level, and each man thinking himself an able divine and politician; hence the prevalence of rigid enthusiasms and conceited notions and practices in religion, and republican and mobbish principles and practices, next door to anarchy, in polity; and hence her frequent feuds and factions in both; and every thing is managed by profound hypocrisy and dissimulation, so that they may, in effect, be called a commonwealth of hypocrites. I speak of the prevailing bulk, who all conspire to keep men of true, sober and honest principles and integrity out of places; and such, indeed, as things go, abhor to have any hand in the publick affairs, the rest having lost all notion of almost any king or kingdom to which they are accountable. This state of things makes multitudes very inquisitive after better principles, and many, from too much indignation, run into the wild extremes of boundless latitude and free thinking, while many (I hope the most of those that are inquisitive) seem disposed to set down in the golden mean, the Church of England, if they could be provided for; so that it is of the utmost importance for the best weal of that colony, and its eastward neighbours, that the Church be propagated, and, if possible, be supported; and if, at the same time, their charters were demolished, and they could be reduced under the management of wise and good Governors and a Council appointed by the king, I believe they would in a little time grow a good sort of people, and the best of all the provinces.

And now, my Lord, I return homeward. Westchester and New-Rochelle, in this province, have both lost their ministers, who had been disabled for some considerable time before, and Rye hath lately suffered a grievous loss by the death of good Mr. Wetmore, of the small-pox, so that there is not one Clergyman in all that county or the county above. Rye has been trying to prevail on Mr. Dibblee, of Stamford; but he, good man, though in great need of better support, and apprehensive of the great detriment it would be to that Church, has refused; being also made to hope for the enlargement of his salary, which he truly deserves, and if it can be done, I earnestly wish it may. They think next of trying for Mr. Sturgeon, but I hope they may unite on a worthy son of Mr. Wetmore's, who is preparing for orders; and, I believe, these vacancies must wait till our candidates, three or four of them, are ready. Westchester was sadly disappointed in Mr. Greaton's failing them, and I hope they will unite on one Davies, a good, sensible young man, who will go the next fall, and, perhaps, another.

I am now, my Lord, though not without some danger, returned to my College, ever since the middle of May, and have lately held a Commencement, which was generally well approved, when six were graduated Bachelors, none having, till next May, sufficient standing for Masters. My absence, together with the long sickness and death of my best tutor, has been a great damage, five or six having left the College. I conclude your Grace has had our letters, earnestly begging your assistance in providing two more tutors, one that may be qualified to succeed me, and the other to succeed him that is dead, in teaching mathematics and experimental philosophy. This latter is now extremely needed; and I beg, if possible, he may be sent, though it be late in the fall, for we must entirely suspend those parts of learning till he comes.

Our house, all at present intended, is now near finished, and is a very neat and commodious building, one hundred and eighty feet in length by thirty, three stories high, in a very delightful situation, near Hudson River, opening on the harbour. This is designed for one side of a quadrangle, to be carried on and completed in time, as we need and shall be able, but we cannot go on any further without a collection at home, which we hope, ere long, may be obtained. I now long for Dr. Bristow's library, having got a good room ready for it. Our College has also lately suffered an unspeakable loss in the death of the best and most active of its Governors, in meridian of life, one Mr. Nicoll, a lawyer of great note, who was my son-in-law, than whom no man was ever more lamented throughout this province. Under these losses and difficulties, I humbly beg leave to recommend both it and myself to your Grace's prayers and blessings.

By a letter I had lately from Dr. Smith, of Philadelphia, he puts me upon humbly requesting of your Grace, the honour of a Doctor's degree for the worthy Mr. Barclay, wishing, with me, that if it cannot be procured from Oxford, it may come from Lambeth. I was surprised and very sorry to be told by him, upon my inquiry, that he had not yet then prepared the draughts he was to make and transmit to your Grace, for which I furnished him with some materials from Connecticut, and expected it to have been done last fall; he again promises to do it soon.

And, my Lord, I again beg your pardon for this tedious letter, and whatever improprieties there may be in it,

And remain, may it please your Grace,

Your Grace's most obliged, most dutiful,

And devoted humble servant,

SAMUEL JOHNSON.

Kings College, New-York, July 13th, 1760.

July 30th.

P. S.—This letter, my Lord, having waited thus long for an opportunity, and may yet wait some days, I humbly take occasion to inform your Grace, that this day died, very suddenly, our Lieutenant-Governor, De Lancey, so that we shall need to have a Governor soon sent us; and I need not suggest to your Grace of how much importance it is to us, that he be not only a good statesman but a friend to religion and the Church, and exemplary in attendance on her publick offices, for want of which, religion hath suffered extremely in this province. If, therefore, your Grace can have any influence in the next appointment, I doubt not it will be duly exerted that we may have such an one. As Mr. Standard is dead, and Westchester people are about applying to your Grace for another minister, I question whether a more suitable man can be found than Mr. Milner, by whom I wrote to your Grace, and who, I conclude, is now at Oxford. I could therefore wish, if the Society think proper, that he may be appointed to supply that vacancy.

I am, my Lord, &c.

[*Rev. Mr. Winslow to the Secretary.—Extract.*]

Stratford, New-England, July 14*th*, 1760.

Reverend Sir,

I have the pleasure to say, as to the general state of this parish, that our congregation continues to maintain their steadfastness to their profession, and their endeavours to adorn and to recommend it by unity and peace among themselves, and prudence and charity toward their neighbours, and by a becoming zeal for the purity of the faith of the gospel, and for its due influence toward their own improvement in Christian knowledge and virtue, and toward the like improvement of their families. This will, I hope, by God's blessing, ever be the increasing fruit of the Society's pious care toward us, and wherever it is extended in these colonies, and that by the same divine blessing we that are employed in the Society's service may be enabled, wisely and faithfully to discharge our important duty to them and to the people of our charge.

It has pleased the Supreme Dispenser of all events, to make an effacing breach upon us, in the death of the late Reverend and truly worthy Mr. Wetmore, a gentleman of extensive influence and usefulness, a father and exemplary pattern to the Clergy in these parts. We have also much to regret the necessity Mr. Camp has thought himself under, to remove from his mission at Middletown and Wallingford, as at this time it is peculiarly unhappy that those places, especially the latter, should be destitute, this being the chief seat of the religious controversies now agitating in this colony; and where, if the people could be properly attended, a very flourishing Church would soon be established, to which their being destitute, may, I fear, prove some obstruction. Upon their application to me, I have engaged, as often as I can consistently with my proper duty, to give them all the assistance in my power, until they are provided for.

I have formerly taken the freedom to observe to you the grounds of the contentions in this colony, and chiefly among the teachers; these they are still warmly engaged in, and are increasing confusions among themselves, which have already had, and must more and more produce the effects to awaken the consideration of many of the serious and thinking part among them, and put them for seeking an established foundation whereon, with some security, to settle themselves and enjoy the regular administration of the means and ordinances of religion.

At a late convention of the Clergy of our Church in this colony, at New-Haven, a sermon was preached by the Rev. Mr. Beach, wherein, much to his own reputation, and, I trust, by the Divine blessing, to the credit of religion and advantage of the Church here, he has with great zeal and faithfulness endeavoured to vindicate and establish the important fundamentals of the Sacred Trinity, and the divinity of our blessed Saviour; his atonement and satisfaction; the necessity of the renewing and sanctifying influences of Divine Grace and the eternity of future punishment, and to expose the falsehood and danger of the contrary pernicious errors, which, by means of spreading bad books and other industrious arts of too many men of bad principles in these parts, have been successfully propagated. The Clergy have unitedly taken the occasion of the publication of this discourse to give their testimony against these errors, and to recommend the doctrines therein inculcated as the prime truths of the gospel, and the foundation on which the whole structure of the articles and liturgy of the Church is framed. I hope Mr. Beach has, by this service, atoned in some measure for the ill effects of his former unhappy mistake, and that it may prove a seasonable means to preserve our people in their steadfastness, and to guide our dissenting brethren to that refuge from their various distractions among themselves, both about doctrines and discipline, which they must needs wish to find. You will receive a copy of this sermon from Dr. Johnson.

How greatly, Sir, are we indebted to my Lord of London, for the further instance we have lately received of his pious regard to us in the distribution of so large a number of copies of the second volume of his most excellent discourses, so extremely well calculated for our circumstances and for general instruction in knowledge and direction in practice. May a distinguished crown of glory be the reward of his usefulness.

I beg leave to offer my due regards and best wishes for your health, and respectfully subscribe myself,

Reverend Sir, the Society's

And your most obedient servant,

EDWARD WINSLOW.

[*Rev. Mr. Winslow to the Secretary.—Extract.*]

Stratford, December 29th, 1760.

Reverend Sir,

During the past six months have been baptised here and at Wallingford nineteen white infants and two negro children, and several persons added to the communion of this Church. The present number of communicants is near one hundred and fifty, and I have still the satisfaction to be able to acquaint you that our people continue steadfast in their attachment to the Church, and, in general, careful to evidence the purity of their profession, and their sincerity in it, by endeavouring to make its substantial fruits and ornaments appear in their own personal improvement, in maintaining a union among themselves, and in giving no occasion of offence to others. By this means, through the divine blessing, the Church in this town preserves its ground, notwithstanding a restless spirit of opposition is but too visible in some of our dissenting brethren of authority and influence among us. This has an unhappy tendency to keep up the prejudices of many who are really otherwise not ill affected to the doctrines and worship of our Church, and are much disposed to live in friendship. Much artifice is used by the leading persons among the Dissenters in this colony to prevent their people from attending our service, and to possess them with the absurd notion of their worship and discipline being an establishment here, from which ours is a separation; but their own late divisions and distractions among themselves, with regard to doctrine and discipline, have already unsettled so many, and must necessarily have the like effect with others, that, I doubt not at all, there will be seen numbers gladly embracing the refuge from these confusions and those wholesome means for all needful instruction and improvement in Christian knowledge and practice, which our happy constitution will afford them. This is manifestly the present case at Wallingford and in its immediate neighbourhood, where the Church congregation has so far increased that the people think themselves in a condition to make some suitable provision for sending home for holy orders, and for supporting a deserving young man, who has been some time employed as a reader among them. They dare not presume upon the Society's assistance, further than to crave the liberty to apply for part of the salary granted to Middletown and Wallingford, should they in their goodness see fit to allow it. The people who belong to the congregation at Wallingford, and live at some distance, have lately built themselves a small Church for their greater convenience in the winter season, when their families cannot well attend at the other. I continue to officiate at Wallingford about once in six weeks, which, by the reason of the distance of near thirty miles, and the needful care of my particular charge, is as frequent attendance as I am able to give.

I am, Reverend Sir, the Society's

And your most obedient servant,

EDWARD WINSLOW.

SKETCH OF THE SEABURY FAMILY.

[THE following sketch of the Seabury family, furnished at the request of the Editors, by one of its descendants, forms a part of the history of the Connecticut Church, in its brief narrative relating to its first Bishop. It possesses also additional interest from its presentation of the remarkable fact (at least in this country) of four successive generations having each furnished a Clergyman to the Church. It may well be questioned whether our ecclesiastical annals afford any similar instance. If any name, therefore, may be considered as belonging to the history of the Church at the North, it is that of Seabury. We are glad to have it in our power to present the following from the pen of a great-grandson of the Bishop.—EDITORS.]

THE name of *Seabury* appears at a very early date in our Colonial history. The family came from England and settled first in the Colony of Massachusetts, and was thence spread to Connecticut and New-York. *John Seabury*, the first of the name in this country, resided in Boston in the beginning of the seventeenth century. His son *Samuel*, born in 1639, was a surgeon, and lived at Duxbury, Mass. He is spoken of as a man of some note in his profession.

His son, *John Seabury*, removed from Duxbury a little before the year 1700, and settled at Stonington, Connecticut. In the year 1704 he exchanged his farm in Stonington for one in Groton, a small place on the River Thames, opposite New-London, where he resided for many years; removing, in the latter part of his life, however, to Hempstead, L. I., at which place he died, on the 17th day of December, 1759.

Mr. John Seabury married, in 1697, Elizabeth Alden, a grand-daughter of the famous John Alden of the May Flower, by whom he had eight children, and who survived him many years, dying on the 4th of January, 1771, at the advanced age of ninety-four. She was interred at Stonington, where it is recorded, on her tombstone, that she lived to see the fourth generation of her descendants.

From the religious customs of the colony where he was born, as well as of that in which the greater part of his life was spent; from the ignorance and hatred of the Church, which, at that time, were in these places almost universal; and from the associations of his marriage, we might naturally expect to find Mr. Seabury the staunchest of staunch Puritans.

Accordingly, we are not surprised to read that he lived in the practice of the Congregationalist sect; that he was a prominent member and Deacon of the Society of that persuasion in Groton; and that he trained his son to be a preacher of the doctrines to which he himself had been trained to listen.

Samuel, the fourth son of Mr. John Seabury, was born at Groton, on the 8th of July, 1706. He was educated at Harvard College, graduating in the year 1724, at the age of eighteen years, and soon after graduating was licensed to preach as a Congregationalist minister.

For several months during the year 1726, he preached to the Congregationalists at North Groton, but in this position he could not long remain. The doctrine and order of the Church, hitherto almost unknown, were then beginning to emerge from the obscurity with which ignorance and prejudice had shrouded them, and the Congregationalist minister of Groton was among the first who came within their light.

The famous controversy between the president and professors and the trustees of Yale College, had but recently been followed by the conformity and ordination of Dr. Johnson and others, and their learned and pious illustration of the faith of the Church led many to reflection, and laid the foundation of the subsequent prosperity of the Church in Connecticut.

The study and reflection of Mr. Seabury convinced him of the invalidity of his orders; he declared himself a convert to the doctrines of the Church of England, and, in the year 1731, crossed the ocean and received Episcopal ordination from the Bishop of London. Returning to America, he soon afterward received a commission from the venerable Society for propagating the gospel in foreign parts, to exercise his sacred functions in New-London, at a yearly compensation of sixty pounds, "with an arrearage or payment backward from the Feast-day of St. John the Baptist, which was in the year 1730."

The Rev. Dr. McSparren, a missionary of the Society, who resided for many years in the Narragansett Country, was probably the founder of the Church in New-London. Services were held there by him, and a subscription fund was started, so early as the year 1725, for the erection of "a Church or decent edifice for the service of Almighty God according to the liturgie of the Church of England, as by law established," but it was under Mr. Seabury that this Church attained its first organization in a permanent form. He met with those gentlemen in New-London who had interested themselves in the establishment of the Church, on the 10th of April, 1732, and by the choice of Wardens and Vestrymen, the parish was then first organized as "the Episcopal Church of New-London," the style which continued until the year 1741, when it begins to be designated as "St. James' Church," under which title it has attained its present flourishing condition.

Mr. Seabury's commission bears date in May, 1732, one month after the organization of the Church. In the autumn of the same year, the building erected by the parish was opened for divine service, and from that time for a period of about eleven years, Mr. Seabury continued to officiate there, faithfully guarding the infancy of the parish, which, in its maturer growth was subject to the ministrations both of his son and grandson, and in which his great-grandson also has more than once officiated.

In the year 1743 Mr. Seabury was transferred by the Society, whose commission he held, to Hempstead, Long Island, a removal which was made at the request of the people of that place, and with his own consent. Here he spent the remainder of his life, occupying a small farm, and adding the duties of teacher to those of pastor.

It was during his residence at Hempstead that an effort was made to establish the Church in Dutchess County, and at the request of certain gentlemen of that county, he wrote to recommend them to the care of the venerable Society. The Society replied by promising to establish a missionary there when there should be provision made for the erection of a Church building, and in the mean time directed Mr. Seabury to give the people of Dutchess as much of his care as was consistent with his regular duties; in accordance with which, Mr. Seabury for some time officiated at Fishkill and probably at other places in the country, as opportunity offered.

He is said to have preached his last sermon at New-London while on a visit to his relatives and former parishioners. He returned to Hempstead from this excursion, and being taken sick soon after, died on the 15th day of June, 1764, leaving behind him (says Dr. Chandler, in his life of Johnson) a character that is held in high esteem, and an example that is worthy of all imitation.

Mr. Seabury was twice married; the first time to Abigail, daughter of Mr. Thomas Mumford, of New-London, the second son of which marriage was *Samuel*, afterward Bishop of Connecticut and Rhode Island, who was born on the 30th of November, 1729, and whose history requires a more extended notice than comes within the limits of this sketch. He was graduated from Yale College in 1748, and soon after was appointed by the venerable Society a Catechist, to act under the direction of his father, at Huntington, a place about twenty miles from Hempstead, L. I. He subsequently studied medicine in the University of Edinburgh, acquiring a knowledge which he found very useful in the course of his clerical ministrations.

Whether he studied the medical science only with a view to this usefulness, as some have said, or whether he intended to live by the practice of it, is not known. However this may have been, he put aside his medical studies for the study of Theology; became a candidate for holy orders, and on Friday, December 21st, 1753, was ordained Deacon, by John, Bishop of Lincoln, acting for the Bishop of London. He was admitted to priest's orders, by Richard, Bishop of Carlisle, acting for the Bishop of London, on Sunday, the 23d day of December, 1753, and was on the same day, by Thomas, Bishop of London, licensed and authorized to perform the office of a priest in the Province of New-Jersey, in America. The venerable Society gave him the appointment of missionary at New-Brunswick, in that colony, and he entered upon his duties there in 1754.

On the 12th of January, 1757, he was collated and inducted into the Parish of Jamaica, L. I., by Sir Charles Hardy, Governor of New-York.

By the mandate of Sir Henry Moore, bearing date December 3d, 1766, he was instituted Rector of St. Peter's Church, in Westchester County, and, in pursuance of this mandate, was formally inducted to the office, at Westchester, on the 1st day of March, 1767, by the Rev. Myles Cooper, D. D., President of King's College, New-York.

In this parish he continued to officiate until the troubles of the Revolution interfered with his ministrations. Firmly adhering, during this period, to his loyalty to his Sovereign and his fidelity to his Church, he was at all times troubled, at one time seized and imprisoned, and finally, after an edict was published at New-York, making it death to support the King or any of his adherents, fifty armed men being sent into his neighbourhood to enforce the same, he shut up the Church, and, with difficulty, effecting his escape from Westchester, retired to the City of New-York, then in possession of the British. The returning forces of the patriots, whose temporary withdrawal had afforded him the opportunity of escape, damaged his property to a considerable extent, subjecting the members of his family to insult, and to the breaking open and injuring the Church.

It being impossible for Dr. Seabury* to resume his parish duties, he continued to reside, during the war, for the most part, in the City of New-York, where he supported himself by the practice of medicine. He also served as chaplain in the King's American regiment, to which position he was

* He was made *Doctor of Divinity* by the University of Oxford, Dec. 15, 1777.

appointed by Sir Henry Clinton, on the 14th of February, 1778.

After the independence of the colonies and the consequent removal of the authority of the Church of England from them, the Clergy of Connecticut were the first to realize the necessity of an American Episcopate, and to inaugurate the measures necessary to obtain it. They chose Dr. Seabury to become their Bishop, and, in compliance with their choice, he set sail for England in the year 1783, to obtain consecration.

This, however, he could not obtain there. The existing law prevented the consecration of a Bishop who could not swear allegiance to the King, and a policy hostile to the interests of the American Church forbade the repeal of that law. The English Bishops, therefore, feeling themselves bound to refuse his application, Dr. Seabury turned to the Church of Scotland; a Church which, while it preserved unimpaired the Apostolic faith and order, enjoyed also an entire immunity from the restraints which fettered the legal establishment of the Church of England. His application here was favorably received, and on the 14th day of November, 1784, Dr. Seabury was consecrated at Aberdeen, by Bishops Kilgour, Petrie and Skinner. He immediately returned to Connecticut, and entered upon the discharge of his Episcopal functions, which he continued to exercise in that State, and afterward, also, in Rhode Island, until his death.* He had his residence in New-London, and, in connection with the duties of the Episcopate, filled the position of Rector of the Parish of St. James. He died very suddenly on the 25th of February, 1796, in his sixty-seventh year.†

Bishop Seabury married, on the 12th day of October, 1756, Mary, daughter of Mr. Edward Hicks.

---

* Bishop Seabury, on his return from Scotland, landed at Newport, R. I., on the 20th of June, 1785. On the next Sunday he preached the first sermon of an American Bishop in America, from Heb. xii., 1st and 2d verses.

† The tablet to Bishop Seabury's memory, in New-London, gives his age as 68. It appears from the town records of Groton, as reported by Miss Caulkins, in her valuable history of New-London, that he was born in 1729. The statement of the tablet is, therefore, in this respect, erroneous. The exact age of the Bishop, at the time of his death, having been 66 years 2 months and 25 days.

Charles Seabury, the youngest child of Bishop Seabury, was born at Westchester, on the 29th day of May, 1770, residing with his father at New-York; he removed with him, after his consecration, to New-London. Deterred from applying for admission to Yale College by the opinion that the religious prejudices there prevailing would have subjected him to discomforts which would have more than counterbalanced any advantages to be derived from the Collegiate Course, he pursued his preparatory studies with the Rev. Richard Mansfield, D. D., at Derby, Conn., and afterward at Narragansett with the Rev. William Smith, D. D., and then devoted himself to the study of Theology under the immediate supervision of his Right Reverend father, by whom, upon the recommendation of the Clergy present at the Convention of the Diocese of Connecticut, in Christ Church, Middletown, he was admitted to the holy order of Deacons on the 5th of June, 1793. He resided in New-London until 1795, accompanying his father on several visitations, and in the winter of 1795–'6, he officiated at Grace Church, Jamaica, L. I.

Within a month after the decease of his father, he was called to the Rectorship of St. James' Church, New-London, of which parish he continued to be Rector until about the year 1813–'14.

On the 17th of July, 1796, he was admitted to the Priesthood by Bishop Provoost, at St. George's Chapel, in the City of New-York. He married, on the 13th of June, 1799, Anne, fourth daughter of Mr. Rosewell Saltonstall, of New-London, and by her had six children, the eldest of whom was the Rev. Samuel Seabury, D. D., of New-York. About the year 1814 he removed from New-London to Setauket, L. I., and became the Rector of Caroline Church at that place, where he spent the remainder of his life. He removed under the expectation of a salary of two hundred and fifty dollars, and an annual allowance from Trinity Church of a like amount. Trinity Church having discontinued the allowance, and the promised salary having been from time to time diminished, Mr. Seabury, in 1816, accepted a stipend of two hundred dollars from the Missionary Society of the Diocese, and had the field of his ministrations enlarged by the addition of St. John's Church, Huntington, where his grandfather had in his lifetime regularly officiated, as did afterward his son; and the parish at Islip, the one at a distance of seventeen, the other of twenty-four miles from Setauket.

The Huntington Parish was only a short time attached to his mission, but he retained the charge of the other two parishes until the infirmities of advancing years compelled him to give up the one at Islip. From that time he went seldom from Setauket, continuing to devote himself to the services of the Church in that place until his death, which happened very suddenly, on the 29th of December, 1844, and which found him still discharging the duties of a ministry, maintained for more than half a century, with a zeal and ardor which trouble and privation could not abate, and age could scarcely chill.

[Of the present clerical representation of the family of Seabury, the Rev. Samuel Seabury, D. D., of New-York, little need here be said, inasmuch as his well-earned reputation is well known to the members of the American Episcopal Church. He is at present Rector of the Church of the Annunciation, and "Professor of Biblical Literature and Interpretation of Scripture," in the General Theological Seminary of the Protestant Episcopal Church in the United States.—Eds.]

www.ingramcontent.com/pod-product-compliance
Lightning Source LLC
LaVergne TN
LVHW020218110826
845151LV00003B/750

* 9 7 8 1 4 2 5 5 3 3 7 8 6 *